Karl Marx and the
Future of the Human

Raya Dunayevskaya Series in Marxism and Humanism

Series Editors: Kevin B. Anderson, Purdue University
Olga Domanski, News and Letters Committees
Peter Hudis, News and Letters Committees

The Power of Negativity: Selected Writings on the Dialectic in Hegel and Marx
Edited and Introduced by Peter Hudis and Kevin B. Anderson
Philosophy and Revolution: From Hegel to Sartre and from Marx to Mao
by Raya Dunayevskaya
*Helen Macfarlane: A Feminist, Revolutionary Journalist, and Philosopher
in Mid-Nineteenth-Century England*
by David Black
Karl Marx and the Future of the Human
by Cyril Smith

Karl Marx and the Future of the Human

Cyril Smith

LEXINGTON BOOKS
Lanham • Boulder • New York • Toronto • Oxford

LEXINGTON BOOKS

Published in the United States of America
by Lexington Books
An imprint of The Rowman & Littlefield Publishing Group, Inc.
4501 Forbes Boulevard, Suite 200, Lanham, Maryland 20706

PO Box 317
Oxford
OX2 9RU, UK

British Library Cataloguing in Publication Information Available

Library of Congress Cataloging-in-Publication Data

Smith, Cyril, 1929–
  Karl Marx and the future of the human / Cyril Smith.
    p. cm.
  Includes bibliographical references and index.
  ISBN 0-7391-1026-8 (cloth : alk. paper) — ISBN 0-7391-1027-6 (pbk. : alk. paper)
  1. Marx, Karl, 1818–1883. 2. Communism—History. 3. Socialism—History. I. Title.

  HX39.5.S558 2005
  335.4—dc22   2004025094

Printed in the United States of America

♾™ The paper used in this publication meets the minimum requirements of American
National Standard for Information Sciences—Permanence of Paper for Printed Library
Materials, ANSI/NISO Z39.48-1992.

I pondered all these things, and how men fight and lose the battle, and the thing they fought for comes about in spite of their defeat, and when it comes turns out not to be what they meant, and other men have to fight for what they meant under another name.

—William Morris, *A Dream of John Ball*, 1887

Contents

Preface

This book contains some of the contributions I have made toward understanding the ideas of Karl Marx since I published *Marx at the Millennium* in 1995. As such, it contains an account of some of the mistakes I have inevitably made along the way. Upholders of the rule of capital had been relieved to hear that "Marxism was dead" and were very upset by any attempt to distinguish it from the work of Karl Marx. They much preferred to go on smearing him with responsibility for the monstrous regimes in Eastern Europe. Meanwhile, the dwindling and aging band of "orthodox Marxists" pointed to the obviously obnoxious features of the world after the fall of the Wall, and loudly denounced every attempt to question our old beliefs as "revisionist betrayal."

Nine years on, the situation has changed considerably, and the idea that "Marxism" totally misread Marx is quite often repeated. However, I believe the intensity of the opposition between the two is still not grasped by many people, who still think of Marx as a "theorist" who was also—incidentally—a revolutionary. This hides the radical nature of what Marx, the revolutionary humanist, was trying to do.

While the idea of the impossibility of life without the market still predominates, my own position has if anything hardened over the past nine years, and I hope some issues are a bit clearer. In particular, I soon came to see that I had gone too far in my attempt to absolve Engels of all blame for the Marxist distortion of Marx, and blunted my attack on the old orthodoxy. To make amends, I wrote a paper on "Friedrich Engels and Marx's Critique of Political Economy" (*Capital and Class* 62, Summer 1997), showing that even that great and devoted upholder of Marx had not really grasped what his friend was trying to do.

During these past ten years, socialism has begun to escape from the shadow of the revolution of October 1917 and its betrayal, but little more than that. It is impossible to exaggerate the extent to which this long historical detour affected the entire socialist project. Understanding of the struggle for a new social order or even its possibility was pushed back in the thinking of millions. When the end of the Russian revolution was finally placed beyond doubt, the disappointment of many "leftists" was great. But it meant that a new generation could begin to face the challenge of fighting against the old order without the dogmatic straitjacket worn by its elders.

In this book, investigating the origins of Marx's fundamental ideas yet again, I want to demonstrate more clearly that his humanism, clearly stated in his early writings, was developed throughout his life, and was never abandoned, or replaced by what Marxism had called a "scientific world outlook." In particular, I want to probe further the relation between Marx's three concepts: "truly human," "science," and "critique." Without understanding what he meant by humanity and inhumanity, the contrast between his own critical science and what is generally called "science" is lost. Herein lies his crucial relevance to today's problems.

Marx's critique of philosophy, of political economy, and of socialism was made from the standpoint of "human society and social humanity." Only from this angle can the inhuman character of modern society be comprehended and the social categories of science criticized as embodiments of inhumanity. Only then can they be transcended in conscious practice. What is at stake here cannot be overstated, for it involves the very survival of what it means to be human.

But that is not all. "Human being" is not just a biological term, which can be applied to an individual, or even a single species, but much more. In working on nature, the human takes on the character of a universal being. As such, humanity is both individual and social, and this leads us to bring up questions, which have been the prerogative of what "Marxism"—but never Marx— would have dismissed as the "mystical." These people were groping after what in Marx's terms he called a truly human society.

The first chapter in this volume emphasizes the gulf between Marx's attitude and nearly all the various meanings given to the word "socialism." I hope that, at this time when the very notion of a world of social relations freed from the domination of the market is widely rejected, this will help to press the reader even harder to grasp the radical nature of what Marx is up to. He is neither propounding a scientific doctrine nor constructing a model of how he thinks the world works. Nor is he setting out a Utopian "vision" to which he thinks the world ought to conform. His central aim is "universal human emancipation," so that *in principle* there can be neither a blueprint for freedom, nor a "doctrine of freedom." Marx's critique of all blueprints and doctrines constantly strives to strip away the obstacles to freedom, as they exist both in our heads and in the way we live. That is the aim of his critique of all forms and categories of "social science."

Chapter 2 is an attempt to separate Marx from the commonly repeated idea that he was the author of something called "historical materialism," a way of "explaining" history and social change. Marx never used this term, which implies something quite opposed to his own understanding of his work. When the journal *Historical Materialism* was started, I submitted an earlier draft of this paper to the editors. Two years later, it became clear that they were never going to agree to publish it. Eventually, one of them told me—quite correctly— that I hadn't discussed "the secondary literature." At this point, I gave up the unequal contest, and the article appeared in *International Socialist Forum*, volume 1, number 3.

Chapter 3 reprints an article I wrote in 1998, when there were many commemorations of the 150th anniversary of the publication of the Communist Manifesto. This also appeared in *International Socialist Forum*. One of its aims was to correct some of the many "orthodox" accounts of the origins of this vital document, repeating the old mythology, for example, that rehashed in the Introduction to the Verso edition of the *Manifesto*, contributed by Eric Hobsbawm.

Part 2 of this book consists of an investigation of the relation between Marx and the tradition of political philosophy. In writing this essay, I was prompted especially by a book which received hardly any attention when it appeared. Gary Teeple's *Marx's Critique of Politics, 1842–1847* (Toronto, 1984) was very important for me because of his careful account of the way that Marx's concept of critique developed in his early work. I then found that, in order to understand this, I had to return yet again to the contradictory relation between Marx and Hegel, and to reexamine it in the light of the history of political philosophy as a whole. As such, the position with regard to democracy held by philosophy as a whole is found to be one of hostility.

Part 3 is the most recent section. It deals—very partially—with what I now regard as the heart of the problem; the question of what *is* the human. Chapter 10 is an attempt to give an account of the development of this category, which in Marx's work toward what he called communism, or a truly human society he identified with human self-creation. Chapter 11 is a brief account of the relation of Marx's conceptions with those of William Blake, which I at any rate found helpful.

I know some readers will complain about my immersion in what they will call "academic" questions. But I believe more strongly than ever that Marx's main work was to cut away those mental forms embodying the forms of oppression.

Only then can the "real movement" find its "mouthpiece," and any attempt to introduce "politics" before this will lead us to disaster. My apologies are also due for all kinds of repetitions and contradictions: they are unavoidable. Any other defects must be attributed to my state of health.

While doing this work, I have tried to draw my old comrades into discussion, but with little success. In the main, they have preferred to take up simpler matters, which they see as getting on with the "real job," as they variously understand it. Still, my campaign has forced me to clarify some important questions, and for that I am grateful. My discussions with the late Don Cuckson were invaluable, especially in pulling up by the roots any remaining vestiges of Leninism. Hayo Krombach has continued to place his knowledge of Hegel's system at my disposal. Geoff Barr and Christian Heine read an earlier draft of part II and their criticisms and comments were vital in making me attempt to express more clearly what I was trying to achieve. Discussions with Ute Bublitz have left their mark on these pages. Several arguments with Massimo De Angelis have also forced me to reconsider many issues. These and many other discussants have helped me in this work, while being entirely innocent of responsibility for its shortcomings.

I must also thank Glenn Rikowski for the title of this book. When he presented his paper "Marx and the Future of the Human" to a meeting of the seminar on "Marx: Individuals and Society" at Birkbeck College, London, I agreed with some aspects and disagreed with others, but I realized that its title expresses just what I was trying to do. So I asked him if I could purloin it, and he very kindly allowed me to do so. I should like to mention also Melissa McNitt and Rob Carley of Lexington, without whose help this volume would not have appeared.

Part One

MARX'S CONCEPT OF THE HUMAN

... endeavouring to shut out of the Creation, the cursed thing, called Particular Propriety, which is the cause of all wars, bloud-shed, theft, and enslaving Laws, that hold the people under miserie.

> Signed for and in behalf of all the poor oppressed people of
> England, and the whole world.—Gerrard Winstanley, 1649

Chapter One

The Prospects for Socialism

In olden times—twenty years ago, say—I should have understood the title of this chapter quite clearly, and written pages on the subject without the slightest difficulty. I would have used a vocabulary and categories well known to whoever might have happened to read them. Words like "socialism," "class," "property," "struggle," and "crisis" would have tripped smoothly from the keyboard, and I should have wasted little effort asking myself what they meant, because "everybody knew."

Basically, for people like me, socialism meant an economic system in which state ownership and democratic planning replaced the anarchy of private ownership in the organization of production. As a Trotskyist, I might have explained how 1917 marked the beginning of the world transition from capitalism to socialism. The degeneration of the Russian revolution had held things up, and I knew that what others called "actually existing socialism" was really a monstrous, oppressive, bureaucratic nightmare. But I could explain this degeneration, and the rise to power of the Stalinist bureaucracy, as results of the isolation of the revolution in a single backward country. The spread of the proletarian revolution to the "advanced metropolitan countries," as we called them, would soon make possible the overthrow of the bureaucracy and then the advance to a new social order would be resumed. All that was needed was a world party, founded on the scientific truths of Marxism-Leninism, which in each country would lead the working class to "take state power."

And what about "prospects," or "perspectives," (the nonexistent English plural, into which the Comintern had translated the Russian word *perspektiviy*). This was something like a historical weather forecast. The course of history was law governed and so amenable to scientific investigation by those who employed the "correct" method. (We were always keen on being "correct." It

3

meant conforming to a body of orthodox theoretical knowledge whose truth we asserted.)

There were other people who also thought of socialism as a change in the economic order. They assumed that capital and its power would disappear in the course of a long series of parliamentary elections, each of which would move things along a little bit with another small encroachment on the power of wealth. As a result, people would treat each other progressively better and inequalities would gradually get evened out, both within and between nations. As a serious prospect, such ideas died out long ago, replaced with various kinds of electoral gimmicks, as exemplified by the corruption of Blair's elusive "Third Way." To find traces of parliamentary socialism as actually aiming to get rid of capital, you'd really have to look back more than a couple of decades. (My father, like many of the generation which came through the First World War, saw politics in that way.) In so far as there was any theory behind such notions, it would have been some variant of liberalism. I should have called it "social democracy," and thoroughly disagreed with it. However, paradoxically, it had something very basic in common with my own "revolutionary" views: like we Leninists, these "reformists" also thought in terms of an elite which would take political power and do good things for working people.

Between them, these conceptions of socialism, the revolutionary and the reformist, attracted the devoted support of millions of working men and women and their allies, including some of the finest human beings of the twentieth century. But, after the passing of that terrible century, I believe that their ideas have now clearly shown themselves incapable of answering the problems of humanity.

Of course, any theoretical framework whose categories have been frozen solid gets into difficulties when the world exhibits its embarrassing habit of changing. Even if it had been true before the change, upholding it under the new conditions would demand some fancy theoretical footwork. (Did somebody mumble something about "dialectics"? Then you can be sure of trouble.) I don't think I have to prove that the world has indeed profoundly changed and that those old ideas just can't be patched up to fit the new world situation. Those who try to convince themselves otherwise are clinging to the old "Marxist" language like a comfort blanket, under which they can hide from the horrors of the modern world.

Certainly, some things are the same. More than ever, money itself, and not just its owners, exercises inhuman power over all forms of sociality and of social production. Capital is even more powerful than before, distorting and destroying the lives of billions of people, whatever their living standards. Global deterioration of their well-being accompanies the ever-accelerating advance of technology. While the productivity of labor races forward, a hundred million children go to bed hungry each night. The omnipotence of the market invades every aspect of life and culture. State power takes the shape of tyrannies of appalling brutality. The threat of war involving nuclear destruction and biological devastation still hangs over the world. Trotsky's description of "a crisis in human culture" is even more apposite than it was in 1938.

But the forms of this "crisis" are not those of thirty years ago, and we must stop pretending that they are. Transnational corporations now hold unprecedented power, rivaling that of states; industry has massively translocated to new areas of the world, in some of which it produces under near-slave conditions; production is controlled by purely financial enterprises of a wholly new kind, which decide the fate of entire continents; profit-driven technology threatens to degrade the natural environment and to disrupt life-support systems; developments in the former bureaucratic states show Mafia-type gangs dominating the state and financial systems; national and ethnic conflicts reach increasing levels of brutality.

These and other changes have basically altered the conditions for any possible social and political transformation, and thus demand a fundamental re-examination of the way the socialists used to look at their tasks. Both the power of the existing world order to destroy us all and the possibility for human advance are quite beyond anything the old Marxism considered. That is why, I believe, the traditional categories of Marxism now show themselves quite inadequate to grasp the twentieth century, let alone the twenty-first. Indeed, they have become a major obstacle to finding any way to grasp possibilities for fundamental social transformation.

Of course, struggles against the more obviously repulsive aspects of modern society have never stopped. Militant trade union activity has arisen in places where it was previously unknown, notably in the new sweatshop areas of capitalist development. It is also found among migrant workers in the older industrial countries, who sometimes reinvigorate the old trades unions. In alliance with these struggles, a new coalition of environmentalists, feminists, motorway campaigners, and human rights activists emerged in the 1990s. It became particularly prominent in demonstrations like those which disrupted the meeting of the World Trade Organization in Seattle, and that of the World Bank and the International Monetary Fund in Prague.

This movement, which sometimes thinks of itself as "anticapitalist," has some very encouraging features. It is healthily antipathetic to old ideas of leadership and program and its activities are organized without hierarchy. Unlike the old Leninist attitudes, which kept means and ends, method and goal rigidly apart, it regards its forms of activity as themselves being the precursor of new social forms. No wonder that the forces of the "old left" has been as highly suspicious of this movement as it has of them. The old slogans had no relevance for the "anticapitalist" marchers and Vladimir Ilyich Lenin had no place on the streets of Seattle last November. But, I shall argue, whether or not the demonstrators saw it this way, Karl Marx was well to the fore in Seattle. For the marchers were seeking a mode of struggle for a free association, but one which was itself already a free association. As we shall see, that was his aim too.

But, however much we might welcome the emergence of this movement, its ideas can only be described as confused and superficial. This is partly because it is a loose coalition of disparate forces—trades unionists, feminists, environmentalist, fighters for the rights of minorities and others—and because it is posing problems which have never been confronted before. But, for all their rhetoric, these "anticapitalists" never explain what they mean by either "capitalism" or by "anti." They are thus left only with protest against the symptoms of social ills or the policies of particular states. They refuse to face the fact that the actions of their enemies, the transnational corporations and financial institutions, are not simply the expression of the unlimited greed of their personnel—although this certainly is there for all to see. But what is the reason for this greed and its power? It is the working out of the logic of a complete way of living, specifically, of the nature of private property and its money form. Only by tracing this lunatic logic to its source can humanity assure its future.

So to bring about the changes in the world sought by the "anticapitalists" demands the most drastic transformation of human society. And, since that change must also be quite conscious, it also requires the greatest possible clarity of thought. It makes necessary nothing less than a complete reexamination of the meaning of humanity and of its inhuman way of living. Only this could match up to the magnitude of the task of learning to live humanly, without private property or state power.

What is humanity? In this age of genetic engineering and artificial intelligence, biological definitions are not much use. What is most importantly specific about homo sapiens is not our DNA or our intellectual talents—these we can take for granted—but our forms of social life and communal ways of satisfying our material and spiritual needs. To be human means, first of all, to participate freely in social production and to work as free individuals for each others' well-being. All of this is denied by the fact that we live under the sway of the market.

Living under the control of impersonal "market forces" is crazy. How have we fallen under the sway of such powers? To answer such questions, we must turn for assistance to an unknown writer of the nineteenth century: Karl Heinrich Marx.[1] Discovering his ideas is not as easy as you might expect. For the millions of words devoted to "Marxism" over the past century and more, rather than helping us to understand Marx's ideas, in fact built a massive ideological barrier, which must be penetrated if we are to find out what he was trying to do.

First, let us say what he was not doing. He was not an economist, making theoretical "models" of "capitalism." He was not a philosopher, with a unified "theory of history." He was not a sociologist, developing a science of social structure. He certainly did not manufacture "an integral world outlook," "cast from a single sheet of steel." Neither was he the draughtsman of a utopian blueprint for an alternative kind of economic system. (It is interesting that Marx himself rarely used the term "socialism," except as a label for ways of thinking and acting which he was criticizing. As far as I know, he never spoke about "capitalism" either.)

An important part of what he wanted to achieve was a demonstration that all such "theoretical" projects were themselves symptoms of a false, "alienated" way of living. They were alienated forms of thought because they saw themselves in opposition to their objects. They thus reflected a world in which the social relations between us dominated our lives independently of our wills and consciousnesses. Built into their foundations is a hidden assumption: that the actual producers, the "doers," have to be directed by an elite group, who are the "thinkers." Universal human self-emancipation—and Marx's concern was nothing less than this—could not be grasped by theorists, for it was a practical task, in which the masses would become the subjects of history.

"Philosophers have interpreted the world in different ways" for a long time. A few of them have still not quite given up. But this activity is itself alienated, governed by its own products, as are the productive activities of wage workers. Instead of trying to be theorists, stuffing the world into our preconceived categories, and then giving up in despair when it obstinately refuses to fit, Marx tells us to undertake the strenuous effort of allowing reality to unfold itself, objectively showing the origins and the defects of all categories. Only then will it reveal its human meaning. As he explains in the Theses on Feuerbach, he takes as his standpoint "human society and social humanity."

Marx's achievement is precisely to distill, by means of his critique of philosophical science, the conception of humanity, and thereby inhumanity, for which the philosophers had sought in vain. "Communism is the riddle of history solved." Humanity is not a fixed essence, but is in essence freely and socially self-creating, and, only because of this, self-conscious. Humans are parts of nature, which engage consciously in the production of the objects to satisfy their needs. At the same time, they transform these needs in ways which mark them as specifically human.

Among the questions with which Marx was concerned, four stand out:

What is humanity?

How have we humans come to live inhumanly, treating ourselves as things?

How can a truly human life, a free association of individuals, emerge out of this internal conflict between humanity and inhumanity?

How can a scientific understanding be established which can grasp the collective and individual tasks implied by universal freedom?

Alienated life is dominated and fragmented by private property and money. Especially in its bourgeois mode, it denies everything that is characteristically human. That is why, as Marx said (*Capital*, volume 3), it was not "worthy and appropriate for our human nature." Human productive powers are encased within social forms alien to humanity, forms which restrict and pervert their content. All the struggles of society may be seen as expressing the efforts of this human content to free itself from its inhuman shell. To live humanly means undertaking as a conscious piece of work the formation of a free association of social individuals. (It is interesting to recall the famous words of Montaigne: "To live properly is our greatest masterpiece.")

So Marx did not study an economic system called "capitalism" and seek its replacement by a different one called "socialism." His subject was capital, which stands over us all as an omnipotent, inhuman social power, but which is the falsified form of truly human social relations. It determines the way that humans treat each other, and themselves, not as free ends in themselves, but as mere means, as things. Conversely, things—for example money or machines—take on the character of subjects, dominating individual human lives. The life activities of individuals, their human creative potentials, are subsumed under these inhuman powers, and are turned into enemies of their own humanity. In chapter 1 of *Capital*, Marx describes this as "insane" (*verrückte*).

Implied in every part of Marx's study of capital is the possibility of our emancipation from it, and this went far beyond the many schemes and Utopias which went under the names "socialism" and "communism" long before Marx came on the scene. Rather, his work is directed to clearing a way through the ideological rubble, which blocks the path of human liberation. The producers of wealth, those engaged in human creative life activities, can take conscious control over their productive powers. Then, the free development of each individual will become the condition for the free development of all.[2]

At the end of the twentieth century, in some ways for the first time, we can see the possibility that these fundamental notions of Marx, can be realized, not just in our heads, but within the horrors of global capital itself. The scale, global scope, and speed of technological advance have brought misery to millions and increased the dangers for the survival of human life posed by the continued power of capital. But they have also given us the material potential to answer many of our traditional difficulties. If we search for universal human emancipation from private property we will begin to find the potential for freedom within the forms of the globalized world order. Theorists in the "postmodern" fashion insist that the many separate forms of resistance to "neoliberal" economic policies and their attacks on human values can never amount to a wholesale re-creation of truly human life, and they point with delight to the collapse of the old "Marxist" dogmas. On the contrary, this collapse gives us the chance to "strip off the mystical veil," which hides the reality of these struggles, and to reveal their meaning. Contained implicitly in each of them is the striving for "universal human emancipation" against the inhuman shell in which it is imprisoned.

But we can never become conscious of this meaning so long as we try to impose some external shape on reality. "Marxism" kept revolution and emancipation rigidly separate. Convinced that it was the sole proprietor of "socialist consciousness," and vigorously combating all competition, it tried to keep each struggle for freedom under tight control. It failed. Clinging to the old ideas of revolution makes it impossible to grasp any "prospect for socialism," even when it is right under your nose. And the social, political, and economic forms in which the new world makes its appearance cannot be predicted, for they can only emerge from the free creative activity of masses of people.

Some readers might be upset by the cavalier way that I dismiss or ignore the contributions of many authoritative writers who have discussed the work of Marx. Dozens of "interpretations" of his ideas are to be found on the library shelves, and some of them have undoubtedly been of great value, helping to keep Marx's writings in print and throwing light on his works. But, whether they were revolutionaries or academic "Marxologues," I am convinced that these writers are separated from Marx himself by a huge gulf. My aim in this book is not to add yet one more "interpretation" to this list, but to look at the inhumanity of the way the world lives and to see what light Marx's ideas throw on the struggle for humanity. (By the way, if anyone thinks the way the world lives is more or less OK, this book is not for them, and there is not the slightest chance of them understanding anything that Marx wrote. Sorry about that.)

The ideas of Karl Marx, declared dead by large numbers of "official" commentators, are only now coming into their own. Of course Marx can't answer the problems of the coming century. His task is rather to make it possible for those engaged in the coming struggles to comprehend the real significance of their own actions. The world does not need some new "program," to be realized by a historical computer. Instead, as the contradictions between humanity and inhumanity thrust millions of people forward to fight for control over their own lives, we have to redevelop the ability to grasp the new world within these struggles. Whatever their immediate aims, they are actually struggles for humanity against the inhuman power of capital.

But for that, a lot of thinking is necessary, and for that two opposite tendencies must be avoided. On the one hand, those who try to talk in the language of the old "Marxist" tradition are walling themselves off from seeing the significance of the newer forms of struggle. On the other hand, those well-meaning activists, who imagine that their devotion makes it unnecessary to do more than adopt some clever slogans, will end up adapting them to the existing social order.

Marx's ideas are totally foreign to every kind of dogmatism. He grasps his own work as the conscious expression of the battle for universal human emancipation. At bottom, the old order of oppression and exploitation is held in place by ideological and spiritual forces, which make brutality look "natural." The drive to be human has to break through the categories which form the framework of this prison of lies. That is why the battle for freedom cannot get to the heart of this monster without the deepest and most radical critique of the entire tradition of thought in which the history of class society found its expression.

If those of us who have survived from the "old" socialist movement can listen to Marx critically, he might yet help a new generation to go beyond him and to break through the "mind-forged manacles" which have bound us all for too long.

NOTES

1. In *Marx at the Millennium* (London: Pluto, 1996), I tried to show how Marx's revolutionary humanism had been completely lost in the Marxist tradition, even while Marx was still alive, and how relevant it was to the problems of our time. See also my paper, "Friedrich Engels and Marx's Critique of Political Economy," *Capital and Class* 62 (June 1997).

2. To get back to Marx's conception of what a human relation between individuals and social relation would be like, his continuity–discontinuity with Hegel is very important. "Marxism" got this completely wrong. For some ideas about this, see my contribution "Hegel, Economics and Marx's Capital," in *History, Economic History and the Future of Marxism: Essays in Memory of Tom Kemp* (Porcupine, 1996).

Chapter Two

Marx versus Historical Materialism

This title is not merely intended to provoke. It also aims to draw attention to the direct opposition between the body of theory traditionally known as "Marxism," and the essence of the work of Karl Marx. If you try to discuss what Marx was doing, without placing the struggle for his conception of communism as a "truly human society" right at the center of the picture, you surely falsify him. But that is precisely what "Marxism" does. Elsewhere,[1] I have discussed the significance of this contrast for Marx's work as a whole. Here, I concentrate on showing how far the "Marxist" tradition has misread Marx's conception of history.

I believe it is vitally necessary for this discrepancy to be made explicit. The falsification deeply embedded in traditional accounts of Marx's ideas, particularly of his understanding of historical development, is a major obstacle to the regeneration of the revolutionary tradition. "Marxism" was an attempt to set up a philosophical doctrine, a philosophy of history, which would explain how society made transitions from one stage to another. This misunderstanding obscured what was crucial for everything Marx did: the necessity for social consciousness to break out of its existing, fetishized forms to the level necessary for communism. This was not a matter of replacing one way of thinking with another, for it implied what Marx called "the alteration of humans on a mass scale."[2] Instead of this understanding of the revolutionary transformation of humanity, "Marxism" set up a system of thinking which assigns to special people—radical philosophers, or social scientists, or economists, or the Marxist Party—the task of "interpreting the world in various ways" on behalf of the rest of us. In a quite separate operation, their conclusions could then be communicated to the benighted masses.

The basic notion of historical materialism is well known. Georgi Plekhanov, one of its chief founders, puts it like this:

> (I)t is the economic system of any people that determines its social structure, the latter, in its turn, determining its political and religious structures and the like. . . . (T)he fundamental cause of any social evolution, and consequently of any social advance, being the struggle man wages against Nature for his own existence. . . . Marx's fundamental idea can be summed up as follows: 1) the production relations determine all other relations existing among people in their social life. 2) the production relations are, in their turn, determined by the state of the productive forces.[3]

> The basic principle of the materialist explanation of history is that men's thinking is conditioned by their being, or that in the historical process, the course of the development of ideas is determined, in the final analysis, by the course of development of economic relations.[4]

So, whatever the details of the mechanisms proposed by any of its many versions, historical materialism claims to be a way of *explaining history*. It deals with the causes of social evolution, stressing that history is governed by necessary laws, laws that are as immutable as laws of nature.

When Plekhanov talked about "materialism," he wanted to conjure up those eighteenth-century French thinkers like Holbach and Helvetius, who argued that human thoughts and actions had their roots in material conditions of the lives of individuals. What they called "matter," defined as "what acts in one way or another on our senses," caused us to feel and think, and so to act, in specific ways. Plekhanov and Kautsky thought that Marx's "materialist conception of history" was an extension of this outlook to the explanation of history. In his eagerness to extirpate all forms of idealism, one of their disciples, V. I. Lenin, was led to write about "the analysis of material social relations . . . that take shape without passing through man's consciousness."[5]

Historical materialists "explain" the transition from one stage of social development to another by the conflict between productive forces and social relations. Some practitioners here take productive forces to mean a discrete mixture of two things: means of production plus labor power.[6] The question they ignore is *why* are they two? Here are the two aspects of social life, one the human power to produce, the other the social connections within which this power operates. But why are they separate? Why are they at war with each other?

If you explain something, you have to stand outside it. A "materialist" explanation involves hypotheses about how some things external to the explainer cause other external things to happen. Here is the basic paradox: when the object to be explained is human history, it includes the wills and consciousnesses of the historical agents, not to mention the will and consciousness of the explainer. In general, they considered historical forces as determining the changes in social forms, as though history had nothing to do with the strivings of living men and women. Many devotees of historical materialism believed strongly in a socialist future and devoted their lives to struggling for it. Did they stand outside the causal process they imagined governed history, somehow immune to its influences?

Some might think that Plekhanov's statement of historical materialism does not give a fair account of the theory. What about other, more sophisticated "Marxisms"? However, I think that Plekhanov, for all his crudity, actually gets to the heart of the matter. At any rate, he has the not inconsiderable merit of stating clearly just what he means. Since his opinions formed the basis for the outlook of Lenin and his followers, and therefore came to predominate in the Communist International, their influence on all later work is undeniable. When Stalin produced his obscene caricature, *Dialectical and Historical Materialism*, in 1938, Plekhanov certainly provided him with his model, one well adapted to bureaucratic requirements.

So, while not everybody using the term "historical materialism" means exactly the same thing by it, they all have at least one thing in common: they each have in mind a way of explaining history. This also applies to the various schools of "Western Marxism," who often use the expression, although, they lack Plekhanov's virtue of spelling out just what they think it means. (Karl Marx himself, let us recall, never used the term at all.)

Lukacs' *History and Class Consciousness*, the origin of all such thinking, contains his famous lecture "On the Changing Function of Historical Materialism," delivered in 1919 to his Budapest Institute for Research into Historical Materialism. Early in the lecture, he comes near to giving a kind of definition:

> What is historical materialism? It is no doubt a scientific method by which to comprehend the events of the past and to grasp their true nature. In contrast to the historical methods of the bourgeoisie, however, it also permits us to view the present historically and hence scientifically, so that we can penetrate beneath the surface and perceive the profounder historical forces which in reality control events.[7]

But what "forces" are these? How do they "control events"? Why are they "beneath the surface"? Although Lukacs goes on to relate this to his conception of "proletarian class consciousness," (by which, do not forget, he does *not* mean the consciousness of the working class), he does not take issue with Plekhanov's ideas. But then, from the time he joined the Communist Party,

Lukacs was incapable of disagreeing openly with Lenin and thus, on this topic, with Plekhanov.

The story of the Frankfurt School is more complex. Before 1933, when they considered themselves Marxists, they used the term historical materialism fairly frequently, although assuming its meaning to be too well known to their learned readers to require elaboration. Later, as they moved to the right along their various trajectories, they expressed differences with the theory, but still without explaining exactly what they were disagreeing with.

In 1932, within a few months of the first publication of Marx's *Paris Manuscripts*, Herbert Marcuse's extraordinary essay on them appeared. It is one of his most brilliant works, and undoubtedly completely original, since nobody had yet commented on the *Manuscripts*.[8] But we would search it in vain for a direct reference to the topic announced in its title: "New Sources of the Foundations of Historical Materialism." When *Reason and Revolution* came out in 1936, Marcuse had just as little to say about the subject.[9] Nor is his 1958 *Soviet Marxism: A Critical Analysis*[10] any more helpful on this point. In that book he treats Stalinist "theory" as a kind of Marxism, although he sometimes hints at its great distance from Marx himself, and Marx's own ideas are not discussed in detail.

Finally, let us mention two of the later representatives of the Frankfurt School. Jurgens Habermas, who once wrote extensively on historical materialism, clearly assumed it to be a theoretical explanation of history. Significantly, he recommends Stalin's 1938 essay as "a handbook of historical materialism."[11] Alfred Schmidt's *History and Structure* is an attack upon Althusser's antihumanist adherence to the Plekhanov story. He declares that his aim is to speak about "the cognitive primacy of the logical over the historical, without abandoning the materialist basis."[12] I cannot claim to have understood what this means. Maybe it is something like the view I am arguing for in this article, but I am not sure.

Marxism believed that it possessed a theory of history, a set of general explanatory ideas to "guide revolutionary practice," while the theory's truth remained essentially outside any kind of practice. Of course, Marx himself is sometimes interested in explaining the world, but this is never his primary concern. His famous declaration that "the point is to change" the world is not a recommendation to alternate a bit of thinking with some "practice," although that is the way some Marxists understood it. (Generally, by "practice," they just meant "activity.") It is an insistence that the objective truth of thinking is essentially bound up with the relations between human beings.[13] (See Aristotle's use of the word *praxis*.) That is what I mean when I argue, in *Marx at the Millennium*, that Marx *did not have a theory*.

Certainly, he is keenly interested in theoretical ideas. But when he examines a theory, it is to criticize its categories, and to investigate them as symptoms of social illness. And why does history need explanation? *Only because it is not made consciously.* Some time ago, many people gave up the idea that the course of history is determined by God's will, and accepted that it can only be made by the willed acts of living men and women. But then we are faced with a problem: why are the outcomes of these acts so different from what any of the actors envisaged? History appears to be something that happens to us, not something we do. God's ways used to be beyond our understanding, but now historical theory thinks it can penetrate the mystery of historical development. However, it can't explain the source of that mystery, since its own categories are taken uncritically from the existing setup. Marx's task is not just to solve this riddle "in theory," but to uncover the reasons why our way of life is shrouded in mystery. Only then can he ask: what must we do to live otherwise?

In the light of the outcome of the French Revolution, the questions which Hegel asked also involved the relation between scientific thought and the world it tried to explain. He answered in terms of the cunning irony of History. Spirit, "substance which is also subject," "the 'I' that is 'we,' the 'we' that is 'I,'"[14] worked out its dialectical logic, "behind the backs" of individual consciousnesses. Although we have made society ourselves, it appears to us as if it were beyond ordinary thought, under the control of alien powers. Only philosophy, thought Hegel, can reveal what the human Spirit has achieved, and this only after Spirit's work is done, when it is too late for the philosopher to tell anybody what to do about it.

The old scenario about "Hegel the idealist" and "Marx the materialist," in which Hegel was dressed up as Bishop Berkeley, and Marx as Holbach, or even as John Locke, totally mystified the relation between Marx and Hegel. For Marx, it was precisely Hegel's idealism, which enabled him to give an account of history, that is, history in its modern, "alienated" form. This was because Hegel's account was itself "alienated," set against its object.

> Hegel . . . has only found the abstract, logical, speculative expression for the movement of history, which is not yet the real history of man as a given subject, but only the act of creation, the history of the origin of man.[15]

Marx agreed with Hegel that that history had indeed operated blindly hitherto, but contended that this was because it was the history of a false, inhuman way of life. A "truly human" life, now coming into being, will be quite different. Our social relations—and, centrally, our own consciousness of them and of ourselves—will be transparent to us. This was where Marx's critique of Hegel's dialectic began. A theory, even one as powerful as that of Hegel, assumes that its object is inevitably just what it is:

> For it is not what is that makes us irascible and resentful, but the fact that it is not as it ought to be. But if we recognise that it is as it must be, ie that it is not arbitrariness and chance, then we also recognise that it is as it ought to be.[16]

"Critique" is a word which occurs in the title of almost all of Marx's major works. Marx turns questions of theory against the reality of the life which gives rise to them, demonstrating that this reality is *inhuman*. For him, the critique of philosophy, like the critique of religion,

> ends with the teaching that man is the highest being for man, hence with the categorical imperative to overthrow all relations in which man is a debased. enslaved, forsaken, despicable being.[17]

Any attempt to describe this contradictory world in a theory is certain to run into difficulties. But these deficiencies may be taken as signals that questions had been raised which no theory is able to answer. This is because to answer them would mean making actual changes in the world, not just in our heads. Then theory's equipment, the "weapons of criticism," must be exchanged for "the criticism of weapons." Let us take two examples of critique, frequently linked by Marx: first religion and then economics.

He did not devote any effort to finding out whether religious beliefs were "true," but he was very interested in the question: why do people so obviously show a need to believe them? He concluded that society produces religion, "an inverted world-consciousness," because it is "an inverted world." Religion is the heart of the world, so its very existence demonstrates that this is a world with no heart.[18]

Marx admired the political economists who strove to explain why economic life works in the way it does. But the very existence of political economy as a science pointed to a mystery at the core of those economic activities in which everybody is engaged, which nobody can control, and which therefore are at the foundation of all social life. Here is where Adam Smith's "invisible hand" does its work, the counterpart to Hegel's Spirit. However, political economy cannot imagine the possibility of a human way of living. (Religion says it knows another way, but that it is not, unfortunately, to be found in this world.)

This is the starting point of Marx's critiques of religion, of socialism, of Hegel's dialectic and of political economy. A critique demands an explicit standpoint, a criterion against which to measure the object under criticism. Marx describes his standpoint as that of "human society and social human-ity."[19] In this, he differs from theorists, the people whose main aim is "expla-nation." They can never evade the task of justifying their premises, and this always leads them into a never-ending spiral of explanations. Above all, they can never explain themselves. Marx starts off with the knowledge that hu-manity is socially self-creating, while it lives in a fashion that directly denies this. This standpoint does not itself need justification, for it is the condition for discussing anything at all. Marx knew a criterion against which to judge history, which he grasped as the process of struggle through which "socialised humanity" and its self-knowledge bring themselves into being. That is why he can say that "communism is the riddle of history solved, and knows itself to be this solution."[20]

Someone who attempts to "explain" history, or, indeed, to do any kind of "social science," tells us that some human action had "necessarily" to take the form it did. But we, in turn, have the right to ask the scientist: "how do you know?" If people's actions are "determined" by some necessity outside them, are you not yourself, along with your "objectivity," "determined" by the same forces? Marxism insisted on calling Marx's conception of history "material-ist." But Marx's materialism has nothing to do with "matter" and "mind," nor is it a "theory of knowledge."[21] Marx knew that the history he investigated was the process of alienated social life, in which consciousness was inhumanly constrained by social being. Knowledge of this process is not something ex-ternal to it, but itself developed historically in the struggle of living men and women to break out of these constraints. Thus Marx's critical science was a part of the coming-to-be of real, of human, self-consciousness. That is why it presaged the coming-to-be of real, human, self-created social life.

Theoretical science, in the form of a particular scientific study, aims to ex-plain some particular aspect of the world. Such a science cannot itself have a scientific explanation, any more than Utopia could explain itself. The great Utopians thought of themselves as scientific students of history. But their standpoint was that of "the isolated individual," not situated within the actual world, but observing it from the outside. Utopianism told the world what it ought to be like. Thus their "materialist doctrine must . . . divide society into two parts, one of which is superior to society."[22]

Once Marx had discovered the historic role of the proletariat, he could clearly set out his alternative to this attitude:

> But in the measure that society moves forward, and with it the struggle of the pro-letariat assumes clearer outlines, they [the "socialists"] no longer need to seek sci-ence in their minds; they have only to take note of what is happening before their

eyes, and become its mouthpiece. So long as they look for science and merely make systems, so long as they are at the beginning of the struggle, they see in poverty nothing but poverty, without seeing in it the revolutionary, subversive side, which will overthrow the old society. From the moment they see this side, science, which is produced by the historical movement and associating itself consciously with it, has ceased to be doctrinaire and has become revolutionary.[23]

Science which takes immediate—inhuman—appearance as its given object cannot envisage a human kind of world. Its task is to show, by means of some mental image or logical model, that this appearance has to be just as it is. Hegel's dialectic aimed to reconstruct within his system the development of the object itself, and of its relations with other objects. This was a huge advance. However, Hegel only saw these relations as ideas. Thus his dialectic, too, was limited, and later came "to transfigure and glorify what exists (*verklären das Bestehende*)."[24]

Marx's standpoint, "human society and social humanity," enables him to do something quite different. He traces the inner coherence of his object— money, say, or the State, or the class struggle. Then he can allow its inhuman, brutal meaning, its hostility to a truly human life, to shine through the appearance of "naturalness" and inevitability. Its own development lights up the road which will lead us to its abolition.

Look again at Marx's view of religion. People's belief in another, heavenly, world points to the inverted, inhuman character of this earthly one. That tells us about religion, but we still have to understand theology, the scientific activity of systematizing and formalizing this belief. Marx, following Feuerbach, grasped this activity as itself a symptom of alienation. Theology, like political economy and historiography, is an upside-down expression of socialized humanity's efforts to become conscious of its own self-creation.

Marx knew that human history was self-creation, "the creation of man through human labor . . . the emergence of nature for man."[25] No theory of history whose horizons are limited by bourgeois society can know this. When it tries to describe the events of human self-creation, it remains imprisoned within a mental world that denies that such a process is possible. For communism, says Marx, "the entire movement of history, just as its actual act of genesis . . . is, therefore, also for its thinking consciousness the comprehended and known process of its becoming."[26]

Historians are spokespersons for the process in which humanity comes to be, creates itself and becomes conscious of itself, "within alienation." But this process can only be grasped in terms of humanity as a united whole, and that unity is beyond their horizons. Humanity in its inhuman form appears as a collection of incommensurable, mutually incomprehensible, mutually hostile fragments. That is why, imprisoned within alienation, historians cannot know what they are doing. The historical movements cannot be seen for what they really are: the life activities of individual human beings, struggling to free themselves. The "historical forces," which historical materialism thinks dominate their lives, are seen as *subjects*, while the individuals whose lives are so determined are treated as mere objects. This inversion characterizes the way life is lived and the way it appears, but it is not in accordance with the nature of humanity.

Because he sees humanity as self-producing, Marx knows that productive forces are really the essential capacity of humans to act humanly, that is, to create their own lives. "Man makes his life activity itself the object of his will and of his consciousness."[27] These productive powers grow inside social relations which simultaneously promote and deny human creativity, which pervert and distort it, that is, which are alien to humanity. The successive forms of society are given to each generation, but the development of human productive powers make possible the overthrow of all such forms.

Thus the key conflict is between productive powers, which are potentially free, and social relations which appear in the form of alien, oppressive forces. In a human society, productive forces and social relations would be "two different aspects of the development of the social individual."[28] Today, however, the battle between them permeates every phase of human life. It secretes the poison which runs through the heart of every individual. Communism is the task of transcending this conflict, moving toward a society in which individuals will be able consciously to make their own social relations, so that "the individuals obtain their freedom in and through their association."[29]

There has been considerable controversy among Marxists about the stages through which history has passed. A dogmatic historical materialism fixes an agenda for the movement from slavery, to feudalism, to capitalism, and—only after the completion of this list—to socialism. Those who help to move the list along, are labeled "progressive," while those who call for socialism "before its time," like those classes or nations whose existence does not fit into the schedule, have to be crushed. Many people have pointed out that Marx himself has no such "unilinear" notion. But what is not emphasized sufficiently is that, in that famous passage from the 1859 preface to *The Critique of Political Economy*, which Marx described as the "guideline" (*Leitfaden*) for his study of political economy, he was discussing human "prehistory," history in its inhuman shape.

The Communist Manifesto famously declared that "the history of all hitherto existing society is the history of class struggles." But Marx never forgot that class antagonism is itself one of the manifestations of alienation. "Personal interests always develop, against the will of the individuals, into class interests, into common interests which acquire independent existence in relation to the individual persons."[30]

Every analogy between the proletariat and earlier classes is potentially misleading. The proletariat is unique among classes, in that its historic role is to do away with itself. It is "a class . . . which has no longer any particular class interest to assert against a ruling class."[31] It is the "universal class," precisely because it is "the complete loss of man, and hence can win itself only through the complete rewinning of man."[32] In the course of this upheaval, it could and must "succeed in ridding itself of all the muck of ages and become fitted to found society anew."[33] It challenges the "laws of history" by forming itself into the historical subject.

Marx's famous "base and superstructure" metaphor was distorted by historical materialism into a blind causal mechanism. However, on the rare occasion when Marx used it, he referred solely to that "prehistory," where economic activity dominated by self-interest fragments communal life. In "civil society," "the field of conflict . . . between private interests and particular concerns of the community,"[34] community is shattered. On the one hand, economic activities are perverted, from expressions of human creativity into forms of antagonism, oppression, and exploitation. Forms of life that purport to represent the community do so falsely. So, for instance, Marx claims that the State is "the illusory community."[35] Law and politics, and institutions and ideological forms corresponding to them—religion, art, and philosophy—exist as a "superstructure" upon a fragmented economic basis.

Marx said that "consciousness is explained by the contradictions of material life," that it is "determined" by "social being," and that "the mode of production of material life conditions the general process of social, political and intellectual life." Historical materialism thought that these phrases described immutable laws of human development. Actually, of course, these are features of our inhuman life, its developing essence. While state, law, family, religion, and all other antagonistic forms of life are our own work, these forms of our own social relations confront us as foreign powers, not merely "independent of the will" of individuals, but dominating them as enemies. All history is the outcome of conscious human action. But when human beings live inhumanly, their own social development appears as something outside their control. "The tradition of all the dead generations weighs like a nightmare (*Alp*) on the brain of the living."[36] Alienated history, Hegel's "slaughter-bench of nations,"[37] can appear only as a nightmare.

Only if social relations were consciously made, opening up the space in which individual human creative potentialities can develop, would they be transparent to us. In such a "true community," there would be no "superstructure," and therefore no "basis." Humans freely associating could freely create their own social and individual lives. Living in such a world, individuals could begin to grasp that history was their own process of origin, just as they would see nature as "their own, inorganic, body."[38]

History has never been made by puppets, with "laws of history" pulling the strings. Living men and women have always struggled to tackle the problems of their time. But, constrained by social forms which were both their own handiwork and alien to them, they were unable to see how these problems could be overcome. This is how Marx describes the resulting appearance of historical necessity:

> This process of inversion is merely an historical necessity, merely a necessity for the development of the productive forces from a definite historical point of departure, or basis. In no way is it an absolute necessity of production; it is rather a transitory (*verschwindene*) one, and the result and (immanent) aim of this process is to transcend this basis itself and this form of the process.[39]

When society no longer appears as an alien "second nature," whose laws seem to be immutable, we shall get to grips with the problems of living as part of "first nature," that is, of nature. Natural necessity would remain, of course, to be studied by natural science, to be the collaborator with technology in satisfying human needs. But historical necessity would gradually be overcome and transformed. If this is "materialism," it is certainly not the "old materialism," whose standpoint was that of "single individuals and of 'civil society.'"[40]

In the bourgeois epoch, the possibility arose of creating a new way of living. Within the antagonistic forms of the alienated world, "the productive forces developing within bourgeois society" have already created "the material conditions for a solution of this antagonism," for a world of "free men, working with the means of production held in common, and expending their many different forms of labor-power in full self-awareness as one single social labor-force."[41]

In such a truly human world, a world without "superstructure," without the distortions resulting from the clash between social relations and human forces of production, without the opposition of means of production to labor power, human life would be self-consciously self-created. We could increasingly learn how to talk over the conflicts which have always arisen as part of social life, and collectively make possible the free development of individuality. This movement toward freedom would mean that our social self-consciousness could increasingly "determine" our "social being." Historical materialism only describes the movement of alienated, life, but Marx views the whole of history as a process of overcoming alienation, and that, for him, is the point of studying it.

Relationships of personal dependence (which originally arise quite spontaneously) are the first forms of society. . . . Personal independence based upon dependence mediated by things is the second great form, and only in it is a system of general social exchange of matter, a system of universal relations, universal requirements and universal capacities formed. Free individuality, based on the universal development of the individuals and the subordination of their communal, social productivity, which is the social possession, is the third stage.[42]

Historical materialism transformed a page from the 1859 preface into a "theory of history," while in fact it refers only to the "second stage" of Marx's scheme. For him, the real importance of studying this stage of alienation, the prehistory of humanity, was to help us understand how it had prepared the ground for that "third stage," the stage of human freedom, the beginning of our real conscious history.

Herein lies the direct opposition of Marx to historical materialism. The theorists of Marxism wanted to explain the past or predict the future. But Marx was not chiefly interested in either of these activities. Instead, he studied history, as he studied everything else, to illuminate the struggle between a way of life which required explanation and one which would be "worthy of our human nature."[43]

NOTES

1. Cyril Smith, *Marx at the Millennium* (Chicago, Ill.: Pluto, 1996).

2. *German Ideology: Marx-Engels Collected Works (MECW)*, Vol. 5 (Moscow: Progress Publishers), 53.

3. Georgi Plekhanov, *Selected Philosophical Works*, Vol. II (Moscow: Progress Publishers), 617.

4. Plekhanov, *Selected Philosophical Works*, Vol. III, 45.

5. Vladimir Lenin, *What the "Friends of the People" Are: Collected Works* (Moscow: Progress Publishers), Vol. 1, 140.

6. For example, see G. A. Cohen, *Karl Marx's Theory of History: A Defence* (New York: Oxford University Press, 2000), 32.

7. Georgi Lukacs, *History and Class Consciousness*, trans. R. Livingstone (London: Merlin Press, 1971), 224.

8. Reprinted in H. Marcuse, *Studies in Critical Philosophy* (London: NLB, 1972).

9. H. Marcuse, *Reason and Revolution* (London: Oxford University Press, 1936).

10. H. Marcuse, *Soviet Marxism: A Critical Analysis* (New York: Columbia University Press, 1958).

11. J. Habermas, "Towards a Reconstruction of Historical Materialism," in *Communication and the Evolution of Society*, trans. T. McCarthy (Boston: Beacon Press, 1979).

12. Alfred Schmidt, *History and Structure: An Essay in Hegelian, Marxist and Structuralist Theories of History* (Boston: MIT Press, 1981), 109.

13. Second Thesis on Feuerbach.

14. G. Hegel, *Phenomenology of Spirit,* trans. H. Kainz (University Park: Pennsylvania State University Press, 1994), 101.

15. *Paris Manuscripts: Marx-Engels Selected Works (MECW)*, Vol. 3: 329

16. Hegel, *The German Constitution: In Hegel's Political Writings* (Knox and Pelczinski), 145.

17. Marx, *Contribution to the Critique of Hegel's Philosophy of Law: Introduction MECW*, Vol. 3: 182.

18. *MECW* , Vol. 3: 175.

19. Tenth Thesis on Feuerbach.

20. *Paris Manuscripts, MECW*, 3: 296–97.

21. Neither Hegel nor Marx can have a "theory of knowledge." They both know that knowledge is a sociohistorical movement. A "theory" of this movement would have to include a "theory" of itself, and that is impossible for any "theory."

22. Third Thesis on Feuerbach.

23. *The Poverty of Philosophy, MECW*, Vol. 6: 177–78.

24. *Capital* Volume 1, Afterword to the Second Edition, 103.

25. *Paris Manuscripts, MECW*, Vol. 3: 305.

26. *Paris Manuscripts, MECW*, Vol. 3: 297.

27. *Paris Manuscripts, MECW*, Vol. 3: 276.

28. *Grundrisse, MECW*, Vol. 29: 92.

29. *German Ideology, MECW*, Vol. 5: 78.

30. *German Ideology, MECW*, Vol. 5: 245.

31. *German Ideology, MECW*, Vol. 5: 77.

32. *Contribution to the Critique of Hegel's Philosophy of Law: Introduction. MECW*, Vol. 3: 186.

33. *German Ideology, MECW,* Vol. 5: 53.

34. Hegel, *Philosophy of Right*, para. 289, Z.

35. *German Ideology. MECW*, Vol. 5: 46.

36. *Eighteenth Brumaire of Louis Napoleon, MECW*, Vol. 11:103.

37. Hegel, *Philosophy of World History*, Introduction.

38. *Paris Manuscripts. MECW*, Vol. 3: 275–76.

39. *Grundrisse, MECW*, Vol. 29: 210.

40. Ninth Thesis on Feuerbach

41. *Capital* Volume 1: 171.

42. *Grundrisse, MECW*, Vol. 28: 95.

43. *Capital*, Vol. 3: 959.

Chapter Three

The Communist Manifesto
after 150 Years

How can a book written in one historical epoch have a meaning for another? If the author has tried to answer the questions posed by the way of life of the people around him, what can these answers mean for those living under changed conditions and facing quite different questions?[1] In the case of Karl Marx, we have yet another barrier to penetrate. At the end of the twentieth century, when we pick up a text like the *Manifesto*, we already have in our minds what "everybody knows" about it. Before we even glance at its pages, distorting spectacles have been placed on our noses by the tradition known as "Marxism." And, even today, Stalinism's obscene misuse of the word "communism" still colors everything we read.

The upholders of "Marxism" thought of it as a science, and at the same time declared it to be a complete world outlook. These claims, which clearly contradict each other, make it impossible to understand the task Marx set himself, a task that, by its very nature, no body of "theory" could complete. For his aim was no less than to make possible "the development of communist consciousness on a mass scale." It was not enough just to prepare the overthrow of the ruling class. This particular revolution required "the alteration of humans on a mass scale . . . because the class overthrowing (the ruling class) can only in a revolution succeed in ridding itself of all the muck of ages."[2]

So the first step was not a "political theory," not a "model of society," not simply a call for revolution, but a conception of *humanity*. What Marx aimed at was simultaneously a science that comprehended human development, an understanding of how that development had become imprisoned within social forms that denied humanity, and a knowledge of the way that humanity was to struggle to liberate itself from that prison. Indeed, only through the struggle for liberation could we understand what humanity was. In essence, it was that "ensemble of social relations,"[3] which made possible free, collective, self-creation. He showed how modern social relations fragmented society and formed a barrier to our potential for freedom, while at the same time providing the conditions for freedom to be actualized.

If we want to understand the *Manifesto*, we must read it as an early attempt to tackle all of these issues, set within the framework of a political statement. More clearly than any other of its author's works, it contradicts the "Marxist" representation of Marx as a "philosopher," an "economist," a "sociologist," a "theorist of history," or any other kind of "social scientist." To grasp what he was doing, we have to break through all the efforts of academic thinking to separate knowledge from the collective self-transformation of humanity. Indeed, one of the tasks of the *Manifesto* is to lay bare the source of all such thinking, finding it precisely within humanity's inhuman—alienated— condition. Marx's science situates itself inside the struggle to transform our entire way of living.

Of course, in the past fifteen decades, the forms of capital and the conditions of the working class have changed profoundly in innumerable ways. But we still live in the same historical epoch as Marx, and, if we listen to what he has to say, we shall discover him to be our contemporary. So let us attempt to remove those "Marxist" spectacles, which prevented us from seeing just how original was Marx's conception. Then, perhaps, we shall be able to confront this product of nineteenth-century Western Europe with the agonizing problems of today's "globalized" society. The essence of the *Manifesto* is not merely relevant for our time; it is vital for us, if humanity is to grope its way forward.

THE COMMUNIST LEAGUE

The *Communist Manifesto* was written in a Europe that was on the eve of the revolutionary upheavals of 1848, and that also still lived in the shadow of the revolutionary struggles of 1789–1815. It is a response to both of these, the storm to come and the one that had passed. Between 1844 and 1847, in Berlin, Brussels, Paris, and Manchester, Marx and Engels had encountered the ideas of the various groups of socialists and communists, and had also studied the organizations of the rapidly growing working class. Hitherto, these two, socialism and the working class, had been quite separate from, or even hostile to each other. The achievement of the *Manifesto* was to establish the foundations on which they could be united and transformed.

From this work came a new conception of communism, situated within the historical context of their time. As the *Manifesto* puts it, communism was not "based on ideas or principles that have been invented or discovered by this or that would-be universal reformer." (*Communist Manifesto. MECW*, vol. 6, 498.) It had to be seen as the culmination and meaning of working-class struggle, and this struggle itself provided the key to understanding the existing economic relations. The "Marxists" thought they found in the *Manifesto* a "theoretical" analysis of "capitalism" and a "theory of history." Actually, Marx was scornful of all pretence of having a "supra-historical theory of history."[4] He never used the word "capitalism" and spent his life writing a critique of the very idea of political economy.

Every line of the *Manifesto* is permeated with his conception of communism. This was not a plan for an ideal future social setup, worked out by some reforming genius, to be imposed on the world by his followers. Instead, it was to be the outcome of the development of the working-class movement itself, and therefore arose *within the existing social order*. Marx had turned toward the ideas of communism in 1844, Engels preceding him by two years. For three years, they discussed—and argued—with the many socialist and communist sects in Germany, France, Belgium, and England, but joined none of them. Then, in 1847 they decided to join together with some former members of one of these secret groups, the League of the Just.

The League, which was largely German, and which had mainly consisted of workers and artisans,[5] had more or less disappeared by that time. Its old members had outgrown the ideas of their leading figure, the heroic founder of the German workers' movement, Wilhelm Weitling, and come closer to Marx's view of communism. Marx and Engels, on the basis of their newfound ideas, resolved to bring these people together in a new kind of organization. On one thing they were quite determined: this was not going to be a secret society, like the conspiratorial sects that abounded throughout Europe. It would be an open organization, with a clearly expounded program and outlook. The Communist League was formed at a conference in London, in the summer of 1847. A newspaper, the *Kommunistische Zeitschrift*, issued by the London branch in September of that year, carried the slogan "Proletarians of all Lands, Unite!" In November, a second conference assembled. After ten days of discussion, Marx was instructed to prepare a "Manifesto of the Communist Party," based upon Engels' draft "catechism," the *Principles of Communism*. Marx's work was not finished until early in February 1848. (As usual, he made slow progress in carrying out their instructions, and the delay brought forth an angry letter from the Committee.) Before printing was complete, the insurrection had broken out in Paris.

What role did the Communist League play in the revolutionary events of 1848–49? As an organization, almost none. Its individual members, of course, were to the fore in many parts of Europe. Marx and Engels, in particular were leading figures in the Rhineland, where they produced the *Neue Rheinische Zeitung*. But, as a body, the League itself did not function during those stormy years. In 1850, after the defeat of the movement, exiles in London made an attempt to re-form it, but soon a fierce dispute broke out among them. Willich, Schapper, and others dreamed that the revolutionary struggle would soon break out again. Marx and Engels and their supporters were convinced that the revolutionary wave had passed, and that a long period of development of capital would ensue. In 1851, leading members of the League in the Rhineland were arrested and tried in Cologne. After that, the organization was allowed to disappear. Marx deliberately cut himself off from the exile groups, and did not resume active political involvement for the next twelve years.

THE MANIFESTO AND THE CLASS STRUGGLE

The first thing to note about this document is that it begins and ends with declarations of openness: "It is high time that Communists should openly . . . publish their aims. . . ." and "The Communists disdain to conceal their views and aims" (MECW 6). Marx was always totally opposed to the idea that social change could be brought about by some secret group, working behind the back of society. This tendency, identified with the heroic but ineffectual conspiracies of Auguste Blanqui and his friends, was also the target of Marx's much-misunderstood phrase "dictatorship of the proletariat," first used by him four years later. In "Marxism," the central meaning of this formula was badly distorted. Quite contrary to any modern connotation of tyranny, Marx wanted to stress that the *entire working class* must govern, as opposed to any secret group, however benevolent its intentions.

"The history of all hitherto existing society has been the history of class struggles."So runs the famous opening of the first section, "Bourgeois and Proletarians," but what does this mean? (Engels' 1888 footnote, excluding prehistory from this statement, does not really help.[6]) As is well known, the idea of class struggle as a way of explaining history was not invented by Marx, but had been employed by French bourgeois historians in the 1820s. Marx gives it a totally different content. For him, class struggles are *an aspect of alienated society*, and communism implies their disappearance.

It is quite wrong to read this section as if it presented history as a logical argument, with a deduction of the communist revolution as a conclusion. Ten years later, Marx depicted human history in terms of three great stages:

Relationships of personal dependence (which originally arise quite spontaneously) are the first forms of society. . . . Personal independence based upon dependence mediated by things is the second great form, and only in it is a system of general social exchange of matter, a system of universal relations, universal requirements and universal capacities formed. Free individuality, based on the universal development of the individuals and the subordination of their communal, social productivity, which is the social possession, is the third stage.[7]

Of course, in 1848, Marx was not able to put the matter so clearly, but already the essence of his point of view is precisely that expressed by these lines. The class struggle was for him a feature of the second of these "stages" only, and bourgeois society marked the end of this entire period. This was the phase of "alienated life," where individuals had no control over their own lives. Only in this stage could you speak about "historical laws," since individuals were not yet the governors of their social relations. The *Manifesto's* paean of praise for the achievements of the bourgeoisie refers to their (of course, involuntary) work, which prepares for the great advance of humanity to its "third stage," communism. This will see human beings living as "social individuals," "universally developed individuals," whose social relationships are their own communal relations, and therefore subjected to their own communal control."[8] Thus Marx's entire picture of the movement of history is bound up with his conception of a "truly human" society, and the obstacles to it within our existing way of life.

Marx does not present us with a static picture of bourgeois social relations, as a sociologist might try to do. Instead, he gives a succinct outline of the birth, development, and death of an oppressive and exploitative social order. He shows how "the bourgeoisie . . . has pitilessly torn asunder the motley feudal ties that bound man to his 'natural superiors,' and has left remaining no other nexus between man and man than 'callous cash payment'" (486–87). The class struggle, which has raged over the centuries, has been simplified by the modern bourgeoisie. "Society is splitting up more and more into two great hostile camps, into two great classes directly facing each other: Bourgeoisie and Proletariat" (MECW vol. 6: 485).

This opening section of the *Manifesto* is concerned with the joint historical development of these classes, including the struggle between them, and the stages of this process are related to the development of modern industry. Thus the huge advances of human productive powers since the eighteenth century have taken the form of the growth of "new conditions of oppression, new forms of struggle in place of the old ones" (487). The outcome is that "man is at last compelled to face with sober senses his real conditions of life and his relations with his kind." Just as the development of these "means of production and exchange" outgrew the feudal relations within which they had developed, now, the powers of modern industry have collided with the bourgeois relations that have "conjured them up" (489). Now, Marx describes the growth of the proletariat,

the class of laborers who live only so long as they find work, and who find work on as long as their labor increases capital. These laborers, who must sell

themselves piecemeal, are a commodity like every other article of commerce.
. . . Owing to the extensive use of machinery, the work of the proletarian has
lost all individual character, and consequently all charm for the workman. He
becomes an appendage of the machine. (490)

The account of wage labor given here is far from the developed analysis Marx
was able to make in *Grundrisse*, ten years later, and, after still another
decade's work, in *Capital*, but it still gets to the heart of the matter.

What is unprecedented about this particular form of class struggle, Marx
explains, is that it prepares the objective ground for the transcendence of
classes as such, and of all forms of oppression.

All the preceding classes that got the upper hand sought to fortify their already acquired status by subjecting society at large to their conditions of appropriation.
The proletarians cannot become masters of the productive forces of society except
by abolishing their own previous mode of appropriation, and thereby also every
other mode of appropriation. . . . The proletariat cannot raise itself up without the
whole superincumbent strata of official society being sprung into the air. (495)

Throughout the *Manifesto*, Marx stresses the "cosmopolitan character" of
bourgeois society, reflecting the development of a world market. "The need
of a constantly expanding market for its products chases the bourgeoisie over
the whole surface of the globe." It is because of this that the struggle of the
proletariat, while national "in form," is international "in substance" (495).

Marx's account of bourgeois society as the objective preparation for the
proletarian revolution is bound up with the emergence of the consciousness
necessary for the transformation of the whole of world society. The "Marxists" attributed to Marx a philosophical outlook called "historical materialism," a way of "explaining" the world. This was sometimes presented as a
mechanical model of history in which "material conditions" caused changes
in consciousness. But this directly contradicts what Marx himself was doing.
After all, was he not engaged in the struggle for the development of consciousness, and wasn't communism precisely the way for humanity to take
conscious charge of history?

Bourgeois society, the last possible form of the class struggle, had also to
bring forth the subjective elements needed for its conscious transcendence.
Central to this is "the organization of the proletarians into a class and consequently into a political party," and that means its *self*-organization. But that is
not all. In a vitally important paragraph, Marx describes how the breakup of
the old order, and of the ruling class itself, has another consequence:

A small section of the ruling class cuts itself adrift and joins the revolutionary
class, the class which holds the future in its hands . . . in particular a portion of

the bourgeois ideologists who have raised themselves to the level of comprehending the historical movement as a whole. (494)

This is a remarkable passage. These "bourgeois ideologists" undoubtedly include Marx and Engels themselves. In 1847, how many others could there have been? Never before had an author been able to put himself into the picture in this way, explaining the origin of his own work in terms of the objective conditions it was investigating. Thus the objective, material development of modern industry is bound up with the development of the understanding of the need to emancipate these forces from the perverting power of capital.

When Marx speaks of the proletariat, he does not mean the members of a sociological category, the collection of those who can be labeled as "wage earners." He is talking about a real movement, an objectively founded, living aspect of modern social life. People who sell their ability to labor find themselves involved in an antagonistic relation to the owners of capital, whether they like it or not, and whatever they may think. "The proletarian movement is the independent[9] movement of the immense majority in the interests of the immense majority" (495).

Obviously, many of the details of the picture of the world presented by Marx in 1848 are hardly to be found in the world of today. As Marx himself realized a short time later, his timescale was extremely foreshortened. But, 150 years on, it is amazing how many of its essential features are still at the heart of our problems.

THE ROLE OF THE COMMUNISTS

The second section, "Proletarians and Communists," largely consists of an imaginary dialogue with a bourgeois objector to the idea of communism. It begins by situating the Communists in Marx's picture of the development of the proletariat. Many of its ideas are drawn from the doctrines of previous socialist and communist groups, and also from Engels' draft. But, working from the standpoint set out in the previous section, he transforms them into something quite new.

The members of the League gave their declaration the title *Manifesto of the Communist Party*. They could not anticipate how much misunderstanding this word "party" would cause for future decades, when it had so changed its meaning. For Marx and his comrades, it certainly did not mean the type of bureaucratic structure with which we associate it today, but a section of society, a social-political trend. Again stressing the open, anticonspiratorial nature of communism, Marx declares

The Communists do not form a separate party opposed to other working-class parties. They have no interests separate and apart from those of the proletariat as a whole. They do not set up any sectarian principles of their own by which to shape and mould the proletarian movement. . . . The immediate aim of the Communists is the same as that of all the other proletarian parties: formation of the proletariat into a class, overthrow of the bourgeois supremacy, conquest of power by the proletariat. . . . The theory of the Communists may be summed up in the single sentence: Abolition of private property. (498)

Objects have been privately owned for millennia, so that individuals have been able to say of something, or even somebody, "this is mine." But the latest form of private property is different. *Capital* is "a collective product," set in motion only by "the united action of all members of society . . . not a personal, but a social power" (499). Abolishing this power, capital, is the only way to ensure that "accumulated labor becomes a means to widen, to enrich, to promote the existence of the laborer."

Marx goes on to summarize the communist critique of the false bourgeois conceptions of freedom, individuality, culture, the family, and education, attacking in particular the oppression of women within bourgeois society. After this, he outlines the nature of the proletarian revolution, "to raise the proletariat to the position of the ruling class, to win the battle of democracy," and identifies the resulting state with "the proletariat organised as the ruling class" (504).

The ten-point political program for the first steps of the revolution with which this section ends is interesting mainly for its surprisingly mild character. Clearly, Marx does not consider revolution as a sudden overnight transformation, resulting from some kind of coup d'état, however violent it might be. He refers to the situation following a prolonged historical transition, when "in the course of development class distinctions have disappeared and all production has been concentrated in the hands of a vast association of the whole nation" (504). Then, he anticipates, "the public power will lose its political character." The proletariat will have "abolished its own supremacy as a class. In place of the old bourgeois society, with its classes and class antagonisms, we shall have an association in which the free development of each is the condition for the free development of all" (506).

This latter sentence summarizes a world of ideas Marx has extracted and negated from the history of philosophy and political economy. It embodies his entire conception of what it means to live humanly. Potentially, humans can be free, but only when the freely created life of the whole of society is completely and visibly bound up with the growth of each individual. Private property stands as a barrier to such freedom.

The third section of the *Manifesto* deals scornfully with most of the previous socialist doctrines, all of which have by now long disappeared from history. However, its final pages refer to "Critical-Utopian Socialism and Communism" with great respect. Marx attributes the limitations of the work of Saint-Simon, Fourier, Owen, and others to the fact that it unconsciously reflected the "early undeveloped period . . . of the struggle between the proletariat and the bourgeoisie." While being "full of the most valuable materials for the enlightenment of the working class," they could see the proletariat only as "a class without any historical initiative or any independent political movement," as "the most suffering class." Because, in their time, "the economic situation . . . does not offer them the material conditions for the emancipation of the proletariat," they could do no more than "search after a new social science, after new social laws, that are to create these conditions." That is why they could be no more than "Utopians," who merely painted "fantastic pictures of future society" (515). In contrast to them, Marx insists that communism is a "real movement," not a dream.

THE SUBJECT OF HISTORY

Marx's problem was to discover the possibility for humanity, individually and collectively, to take conscious charge of its own life, and to find this possibility within bourgeois society. Communism would mean that humans would cease to be prisoners of their social relations, and begin purposively to make their own history. In other words, we should cease to be mere objects and start to live as subjects.

But how can history have a subject? The course of the twentieth century, especially its last decades, makes the idea seem quite ludicrous. The world presents the appearance of pure chaos, without the slightest sign of conscious direction or purpose. The lives of its inhabitants are evidently quite out of their control. At the same time as they are ever more closely bound together, they appear more and more like a collection "of single individuals and of civil society,"[10] at war with each other. In other words, they are *objects* rather than *subjects*. People living under capital, both bourgeois and proletarians, are governed by it; people are treated as things, and things have power over people. Capital, not the human individual, possesses subjectivity. Marx starts from the conviction that this way of life is not "worthy of their human nature."[11]

The notion of the "subject" had been central for the work of Hegel. For him, a subject was at the same time a *thinking consciousness* and a *will*. It created objects which stood in opposition to itself and then tried to find itself in them. In this effort, it changed its relationships with them, and so made itself what it really was. This was what Hegel understood by *freedom*: something was free only if it produced its own conditions of existence, and was not governed by external presuppositions. Overcoming the opposition of the objects it had produced, the subject could recognize itself in a world it had made for itself. Subjects, when their individual purposes clashed at a particular phase of development, revealed that their modes of being were deficient. From knowledge of this deficiency, a new set of relations arose, and so a new subject at a higher level.

The efforts of each individual to realize his or her purpose led to results quite different from what they had intended, because a higher subject called "History" played cunning tricks upon them. From civil society, that war of property owners against each other, sprang the State, whose subjective activities reconciled the warriors on this "battlefield of private interest."[12] All of this was the work of Spirit, "the subject which is also substance," described as "'I' that is 'we,' 'we' that is 'I.'"[13] Here is the starting point of Marx's debt to Hegel, as well as Marx's critique of Hegel.

Marx saw that Hegel's notion of subjectivity was an upside-down reflection of something else: although humanity made itself in the course of social labor—"in changing nature, man changes his own nature"[14]—under the power of capital, this took place in an upside-down world. That is, we develop our physical and mental capacities as social beings in the process of production itself, but we do so only as prisoners of our alienated social relations. Trapped by the power of capital, the actual producers are prevented from comprehending or controlling either what they produce, or their own productive activity. Capital is the subject, not the individual, whether bourgeois or proletarian.

This insight into the nature of bourgeois society, and the position of the producers within it, enabled Marx to go beyond Hegel's understanding of history. The conscious, united action of the workers against capital would lead to the abolition of private property. They could become conscious of their own humanity, and break out of that inhuman situation in which it was denied. Transforming itself from a class "in itself" into a class "for itself," the united proletariat would become the *subject of history*, and in this it differed from all previous, propertied, classes. The cunning which enabled Hegel's "History" to play tricks on humanity could be defeated. The way would be opened to a human society, where life would be made consciously, by individual humans who no longer clashed with the collective will of humanity as a whole.

These conceptions are hostile to any form of dogmatism. However, what "Marxists" used to call "theory" was no more than dogmatic assertion, for it could never explain its own origin. Even during Marx's own lifetime, he saw his ideas being reduced to dogma, and later things became much worse. In the hands of the Stalinist bureaucracy and its devotees, "Marxism" became a kind of state religion. Even those who fought against Stalinism, notably Leon Trotsky, found themselves trapped inside this conception of the "Marxist Party," which was equipped with a set of correct theories or "doctrines."[15] They were led, often unconsciously, to see "revolutionary leadership" as the substitute for that "development of communist consciousness on a mass scale," which was Marx's aim. As we have seen, the *Manifesto* explicitly opposes the conception of such an organization.

Thus the famous formulation of Kautsky and Lenin, that "socialist consciousness" had to be brought into the working class "from without," was a barrier to the central meaning of the *Manifesto*. But even those who did not accept this formula lost sight of Marx's starting point for the movement of the proletariat, the standpoint of "human society or social humanity."[16] Marx argued that the communists, participating in the real movement, could become its mouthpiece, illuminating the self-activity in which the class will "become fitted to make society anew."[17]

The "Marxist" conception, that the revolution was the work of a party, was closely bound up with the way the "Marxists" viewed state power. For them, the first step was the "seizure of power" by their "party." They tried to portray Marx as a "state socialist," just as his enemy Bakunin claimed he was. They often remarked that, in the *Manifesto*, Marx's understanding of the state was "incomplete." (Marx would have agreed with this, at any rate, for, as we have seen, he regarded his own ideas on any subject as essentially incomplete.) His remark that "the first step in the revolution by the working class is to raise the proletariat to the position of the ruling class, to win the battle of democracy," was certainly troublesome for many "Marxists." In fact, Marx came to envisage the rule of the proletariat as operating through local communes, not through a centralized state power. This conception, reinforced by the experience of the Paris Commune of 1871, was essential to his notion of communism as the self-movement of the proletariat.[18]

Thus "Marxism" came, in effect, to treat both the workers' state and the revolutionary party as if these were the subjects of history. They were thought of as moral agents, operating independently of the individuals whose life activity actually comprised them. This outlook was directly opposed to the view for which Marx fought. For him, only the proletariat, united as a class, can become conscious of its own historical situation, and consciously transform it. No other social formation can take its place—not the nation, not any earlier class, not the Party, not the family, and certainly not the individual genius. Such entities purport to be self-creating subjects, but Marx shows that these were illusions, which necessarily arise out of alienated life itself. In particular, living under bourgeois private property, isolated individuals see themselves as independent subjects and the state as the community. These are misconceptions, "false consciousness."

This, then is how Marx sees the question of subjectivity. Private property breaks up the community, and this renders it impossible for individuals to control their own lives. But, in its struggle against capital, the proletariat can transform itself into a self-conscious subject. After class divisions have been abolished, the proletariat will transcend itself, and dissolve into humanity as a whole. Then we shall have a free association of social individuals, that is, individual subjects, each of whom directly embodies the whole community, in which, the *Manifesto* says, "the free development of each is the condition for the free development of all."

Look again at this famous phrase, which so clearly expresses Marx's fundamental notion of humanity. It was a symptom of the widespread misunderstanding of Marx, that it should have been read back to front, as if it made the connection between individual and collective precisely the other way round. Communism means that the well-being of the individual, the possibility for him or her to develop freely all their human potential, is the condition; the good of the whole community is the consequence. While Marx criticized the political economists for their celebration of the "single individual in civil society," his critique did not merely reject this entity. The overthrow of the power of capital will open the way for the flowering of true individuality, but now in a shape where it no longer precluded collective well-being, but made it possible. The individual subjects who live in a human world will not be "isolated individuals" but "social individuals."[19]

That is why Marx's work, both scientific and practical, was not a matter of propounding a new form, one which the world had then to adopt. Instead, it concerned the removal of the inhuman covering (*Hülle* = integument) which encased and constricted a truly human life. Communism was not a new "mode of production," to replace the existing one, but a release of individuals' lives from the straightjacket of private property.

> Private property has made us so stupid and one-sided that an object is only *ours* when we have it. . . . In the place of *all* physical and mental senses there has come therefore the sheer estrangement of *all* these senses, the sense of *having*. . . . The abolition of private property is therefore the complete *emancipation* of all human senses and qualities.[20]

Thus this emancipation, spearheaded by the subjective action of the proletariat, the "universal class," implies far more than can be summed up as "the overthrow of capitalism," or a new economic and political system. It means a new way of living, in which individual and universal no longer collided.

MARX IN THE TWENTY-FIRST CENTURY

Today, millions of people greet the new century with apathy, fear, or despair. A deep malaise grips world society. Science and technology bound forward, bringing new marvels at every stride, but the outcome is mass unemployment, environmental destruction, and the ever-present menace of nuclear war. Those shrill cries about "the End of History" and "the New World Order," which filled the air only a few years ago, have all died away. Soon, I hope, their authors will be forgotten.

If Marx wrote when Europe was still coming to terms with the French Revolution, we live in the shadow of the Russian Revolution. Millions expected this great event to begin the socialist transformation of world society. But in its aftermath of civil war, bureaucratic degeneration destroyed these aspirations. Finally, the Soviet state collapsed into the chaos of modern capital. Unsurprisingly, the assertion that "Marxism is dead" has become a cliché. However, the chief result of the disappearance of the "Cold War" situation is something quite different. We used to be presented with the false choice between two alternatives: either rigidly centralized state control, or the exploitative anarchy of the market. Now, we can break out of this false dilemma. The path has been opened for the renewed study of Marx's actual ideas.

Just look at the world at the end of the millennium. Every aspect of social, political and economic life is dominated by the dogmatic belief in the miraculous power of "market forces." Money and its surrogates rule supreme throughout the planet, not just in a few bourgeois states. The outcome of this development is clear for all to see. Millions of lives are spent in the shadow of poverty and insecurity, menaced by the constant threat of starvation and disease. Some of the poorest people in the world exist within sight of gleaming office buildings, which house the headquarters of transnational corporations and powerful financial institutions. The export of the latest high-tech weapons of destruction vies with the massive trade in illegal narcotics as the chief sustenance of this soulless structure. The mass media, a major part of the profit-making system, broadcast images of famine and war around the globe, carefully integrating them into the profitable business called "entertainment."

No doubt, the world has passed through similar social crises before. One thing which distinguishes this "New World Disorder" from its predecessors is the way it is intellectually and culturally reflected. Whether the idea is put into words or not, there is a widespread belief that "there is no such thing as society." The conception of humanity itself has been perverted. Auschwitz, Hiroshima, Bhopal are accepted as symbols of Homo sapiens in the twentieth century. Truth, Goodness, and Beauty have not merely vanished: they are loudly proclaimed to be illusions. The possibility of a world where "the free development of each is the condition for the free development of all" has, we are often told, become utterly unthinkable. The hopes of the Enlightenment, the nineteenth century certainty of Progress, the struggle for world revolution after 1917, the dreams of the student revolutionaries of 1968, all are dismissed as outmoded juvenile nonsense. To people whose horizons are limited by "market forces," the corruption we see around us is only an accurate expression of "the human condition," and there is nothing to be done about it.

We have seen the revival of a widespread belief that present-day social relations are the only ones possible, and that the anticipation of "a free association of producers" is incompatible with human nature. But just what is that nature? Many answers are forthcoming. The practitioners of artificial intelligence explain that humans are nothing but rather complex machines. "Just a bundle of selfish genes," "genetically programmed talking apes," intone the high priests of sociobiology. "Self-interested atoms," gibber the economists. "Murderous, natural polluters of the planet, which was getting on quite well until you humans arrived," rage the Greens.

Have the forms of capital not changed enormously? Yes, indeed they have, but only into shapes far more horrific and insane than those of Marx's day. The making of money out of money now appears to dominate those operations of capital in which use values are actually produced, while these forms of capital suck the blood of the producers. During twenty-four hours of every day, billions of dollars are sent over powerful computer networks, bringing massive profits to speculators in foreign exchange. Productive capacity itself is moved rapidly to areas where labor power is cheap. Meanwhile, in the older centers of large-scale production, factories lie rusting, and the communities who depended on them are broken up and left without hope.

Thus the main questions posed by the *Manifesto* face us more starkly than ever. How is it that human productive power—now expanded far beyond the dreams of Marx—can take forms through which humanity's environment is destroyed and its very future existence threatened? How can social relations like money or capital have power over the people they relate to each other? Why do the links that bind the entire productive potential of humankind into a unity, simultaneously shatter it into fragments, setting individuals, classes, and nations against each other, even against themselves? Chatter about "postmodernity," with its denial of humanity, cannot drown out such questions.

Of course, in 1848, and in a brief document like the *Manifesto*, Marx could do no more than point to such problems. Even his work over the subsequent thirty-five years did no more than begin to elaborate answers to some of them, while new dangers have shown themselves only in recent decades. When "Marxist" orthodoxy pretended that these beginnings were a complete theoretical system, it lost sight of its essential point. What Marx was looking for—not inside his head, but within the existing social forms themselves—was the way for humanity to begin its task of self-emancipation, of becoming what it really was. This is what the Enlightenment and the French Revolution had promised, but failed to deliver. Marx was able to transcend this outlook. He did not reject its promise, but revealed that the world of capital, which political economy had portrayed as "natural," was in reality *crazy* (*verrückte*). Looking at the world today, who can deny its madness?

Many of those disillusioned with the socialist idea present their demand to "Marxism," as if they were historical debt collectors. "You promised us a revolution—where is it? The *Manifesto* told us that the proletariat's victory over capital would open the road to freedom. We have been cruelly disappointed." We must totally reject this manner of looking at history. Those who are disillusioned are obliged to investigate how they came to acquire illusions in the first place! In any case, there is no way we can evade the problem of how to live together on the planet. This is not a problem for a set of doctrines to solve, or for a political tendency to answer, but for billions of human beings to tackle for themselves.

The working-class movement has certainly gone through huge changes since 1848, especially over the past few decades. After World War II, the advanced industrialized countries set up systems of state welfare, together with a certain amount of state ownership. Sometimes this was associated with the name of John Maynard Keynes, and occasionally—and quite misleadingly—it was called "socialism." After the period of unprecedented economic growth had come to a shuddering halt in the 1970s, the so-called neoliberalism became the prevailing mood of many governments. There was an idea that state-ownership of industry, or state intervention in the economy, would provide a way to raise the standard of living. By the early 1980s, it had vanished with astonishing speed. Of course, the identification of socialism with state ownership was always false. For Marx, the state was "the illusory community,"[21] a bureaucratic structure which, within the framework of the fragmented, money-driven society, falsely impersonated the community.

A major feature of the world today is the fragmentation of the international working class and its organizations. During the 1980s, many sections of the workers' movement retreated into purely defensive actions. The movement of capital in search of higher profits led to the decline of large-scale manufacturing industry in the older capitalist countries, considerably weakening the trade unions there. This process has led some observers to imagine that "the proletariat no longer exists," or that we are living in the epoch of "postcapitalism."

Of course, such ideas are absurd. The substance remains: capitalist exploitation of labor; only its forms have changed.

New sectors of industry have opened up in what was once called the "Third World." There, the widespread employment of women and children, under the harshest working conditions, have brought back many features of economic life that had been long forgotten in the older centers of industry. At the same time, in these older countries, the work force has been split into two increasingly contrasted sectors. On the one hand, there is a relatively well-paid group, employed in high-tech industries. On the other, a large section is forced into poorly paid jobs, or frequent unemployment. They are pushed to the margins of society, condemned to falling standards of housing, health, and educational provision.

As these changes unfolded in the 1970s and 1980s, new working-class struggles began in Asia, Latin America, and Africa. New masses have been drawn into global battles against the power of capital. Important struggles to defend communities against the effects of changing technology have taken place. But how can the class be reunited? I think that the ideas of the *Manifesto* will prove to be vital in answering this question. When Marx looks at the struggles of workers for a higher price for their labor power, or for a shorter working day, he sees this as a form, the content of which is the struggle of the dispossessed to be recognized as human beings. This demand, the essence of Marx's communism, is the only possible foundation on which to rebuild the working-class movement. In "Marxism," communism and the movement of the proletariat were torn apart, after the *Manifesto* had so brilliantly unified them. To heal this breach is the task facing us today.

It is clear that the difficulties faced by the world are bound up with the breakneck speed of technological advance, and its imprisonment with the constricting framework of capitalist exploitation. The *Manifesto* already compared "bourgeois society (which) has conjured up such gigantic means of production and of exchange" with "the sorcerer who is no longer able to control the powers of the nether world whom he has called up by his spells" (489). Today, this does not merely mean that capital is beset by economic instability. Far deeper problems have emerged as a result of the conquests of science and technology. Every advance in telecommunications, information technology, biotechnology, or medical science sharpens the conflict between the requirements of capital and the needs of humanity. If these powers are not to destroy us, a complete transformation of social and economic life is needed, a total change in the way that human beings relate to each other.

The threat to the environment, a direct result of capital's uncontrolled expansion, can be answered only by the collective action of humanity as a whole. But what is this whole? Where can it be found? The "Green" movement has done important work in drawing attention to environmental issues. However, it often evades the question of just who is going to answer these dangers. Technology is not the enemy, but its perversion by the power of capital. Obviously, Marx could not have had much to say directly about issues which had hardly shown themselves in his time. But we will not be able to search for solutions without his conception of the potentiality of the proletariat to transform itself into a subject and emancipate humanity from capital.

In organizing itself to fulfil its historic destiny, the working class has to achieve the necessary knowledge of its situation, and face its tasks as a class with the highest degree of consciousness. As the international workers' movement rebuilds and reunifies itself, it must continually check its practices against the ideas of the *Manifesto*, not as a biblical text, but as a guide. The movement must also rework and demythologize its past history, both its victories and its errors, while it grasps the changes in the way that capital organizes itself. It must become aware of the latest technological developments, finding ways to answer the problems of working-class communities with knowledge of the most advanced conquests of natural science and technology. The working-class movement must take the lead in fighting to halt the effects on society as a whole of capitalist exploitation of the natural environment.

But for all this, those of us who claim to be communists have to ask ourselves a question. How on earth did we, the "Marxists," so totally misunderstand Marx? Of course, it was not just a matter of intellectual inadequacy. It was really because we forcibly squeezed Marx's notion of what was truly human into an iron framework which was truly brutal. We examined writings like the *Manifesto*, as if they were academic texts, expounding a total, complete, immutable doctrine. We thought that they provided us with a "model" of history, whose components were abstract images of Marx's categories. We were afraid to see them as the concrete expression of the lives of human beings. Only now, after the century after Marx's, do the opportunities open up for a new generation to grasp their real significance. Now is the time to read the *Manifesto*.

Certainly, the working class has still to "become fitted to make society anew."[22] That implies that, in the new millennium, the issues which found their first expression in 1848 face humanity with far greater urgency. Today we can say that we either learn how to live humanly, or we shall cease to live at all.

NOTES

MECW = Karl Marx and Frederick Engel, *Collected Works* (London: Progress Publishers, 1975).

1. That Marx himself was interested in this question seems likely, even if he never had the opportunity to discuss it at length. See the closing pages of the 1857 introduction to *Grundrisse*.

2. *The German Ideology*, written a year earlier, but not published until the twentieth century. *MECW*, Vol. 5: 53.

3. Theses on Feuerbach. Thesis 6.

4. See the letter Marx wrote in November, 1877, to the Russian journal *Otechestvennye Zapisky*.

5. Wilhelm Weitling had been a tailor, like Georg Eccarius and several others. Karl Schapper had been a student of forestry. Heinrich Bauer was a shoemaker. Joseph Moll was a watchmaker. Karl Pfänder was a painter of miniatures. Marx, Engels, and Wilhelm Wolff seem to have been the only intellectuals. My account of the history of the League is based on that of David Ryazanov, which contradicts some of Engels' reminiscences. See Ryazanov's edition of the *Manifesto* (New York, 1930), and his lectures, *Marx and Engels* (London, 1927).

6. Engels's idea of "primitive communism," based on the researches of Haxthausen, Maurer and Morgan, was not really shared by Marx. See *The Ethnological Notebooks of Karl Marx*, edited by L. Krader: Van Gorcum (Assen, 1974).

7. *Grundrisse MECW*, Vol. 28: 95.

8. *Grundrisse MECW*, Vol. 28: 95.

9. A later edition inserted here the word "self-conscious."

10. Theses on Feuerbach. Thesis 8.

11. *Capital*, Vol. 3. Penguin Edition, 959.

12. Hegel, *Philosophy of Right*, para 289.

13. Hegel, *Phenomenology of Spirit*, 1.

14. *Capital*, Vol. 1, Chapter 7. This is where the key opposition—and similarity—of Marx to Hegel, is located. The words "materialism" and "idealism" were used by "Marxists" in a quite misleading way. Marx had no concern with the "theory of knowledge," or with the "relationship of mind and matter."

15. Karl Kautsky wrote a book, once very popular in the labor movement, entitled *The Economic Doctrines of Karl Marx*—but only after Marx's death. Plekhanov and Lenin followed Kautsky in this usage.

16. Theses on Feuerbach. Thesis 9.

17. *German Ideology, MECW*, Vol. 5, 53.

18. See notes on Bakunin's *State and Anarchy*, 1875. See also *The Late Marx and the Russian Road*, edited Shanin.

19. I am indebted to a discussion with Professor José-Carlos Ballon, of San Marco University, Lima, Peru, for this important point.

20. *Paris Manuscripts. MECW*, Vol. 3: 300.

21. *German Ideology, MECW*, Vol. 5: 46.

22. *German Ideology, MECW*, Vol. 5: 53.

Part Two

MARX'S CRITIQUE OF POLITICAL PHILOSOPHY

Sir, I see that it is impossible to have liberty but all property must be taken away.

—Thomas Rainsborough, Putney, 1647

Chapter Four

Marx's Critical Science

How can six billion human beings live on this small planet without destroying each other? Which features of humanity make this question so difficult to answer? Which make an answer seem just possible? Such ways of putting the problem may sound comparatively modern, but, over the past two or three thousand years, some of the greatest thinkers have grappled with more or less the same issues. Of course, their approaches differed, in line with the actual forms the problems assumed in their own times, but several themes constantly reappear throughout the entire tradition of thinking about political life.

How does each individual relate to the social setup as a whole? Why do some people hold power over others? Which ways of living might be considered to be good? Is one way the best? Are social and political forms given "by nature" or by God? Are they the outcome of human decision, either a collective wish or the will of some superhuman Hero? Can either of these make any difference at all?

And is it possible for us to obtain the knowledge needed to answer questions like these? For the past few decades, some of these issues have been ruled out of court by authoritative academics, and our century begins not just without answers, but also with a raucous chorus deriding any attempt to find them. It is fashionable to dismiss such matters as not accessible to systematic thinking, and, indeed, for the past couple of decades, the very notion of the True has been sneered at, along with the Good and the Beautiful. The context for this declaration of intellectual and moral bankruptcy is undoubtedly the eclipse of Stalinism, and the consequent allegation that "Marxism is dead" and the near-unanimous and mindless view that the market is the "natural" way to organize our lives. However, these ways of thinking—or nonthinking—are actually symptoms of much deeper aspects of life at the start of the twenty-first century.

In this chapter, I attempt to look at the ideas of Karl Marx in relation to the tradition of political thought. I do this because I think that clarifying this relationship will illuminate the vital assistance that his work can give us—humans as a whole—in finding our way to a "truly human" way of living. At a time when the very possibility of anything worthy of the name "human" is under threat, many people will shrug off such a quest. To attempt this, it is first necessary to distinguish clearly between "Marxism" and the ideas of Marx. The Marxists—Marx did not count himself one of them!—dogmatically refused to grapple with questions like the ones I have outlined. In general, the would-be followers of Marx thought he was engaged in setting up "models" of society, or economics, or politics, or history. When they (I ought honestly to say: "we"!) claimed that Marx's works were "scientific," this generally meant something like the natural sciences, in which "theories" or "hypotheses" yield predictions, which have then to be checked against empirical data. These theoretical models, it was said, allowed us to gain knowledge of the mechanics of sociopolitical change, and the "laws" which governed the revolutionary transition from one social order to the next.

A single tentative metaphor of Marx about base and superstructure (an extract from the preface to the *Critique of Political Economy*) was misread into a complete "theory of history." It was treated as the diagram of a historical machine, in which an economic basis, pushed forward by the development of productive forces—generally that meant technology—in turn "caused" changes in an ideological-political superstructure.[1] Ideas were "determined" by "material conditions," where "determined" was automatically assumed to mean "caused." Since this presumably included the ideas of the Marxists themselves, this led to difficulties, for "Marxism" pretended to justify its doctrine of social development by appeal to its own special "scientific world outlook," deriving its idea of socialism as a corollary. But how could it know any of this?

A "Marxist" theory of politics went along with this mechanical view, according to which the individuals who make up the ruling class are determined to defend their interests against those they exploit, and are ready to use violent means where necessary. The state was then said to be "nothing but" their instrument for this purpose. "Revolution" simply meant smashing up this instrument, and establishing a new one, just changing the form of state power. "Socialism," largely identified with state ownership, was the next "mode of production" on a preset historical agenda. The conception of revolution flourishing in Marxist circles thus centered, not on the idea of liberation, but on the concept of power. In its Leninist form, Marxism misread some of Marx's formulations and transformed them into justifications for new, oppressive political structures. (For instance, the phrase "dictatorship of the proletariat,"

Marx's most democratic concept, was one such victim.) The phrase "workers' state" became current in Marxist-Leninist circles—Marx himself never used it—even before Stalin had revealed its totalitarian content. The idea was that the transition to socialism would begin when this new form of state power—later revealed to be a pseudonym for the Party—had firmly replaced the old one, and industry was taken into its control.

Even while Marx was still alive, his central notion of "general human self-emancipation" had become almost incomprehensible to his devoted followers. When some of his earlier writings became generally available in the 1950s and 1960s, it was hard to see how they could be fitted into the "Marxist" framework. "Marxists" dodged this difficulty by separating a "Young Marx" from an "Old Marx," the latter being the "scientific" one. When we studied the *Grundrisse*, written when Marx was forty years old, and found it had the same outlook as the *Paris Manuscripts of 1844*, some of us realized that this escape route was effectively blocked. It would not be overstating the situation to say that, right down to the present day, the "Marxists" have been among the most direct and bitter opponents of the ideas of Karl Marx.[2] Above all, they lost all connection with Marx's actual conceptions of human self-emancipation and "free association."

In reality, Karl Marx seeks to construct neither a Utopian "vision" of what the world ought to be like, nor a "scientific" "theory of history." Indeed, he shows how each of these ways of thinking embody the inhuman features of modern life. His aim is no less than universal human freedom, our self-liberation, and, as we shall see, this is something no theory and no mechanical model could ever comprehend. He conceives of communism as "a free association of producers," a "truly human society," where "humanity" means the process of free social creation and self-creation, which implies "the free development of individualities." Social production, material and spiritual, individual and collective, forms the heart of self-creation, what it means to be truly human. But, after developing for millennia, this has not yet been liberated from "alienated" forms of living.

Thus Marx could show how the distortions and falsifications of what is truly human are associated with private property and that this is the basis of the power that some humans have over others. Both property and state power are expressions of forms of social labor alienated from their truly human content. Alienated society is characterized by antagonism between the material interests of individuals, between classes, and between each of these and the collective public life. These antagonisms, which stand in the way of a life "worthy and appropriate for our human nature . . . the true realm of freedom, the development of human powers as an end in itself,"[3] are regarded by Marx as insane.

To achieve a human form of life requires that we collectively accomplish the task of progressively transcending these age-old antagonisms, sanely making the "free development of each . . . the condition for the free development of all." So the required social revolution does not just mean a change of regime, or a new economic system, but "the alteration of humans on a mass scale,"[4] through their own conscious activity. When humanity can consciously confront this as its major task, it already possesses the material conditions to accomplish it, that is, to learn to live without either private property or state power. The "free association of producers" will then live humanly, that is, it will engage in the mutually self-creating activity of social production, free from estrangement, in relationships it has self-consciously made.

Individuals become part of the history of society's metabolic exchange with nature in the course of their productive, that is, their creative activity. In this process, we change our relationships with each other, and thus change ourselves, collectively and individually striving to realize our potential for freedom. However, within the existing social order, founded upon the atomised institutions of private property, we are rarely conscious of what we are doing. Living fragmented lives, estranged from each other and from ourselves, we have fabricated a casing around ourselves which denies freedom, and that means our humanity. We ourselves have constructed the forms of antagonism, oppression and exploitation, the very antitheses of free creation, enclosing us like suits of armor. These social forms rule over the individuals, who treat each other—and themselves—as if they were things, mere means to further "self-interest."

In a world under the power of money, what is good for some is bad for others. Thus the possibility of true community, the condition for freedom, is continually being destroyed, both in practice and in theory. This is how private property works, and especially private ownership of means of production: what belongs to me cannot belong to you. The products of social labor become attached to particular individuals, who often have played no part in their creation or, indeed, in the creation of anything at all. If the needs of the community clash with the needs of its individual components it is impossible to be socially and individually self-governing, that is, to be free. Labor itself comes to be alien to the laborers and their own "life activity" is just a means to "make a living."

People live under conditions that are not of their own conscious choosing and so not fit for humans. But there is a continual struggle of humanity against this inhuman way of life, and this is what shows itself in the antagonisms between individuals, between social classes, and between nations. Marx identifies the struggle of the proletariat, the producers of wealth who are oppressed and exploited, against the power of capital that they themselves create, as the movement that would emancipate humanity as a whole. Their labor, their very life activity as human beings, is hostile to them. They can win their collective fight against this alien power only if they take control over their own human, creative activity. Thus they potentially challenge all forms of oppression and exploitation. This movement must transcend private property, which Marx understands as "the perceptible expression of the fact that man becomes *objective* for himself and at the same time becomes to himself a strange and inhuman object."[5] Correspondingly, the transcendence of private property means "the perceptible appropriation for and by man of the human essence and of human life, of objective man, of human achievements."

An essential part of this understanding of social revolution is that the state must be transcended along with all other forms of antagonistic social power. As individual production and public life cease to be separate processes, the domination of some individuals by others fades away. The claim of the state to act on behalf of the collectivity of individual lives, ruling over them for their own collective good, is false, Marx declares. When the state performs functions like punishing crime, sanctioning morality, or waging war, its pretence to act for everyone is a lie. In reality, the state is an illusory surrogate for the "true community"; in a world where relations between people are ruled by the exchange of private property the community cannot operate directly as a single entity. (One of the most alienated of recent political figures once told us that: "There's no such thing as society." No wonder that she is also often depicted as being unhinged!) Proletarian revolution means smashing this power and releasing human potential in a community of freely developing individual subjects.

All of these notions raise the problem of knowledge: "How do you know?" Living as we do, estranged from each other and from ourselves, how can we get to know how to live humanly? If ideas are generated as part of the alienated life activities of individuals, how can we find the truth? How can we even talk about a new way of living with the language of the old? The new society can only be seen as just a variant of the old one, or as a Utopian "vision," to which the world must be made to conform.

"Marxism" had a sort of answer, and it was not very different in form from the kind of solution attempted by the old Utopians. "Just trust us," we said, in effect. "We who are in the know will provide the necessary 'leadership.' We shall tell you how to be free. Just do as we say."

Marx's answer is nothing like that, of course. As he put it in a letter to Ruge in 1843:

> We do not say to the world: Cease your struggles, they are foolish; we will give you the true slogan of struggle. We merely show the world what it is really

fighting for, and consciousness is something it has to acquire, even if it does not want to.[6]

Before Marx, socialism was a set of opinions or doctrines, arguing from personal feelings or philosophical or religious doctrines to a vision of a better future. Those who have tried to build a socialist movement on such foundations have failed. They have even obscured that vision which has inspired the instinctive movement of impoverished masses of slaves, peasants, or wage workers several times in history.

Marx knows that the agency of the new social transformation has to be conscious of itself, to comprehend itself, to be critical of itself as it arises from the history and structure of the existing order, and Marx's conception of *critique* is central to all his work. At any rate from 1843 onward, what he means by this word is something quite precise. When Marx speaks of the critique of a science he means a demonstration that its fundamental assumptions, categories and methods are expressions of an inhuman way of life. Concrete negation of these assumptions, scientifically and in practice, make it possible to preserve what is human about them in an outlook which transforms the idea of a human society into a *practical task*.

"The critique of religion," "the premise of all critique," is the best illustration of what Marx means by critique in general.[7] Marx is not concerned to develop "irreligious criticism," the kind of abstract atheism which argues against the truth of religious belief, as if it were either a logical mistake, or the result of a lying conspiracy of priests. Instead, his aim is to uncover the roots of such belief in the actual lives of individuals, and to reveal its meaning in their actual oppression and misery. Religion is then seen to be "the heart of a heartless world," and the way is opened for the overthrow of those real inhuman conditions to which it is the illusory response. But this insight is possible only if the conditions of life are themselves internally contradictory.

Alienated social relations rule the lives of individuals and the concepts in which those relations are expressed govern their thoughts. So philosophy, along with religion, is the highest expressions of alienation. Marx's aim is to derive the nature of a truly human society, and thus of an inhuman, bourgeois society, from his critique of the philosophical tradition, a critique whose criterion is "social humanity." Marx's entire life's work is the critique of the highest forms of established knowledge, so as to get to the heart of the struggle of humanity for its emancipation, and to speak for it. How else is it possible to see beyond the horizons of existing society?

In a very important remark in *Capital*, Marx explains that

[r]eflection on the forms of social life, hence also scientific analysis of these forms, takes a course directly opposite to their actual development. Reflection

begins *post festum*, and therefore with the results of the process of development ready to hand.

These forms "already possess the fixed quality of natural forms of social life before man seeks to give an account, not of their historical character, for in his eyes they are immutable, but of their content and meaning."[8] Marx's critique is directed at the highest expression of this "content and meaning." It is significant that the paragraph containing this sentence leads directly to the characterization of political economic categories as "mad" (*verrückte*). (The English translations weaken this to "absurd.") While ordinary thinking does not question these forms, science tries to give a consistent account of the world as a rational structure. But this is precisely the falsehood at the core of the most disinterested science.

For bourgeois society is *not* a rational whole, as all kinds of economics assume. Looked at humanly, this is a crazy way to live, and to "make sense" of money, wages, rent, interest, and profit is to lie. This has nothing to do with subjective intention. Indeed, the more honest and sincere the attempt at rationalisation, the more mendacious. Marx, to break through the natural appearance of existing economic forms, allows the theoretical results of political economy to clash with what is self-evidently human. Thus his critique of the science that glorifies what exists, merges with and becomes the mouthpiece for the practical movement of workers who "know"—without benefit of science—that they are not things, but human beings treated as things. Their suffering expresses the necessity of a revolutionary change. But that is not enough: it also requires the critique of economic science to get to grips with its true cause.

That is not to say that Marx is always quite clear about the meaning of words like "theory," "philosophy," and so on, and it is not surprising the he sometimes calls himself "theorist," "philosopher," and even "economist," but this should not put us off. We could summarize Marx's outlook like this:

1. In class society, individual humans—human beings—are governed by social forms that are alien to their humanity. This is insane.
2. These forms condition the way that they think about themselves and about their social life.
3. When science theorizes social problems, its categories give the alien forms their highest expression.
4. The critique of these categories breaks up their appearance of being "natural," and so opens the way for conscious social practice to release their human content.

Marx's critique of political economy, the only part of his work he came anywhere near to completing, is not a "criticism of capitalism." It aims to

give a coherent account of economic life under the power of capital, while re-
fusing to accept those categories of political economy that express this power.
Precisely because these categories accurately represent the essential structure
of private property, they, like all other forms of "social science," systemati-
cally hide the inhumanity, the "craziness," of its essence. What the best political economists can only present as the realm of freedom and equality, turns
out to be the arena of inequality, oppression and exploitation. (This includes,
of course, the economic interventions of a bureaucratic state, which some
people later misnamed "socialism.") This critique both illuminates and is
made possible by those actual forces unleashed by the contradictions which
political economy has hidden. The critique becomes "the mouthpiece of the
real movement."

Marx shows how uncritical acceptance of the "natural" appearance of
bourgeois private property, of money, wages, and so on, as seen at its very
best in classical political economy, disguised and perverted the human content of all systematic thinking. This is what Marx, always conscious of the
parallels between religion and money, calls "fetishism." Political economy,
by definition, has to accept the form of appearance of bourgeois social relations, founded upon "thing-like (*dinglich*) relations between persons and social relations between things."[9] Working "behind the backs of the producers,"[10] the exchange of private property necessarily leads to the development
of money and its most important form, capital. Once it is a going concern,
capital produces and reproduces itself as an all-pervasive, oppressive, impersonal power, globally linking individuals together by setting them against
each other. This is the power that now threatens all truly human forms.

Wherever labor power is bought and sold, in fact what is already implied
by the simple exchange of commodities for one another, comes into the open:
Individual humans are treating each other and themselves as if they were objects. The resulting forms of productive activity are abstract, encased in alienated relations between the producers. When wage workers fight against capital exploiting them—a struggle essential to the capital relation itself—they
are demanding to be treated as human subjects. On the other hand, the creative potential of social humanity is made to appear to be the productive
power of a subject: capital.

Thus relations dominated by capital engender forms of thinking which disguise the oppressive, exploitative character of these relations. Political economy, even at its best, took these false appearances for granted. Only by taking the critique of its categories and methods to their logical depths could the
inhumanity and insanity of money and of the buying and selling of labor
power be revealed and overcome. So long as it remains dominated by the
forms of the market, thought confuses our character as active subjects with

impersonal objects, means with ends. Under the power of capital, people cannot but participate in creating and recreating that power. They might hate it and grumble about it, but they have no choice but to live with it. Capital appears as a pseudo subject, producing and reproducing itself, using both capitalists and workers as its instruments. This is the subject matter of *Capital*, whose first volume is subtitled "The Production Process of Capital"—although a reader of any one of the English translations might not know this.

How is it possible for humanity as a whole to achieve the consciousness that will enable it to free itself from the bonds of private ownership? For Marx, this was the most practical question of all. A remark in *Grundrisse* helps to see the way that Marx answers it:

> [I]ndividuals enter into relation with each other only as determinate individuals. These *objective* relations of dependence, in contrast to the *personal* ones, also appear in such a way that the individuals are now ruled by *abstractions* whereas they were previously dependent on one another. (The objective relationship of dependence is nothing but the social relations independently confronting the seemingly independent individuals, i.e. their own reciprocal relations of production which have acquired an existence independent of and separate from them.) Yet the abstraction or idea is nothing but the theoretical expression of those material relationships which dominate the individuals.[11]

Entities like state, law, money, family all appear to individuals to be part of the furniture of the universe. Actually, they are the products of human activity, but this is hidden from the actors themselves. The categories of theoretical science polish up these entities, beautifying them and presenting them as beyond criticism. Within the realm of these abstract categories, they are the only way to express such forms of living, precisely because these forms themselves are *abstract*, separated from and antagonistic to the individuals who live inside them.

But this is the nature of all theory, theory as such. It is inherent in every theory devised by theoreticians who imagine that they are separated from the object theorized. (This is what they usually mean when they praise themselves as "objective.") This is a false way of thinking, because is a true expression of a false—inhuman—way of living, of social forms in which humans are estranged from themselves. Thus every effort to establish an "objective social science," as if the scientists were not themselves in the picture, is not just a logical error, but essentially expresses humanity's estrangement from itself.

When Marx claimed that his work was scientific, it was in a special sense, which I contrast with the common understanding of science as theory. Since he was engaged in the critique of every kind of "social science," Marx's critical science necessarily includes self-critique. Theoretical science—by which I mean uncritical science—is incapable of anything like this, as is demonstrated by the futile attempts to construct a "theory of knowledge," or an "explanation of explanation." If this also a theory, it must be a viciously circular "theory of theory." If it is not, what is it? Marx's critique of "theoretical" or dogmatic science stripped away its hidden assumptions. By its very character, theory necessarily assumed that private property, money, family, state, and the enforced division of labor, everything that Marx includes under the label "alienation," were "natural" aspects of human life, since they certainly exist.

Marx's critique of social science reveals the contrary: within any theory, the categories with which it operates cannot be questioned. Thus, inevitably, they are forms of oppression. The possibilities for truly human relationships have developed only inside, and in opposition to these forms. Since we ourselves have constructed these prisons in the course of human history, we humans can—with difficulty—break our way out of them. Since these forms are abstractions, appearing as ideas, critique clears the intellectual space needed for this breakout to succeed. Social and political philosophy operates in this dead world of abstractions, while its critique shows the way to break them up and bring them to life. While there could never be a "theory of freedom," Marx's science opens the way to human emancipation.

Throughout its history, philosophy, and particularly political philosophy, has been the highest expression of private property, class division, state power, and the other alienated social forms. At each stage of its development, it provided the most abstract summary of an abstract way of living, not only in its conclusions, but also in its methods, its categories, and its attitudes to objectivity.

That is why Hegel's work is crucial for all of Marx's ideas. Remaining firmly within the boundaries of philosophy, the Hegelian system reached the very brink of philosophy's self-annihilation. Faced with the conflicts and confusions that convulsed Europe after the French Revolution, Hegel aimed to unify and reconcile them in a universal and all-embracing system of thought. As a whole and in each of its parts, this system purported to reconcile contradictory particulars, by showing that they both made up a universal whole and were given their meaning by it.

Before Hegel, Kant, summing up the Enlightenment, had put his finger on its fundamental problem. He turned the spotlight of Reason on Reason itself and tried to explore its limits. Hegel pursued this question much further, breaking through the limitations of the Enlightenment. Knowledge of the world could not be separated from self-knowledge of the knowing subject, for it too was in the world. The categories with which we gained knowledge and self-knowledge arose objectively as forms of world history, said Hegel. Thus

Hegel's system claims to find itself in its own world picture. It contains its own beginning, which turns out to be the consequence of its end.

Hegel's unifying movement operates in two directions. At any moment, the contradictory aspects of modern society had to form an organic whole. On the other hand, the stages of development of Western philosophy, summing up its categories, formed a single process, the highest summary of Mind or Spirit (*Geist*). The movement of world history was identical with this development of thought, and each stage of the unfolding of the Idea was "its own time expressed in thought." Hegel had shown that social life did not develop in line with some "natural" characteristics with which humans were endowed, but was the outcome of their own work and the struggle to comprehend this work. The development of philosophy was thus the movement of freedom, as humans became conscious that the world confronting them was indeed the outcome of their own activity. In particular, the antagonisms between individuals in "civil society" must be contained by a rational higher power, the state, which seeks to represent the needs of the collective and contradictory activity of society.[12] Hegel calls this activity "Objective Spirit."

Marx's critique of Hegel's system is not a complete, once-and-for-all "epistemological break," as some have alleged. He returns to his battle with his teacher again and again throughout his lifetime. After Hegel had unified the tradition of philosophy into a single system, Marx's critique of Hegel confronts that tradition as a whole. Hegel had revealed the element of reconciliation to be at the heart of philosophy as such. Marx agrees with this assessment, but sees it as the proof that philosophy as such had to be transcended. That is how Marx demonstrates in opposition to Hegel that neither social antagonism nor the state's response is a logical necessity, but the outcome of the power of private property, a particular stage of historical development. Transcending the antagonisms of modern society did not imply a new philosophical synthesis, but a practical revolution in which the state and its basis in private property would be transcended. Marx sees that taking "the standpoint of human society and social humanity,"[13] that is, the standpoint of communism, is the only way to grasp what society is. What his philosophical predecessors faced as their central problem, Marx takes as his starting point.

So, before Marx can begin his critique of socialism and of political economy, he has a great deal of preliminary work to do.[14] To understand the limitation of the political emancipation for which the eighteenth-century Enlightenment had fought so hard, he has to tackle the nature of politics itself. Although he never published any work dealing specifically with the state (he planned one in one of his outlines in 1858), his study of political philosophy, made in the years before 1844, is the essential prelude to all of his later work.

In the celebrated 1859 preface to his *Critique of Political Economy*, he explains the importance of this study as follows:

> The first work which I undertook to dispel the doubts assailing me was a critical re-examination of the Hegelian philosophy of law. . . . My inquiry led me to the conclusion that neither legal relations nor political forms could be comprehended, whether by themselves or on the basis of a so-called general development of the human mind, but that on the contrary they originate in the material conditions of life, the totality of which Hegel, following the example of English and French thinkers of the eighteenth century, embraces within the term "civil society"; that the anatomy of this civil society, however, has to be sought in political economy.

Marx here refers mainly to his incomplete manuscript *Contribution to a Critique of Hegel's Philosophy of Right*. (Although Marx wrote this in 1843, it only became available in the 1950s and 1960s.)[15] Dealing with a section of Hegel's *Elements of the Philosophy of Right* (1820), it is undertaken before Marx has read much about communism and before he has begun to see the proletariat as the force for revolutionary change. Why was the *Philosophy of Right* so important? It was because this, the last book Hegel published in his lifetime, was an attempt to epitomize the entire tradition of political thought, stretching back to ancient Greece. When Marx has finished his critique, he is in a position to understand that private property, whose laws are sought by political economy, form the basis on which political life is founded. A truly human society implies the transcendence of both property and the state, and the critique of political economy, tracing the oppressive laws of private property, is the prerequisite for this.

Marx has convinced himself that all philosophy—philosophical thinking as such—is the deepest expression of alienated, oppressive, exploitative, in short inhuman relations. Hegel had seen philosophy as tracing the path of world history. Now Marx's critique of philosophy can reveal that it is an alienated expression of the course of development of alienated life. In the tradition, important thinkers tried sincerely to further the cause of human emancipation. The works of Plato, Aristotle, Hobbes, Spinoza, Locke, Rousseau, Kant, Hegel, and others probe deeply into the problems of social and political power and contain indispensable insights into the nature of social forms. But all of these great thinkers began, tacitly or openly, with certain assumptions. For each of them, property and political power are necessary features of the life of humans. The age-old separation of mental and manual labor, the division between "thinkers" and "doers," is built into their fundamental categories and into their conception of what humanity is. Whatever the subjective wishes of the philosopher, philosophical thought must take it for granted that relationships between humans are necessarily antagonistic, that some people must have power over others, and that there has to be a division between masters and slaves, rulers and ruled.

It is therefore understandable that, in spite of their varied standpoints, the philosophers were almost unanimous across two millennia on one point: they all rejected any possibility that the whole of a community could govern itself. (Spinoza stands out as the great exception to this generalization.) Democracy would inevitably degenerate into mob rule, they all believed, for inequality, the essence of private property, implied that poor people would take away the property of the rich if they had the chance.

The philosophers believed that to interpret our own collective actions and to penetrate the mysteries of social life, specialists in thinking have to be called in—namely the philosophers themselves. Of course, the questions they asked themselves were vital ones: What is Justice? What is the good life for humanity? What is humanity? How does humanity relate to nature? But they did not think that the answers for which they struggled could be made available to the mass of the population. Indeed, what could the man-in-the-street do with this knowledge if he got hold of it? No, it was those who governed— the "Philosopher King," or the "Prince," or the "Magistrate," who made up their audience. At times when absolute rulers went out of fashion, "the best people" (*aristoi*) were the ones to talk to, and later the owners of large-scale property.

However, over the centuries, attempts to get these rulers to put the results of philosophical thought into practice met with little success. In modern times, forms of "representative democracy" came to be the ideal, designed to accommodate the needs of community to those of private property. (Of course, today's multimillion-dollar contests between public relations agencies, trying to sell us politicians packaged like brands of soap, should not really be given the name "democracy" at all.) Then political philosophy as such ceased to exist, being replaced by various kinds of "political science," theorising the technology of power.

But if they saw the conflict between individual life and the life of the community as inevitable, the philosophers were left with a central mystery: how was human society possible at all? Given the antagonisms necessarily accompanying private property and political power, how could individual humans unite in one community? Very broadly, there were two ways to attempt an escape from this problem: either individuals appeared on the scene already molded by society; or preexisting individuals came together into a community. On the first view, society is an organism whose organs are the individuals who live in it. In general, they can never know how their lives are taken over by laws governing the whole social body. On the second view, the individuals are independent atoms and the interactions resulting from their clashing wills and interests move the whole machine along. In the main, political economists fell into the second group. But then, how is knowledge of the whole picture possible?

Neither view, neither "organicism" nor "individualism," allows the possibility of a consciously self-governing community, in which individuals can freely develop. If the community is an organism, it is not possible for any of its component parts to know anything about it as a whole. If it is a conglomerate of independent individuals, how can any one of them, however intelligent, ever be able to consider the whole as a unity?

We repeat: the confusion resulting from these opposing views of society was not the result of false logic, but expressed the real contradictions of alienated social life. However, the philosophers themselves believed that philosophy was needed to make sense of this conflict. If only they could find the necessary categories and sort them into the correct order, all would be clear. Analogous problems are repeatedly encountered in various forms throughout the history of philosophy: whole and parts, universal and individual, inner and outer, substance and accidents—pairs like these keep cropping up as antinomies. Philosophy is thus itself a symptom of the basic contradiction of society. That is why Marx needs a critique of the categories of philosophy before he can uncover the underlying contradiction. Philosophy appeared on the scene to attempt to dispel the basic mystery. Marx shows that this struggle, philosophy's very existence, is the highest expression of what is actually a problem of practical life. The critique of its intellectual structure is, of course, not itself human emancipation, but it is vitally necessary to achieve it. In the meantime, philosophy is in a blind alley.

Marx's critical reworking of the tradition is far more radical than "Marxism" could have imagined. He is sure that the mass of working people had to govern themselves and that they would, under conditions yet to develop, be able to do it. So his answers are addressed, not to kings and princes, but to all of us. After the scalpel of critique has done its work of dissection on the body of philosophy, the essence of this knowledge can be put into the hands of those who are today without power or property. To actualize the wisdom of the philosophers, those without property or power have to abolish private property and state power, making possible the free association and free development of all humans as social individuals. In his earlier writings, Marx calls this idea "true democracy," and a little later "real humanism." Later (to avoid misunderstandings!), he calls it "communism." The real movement to transform social life was the struggle to "win the battle of democracy,"[16] through the transcendence of private property and the development of human forms of freely productive life. Only when private property has ceased to set individuals against each other can they unite their human creative powers in a free, self-governing community, and this is foreshadowed when they unite in the struggle against capital.

In the next four chapters we shall review—very briefly—the ideas of some important figures in the history of political thought. Each of these great thinkers tried to work out how the community could coexist with the particular form that private property took in his own time. First, we look at central texts that laid the foundation for the entire tradition of Western thought, at the time when Athenian democracy was breaking up: Plato's *Republic*, and the *Politics* of Aristotle, which is inseparable from his *Ethics*. When slavery and money were eroding the old forms of community, the meaning of Justice became a major problem. Under the new conditions, it was no longer clear what kind of constitution would make possible the good life. Thinkers who came after Plato and Aristotle, notably the Stoics, turned away from considering the structure of political life, toward the inner life of the individual.

Next, we jump to the beginning of the modern era. As feudalism was entering its centuries of decline, the study of Greek philosophy was taken up by Christian scholars, trying to find a rational foundation for Christian theology. But, while the name of the pagans Plato and Aristotle were revered in the Church, their ideas were given a content which they might not have recognized.

The philosophers of the sixteenth and seventeenth centuries junked Scholasticism, and threw Aristotle out along with it. As bourgeois economic forms fragmented society into self-interested atoms, the Good was replaced with individual feelings and opinions, and politics became a matter of statecraft. In Machiavelli and Hobbes, the state comes to be seen as a special instrument to exercise power. Following closely behind them, the great anomaly, Spinoza, tries to find another way out of the conflict between the individual and the social, which he calls "democracy." (At one point, he calls this "truly human.") Montesquieu, Rousseau, and Kant begin to reveal the contradictions of modern forms of property, and Adam Smith tries to analyze them in detail and investigate their political and moral consequences.

We examine Hegel's *Philosophy of Right* as the conscious culmination and summary of this entire movement. Then Marx's critique of Hegel's conception of the state can be seen in its historical context, and as the real beginning of his life's work. Finally, we ask what our investigation has told us about Marx's own conception of revolution and its relevance for present-day struggles.

NOTES

1. See chapter 2, "Marx versus Historical Materialism."

2. I have attempted to explore these and other problems in *Marx at the Millennium* (London: Pluto Press, 1996).

3. *Capital*, Volume 3, 896.

4. *German Ideology, Marx-Engels Collected Works, (MECW)*, Vol. 5, 45.

5. *MECW*, Vol. 3, 299.

6. *MECW*, Vol. 3, 144. For a revealing misquotation of this letter, see Lenin's *What the Friends of the People Are*, Collected Works, Vol. 1, 184–85, and 328.

7. *MECW*, Vol. 3, 175.

8. *Capital*, Vol. 1, 168.

9. *Capital*, Vol. 1, 166.

10. *Capital*, Vol. 1, 135.

11. *Grundrisse, MECW*, Vol. 28, 101.

12. For my disagreement with some common notions about the relations between Hegel and Marx, see "Hegel, Economics and Marx's *Capital*," in *History, Economic History and the Future of Marxism*, edited by Terry Brotherstone and Geoff Pilling (London: Porcupine Press, 1996).

13. Theses on Feuerbach, Thesis 10.

14. See Gary Teeple, *Marx's Critique of Politics, 1842-1847* (Toronto: University of Toronto Press, 1984).

15. Riazanov discovered the manuscript, and published it in Germany in 1927. It was reprinted in 1957. I have referred to the translation given in *MECW*, Volume 3, 3. Only the well-known *Introduction* to this work was ever published by Marx, in the *Deutsch-Französischer Jahrbücher*, in 1843.

16. Communist Manifesto.

Chapter Five

Democracy and Property in Athens[1]

Western political philosophy begins, like so many other traditions, in Athens at the end of the fifth century BC, shaped by specific historical conditions at the moment when Athenian society was at a stage of transition. Centuries before, the collapse of the Mycenean Empire had been followed by the "Dark Age," when even writing was forgotten.[2] (The epics of Homer look back to this time.) With the revival of civilization, about 800 BC, communal life in the Greek settlements began to be organized in independent "city-states." (Strictly speaking, neither "city" nor "state" in their modern meanings quite fit. We shall use the term "*polis*" to denote this social form.) Each *polis* had its own form of organization, and that of fifth-century Athens was the most advanced, for here the citizens democratically governed themselves.

When the Athenians talked about *demokratia*, "rule by the people" (the *dêmos*) they did not just mean the election of "representatives," to rule on behalf of the electors, but actual, direct rule by every citizen. An Assembly, which actually took decisions, voted on all major issues, passed laws and voted on foreign policy. When it met, about once a week, every citizen could have his say, speaking for as long as he liked—until people got bored with his speech and pulled him off the platform. When the Assembly voted for war — that happened quite a lot—they knew precisely who was going to have to fight, for the citizens were themselves the army and navy and they elected their commanders. In the courts, the judges who implemented the laws were chosen by lot.

Who made up the body of citizens? Most eighteenth- and nineteenth-century writers, including Engels and Hegel, thought that the citizens were people who didn't work. Today, many people think otherwise,[3] estimating that the majority of citizens were ordinary peasants and artisans. If you had to leave your work to attend the Assembly or the court, you got some money in compensation. There was no government, as we know it today. A Council, chosen by lot, was given the job of preparing the business of the Assembly. In fact, there was no *politics* in the modern sense, that is, no institution separate from the rest of social life. "Economics" (*oikonomia*) meant the management of a household. (*Oikos* was the household, of husband and wife, parents and children, and master and slaves, and the *oikonomos* was the master of the household.) What was good for each citizen was good for the whole community (Latin "*com munis*" = "serving together," Greek *koinonia*), and vice versa. Otherwise, the Athenian type of democracy would not have been possible.

Of course, we mustn't idealize this picture.[4] Citizens were exclusively adult males who had been born in Athens. (Resident aliens—including, by the way, Aristotle the Macedonian—had certain rights, but could not be citizens.) So over 50 percent of the population just didn't count: women were classified with slaves by many thinkers. Over the previous two centuries, money had come to play an increasing part in Greek life, and Athens was an important trading center. So, by the fifth century, there was already considerable inequality in wealth and in land ownership. Some wealthy men, with the time and money to spend on their education, were unduly influential in swaying the decisions of the Assembly.

Most important, there was slavery. However, the story that Ancient Greece was a "slave society" is misleading. It seems that earlier estimates of the numbers of slaves might have been exaggerated. (Some people liked to believe that without a massive proportion of slaves, democracy was impossible.) In any case, an Athenian slave in the fifth century should not be confused with, for example, a slave in Rome, and certainly not a nineteenth-century plantation slave in the United States. Slaves were prisoners of war, many of whom worked in the households of wealthy Athenians. (Slaves in the silver mines, who were brutally overworked, were the exception.) Nonetheless, even the most developed democracy coexisted with money, inequality, slavery, and the oppression of women. During the fourth century, the contradiction between property and democracy sharpened, individual self-interest became more and more opposed to the life of the community as a whole, and the *polis* broke up.

We must also take account of war, widely accepted among the Greeks of this time as the most honorable way of life. The *polis* established its identity by fighting its neighbors. While there was unity between citizens of the *polis*, relations with other cities were governed almost exclusively by local self-interest. This is how Thucydides reports an Athenian telling the men of Melos that they were going to kill them all, if they didn't give in to the greater power:

You, by giving in, would save yourselves from disaster; we, by not destroying you, would be able to profit from you. . . . Our opinion of gods and our knowledge of men lead us to conclude that it is a general and necessary law of nature to rule wherever one can. (*History of the Peloponnesian War*, Book Five)

Many of the tragedies and comedies of the fifth century expressed Athenian pride in the democratic tradition, especially after Athens played the major part in defeating the Persian Empire's attack in 490–480. This was the event that opened the way for Athens' economic supremacy and prosperity, as well as its cultural and intellectual flourishing. But eventually, the Athenian *polis* was brought to an end by war. The Athenian Empire got itself embroiled in the war with the Spartan military dictatorship, the Assembly bungled the whole thing, and Athenian democracy was destroyed.

So Plato, Aristotle, and other founders of political philosophy were concerned about the problems of an organism which was already in terminal crisis. When the *polis* was in its prime, citizens knew the difference between what was just and what was unjust. But when the economic contradictions increasingly broke up the harmony between the individual citizen and the collective life of the *polis*, these great thinkers found it necessary to ask their questions about the vanishing community. They were certainly not satisfied with describing the way humans lived: they could not separate such an enquiry from the question: what forms would make it possible to live well? They were not trying to return to the past they knew that was out of the question—but attempting to confront, in the realm of thought, the conflicts which were tearing the *polis* apart. How could community be compatible with inequality in property and in power?

(a) Plato's Ideal *Polis*

The hatred of the aristocrat Plato for democracy is quite blatant. He happily blames it for all the troubles afflicting Athens in his time. Early on in his most celebrated dialogue,[5] *The Republic*, we encounter all of the forces breaking up Athenian democracy. The dialogue begins in the Piraeus, the commercial center of Athens. We meet a slave in the first few sentences, and money is not long in putting in an appearance. All of these institutions of inequality are accepted as given, and Plato, through his mouthpiece Socrates, tries to grasp their implications for political life. Socrates asks the aged Cephalus, a wealthy arms manufacturer, whether his great wealth consoles him for old age, and receives a wise and balanced answer. But this is not much use philosophically, for Plato will soon explain that he is after a timeless truth, not individual opinion. Soon Cephalus departs (lines 328–31) and leaves Socrates and his friends to conduct their quest for the meaning of Justice (*dike*), more accurately "right conduct." This is no criticism of the old man, but illustrates Plato's contention that philosophy is only for certain people. The rest of us must try to live justly, but it is not necessary for us to know what Justice is. The rest of the dialogue takes place in Cephalus' house.

First, Socrates pretends to take Justice to be a characteristic of the individual. Then he tries out the suggestion that it is synonymous with "giving every man his due." If this is interpreted as meaning that "the just man should harm his enemies and help his friends," it has to be rejected. Next we encounter the objectionable Thrasymachus, a fourth-century Thatcherite (336). He is a Sophist, one who philosophizes for a fee, indeed, he gets paid for his part in these proceedings. He noisily defends the idea that Justice is no more than "what is in the interest of the stronger party," rejecting everything else as sentimental rubbish. (The kind of world recommended by Thrasymachus, a world of greed and self-interest, was, no doubt, presented by Plato as a caricature. For us today, however, it is only too familiar as a realistic portrait of the world we live in.)

Socrates easily ties him in knots. He contends that governing is a special skill, requiring special training, like practicing as a doctor or a musician. In any case, the ruler who feathers his own nest is not a *true* ruler, as judged by the ideal. But Glaucon, from here on Socrates' chief interlocutor, is not satisfied. This is not because he agrees with Thrasymachus' absurd attitude, but because he thinks the arguments against it have not gone deep enough. Supported by his brother Adeimantus, Glaucon now presents a more carefully worked-out case for self-interest as the basis for social life, a kind of "social contract," so that Socrates can deal with it on a deeper level (357).

Self-interest is the motive which all men naturally follow if they are not forcibly restrained by law and made to respect each other's claims. (359)

As becomes increasingly clear in the course of the dialogue, the aim of the inquiry is to free us from mere "opinion" (*doxa*), and to open the way for knowledge (*episteme*). Such knowledge is universal and unchanging, and only because of this is it binding on all freethinking citizens. The justice sought by Socrates does not reside in particular instances of just behavior, or just persons, or just constitutions. Such examples can never be more than pale reflections of the Just itself, something eternal and universal. Only this "Idea" is real Justice. To grasp such a reality demands close attention, the kind of philosophical journey on which Socrates leads his young companions.

As a kind of thought experiment, he begins to invent an ideal *polis*, although the first prototype version turns out to be rather less than ideal. It consists of citizens with different skills, peacefully making the various things the community needs to live, and exchanging the products of their labor. "Society originates because the individual is not self-sufficient," says Socrates (369). There has to be a division of labor—although it is quite different from the kind we shall meet in later centuries. "Will a man do better working at many trades or keeping to one only?" asks Socrates: his criterion is not which way will produce more stuff, but which will produce a result of better quality. Ethical considerations are never absent here. There are also traders, to market the goods produced by the others. These are men who are not fit for any productive activity. But where is Justice to be found in such a setup? "Really, Socrates," Glaucon comments, "you might be catering for a community of pigs" (372).[6] Here, Plato expresses two things: boundless contempt for ordinary people and awareness that commerce is incompatible with the ancient virtues.

Socrates pretends to answer by bringing some luxuries into the picture; then doctors and other professions; and finally, soldiers. "If we are to have enough for pasture and plough, we shall have to cut a slice off our neighbours' territory . . . and that will lead to war" (373). Now, the soldiers called the "Guardians," the watchdogs of the *polis*, emerge as a governing class. In the course of the dialogue their selection and training becomes the chief issue, as some of them are transformed from fighters into "Philosopher Kings." (The rest are called "auxiliaries," who work as soldiers and policemen under the direction of the Guardians proper.)

Those who undertake the control of the *polis* have to be philosophers, who are familiar with those Forms whose reality turns out to be Plato's central answer to the mess into which the everyday world is entangled. They must be unencumbered by property or family, and even their sex lives are eugenically controlled by the Rulers.

Plato does not see the need to justify this inequality between rulers and ruled. As far as he is concerned, it is obviously the way things have to be. Justice is eventually going to reveal itself to center on "everybody doing his own proper job." So, even though all the work of the Guardians must aim "to promote the happiness . . . of the whole community" (420), the running of the *polis* is going to concern only specialists in Justice. "In that way, the integrity and unity of both the city and the *polis* will be preserved," says Socrates (423). Ruled like this, the *polis* "will obviously have the virtues of wisdom, courage, discipline and justice" (427), for "the desires of the less reputable majority are controlled by the desires and wisdom of the superior minority" (431). Included in the inferior portion are "children, women and slaves," and "the less reputable majority of so-called free men."

On one issue only does Plato approach a modern liberal view: he considers that women with the necessary ability should be eligible for education as

Guardians. (Less able women he can't be bothered about.) The Guardians, and only the Guardians, are trained as Philosophers, "Lovers of Wisdom." To rule justly, they must know Justice. But a startling paradox emerges, for one of the main jobs of these "Lovers of the Truth" turns out to be telling lies to lesser beings.

> And surely we must value truthfulness highly. For if we were right when we said just now that falsehood is no use to the gods and only useful to men as a kind of medicine, it's clearly a medicine that should be entrusted to doctors and not to laymen.
> Yes.
> It will be for the rulers of our *polis*, then, if anyone, to deceive citizen or enemy for the good of the state; no one else must do it. If any citizen lies to our rulers, we shall regard it as a still graver offence than it is for a patient to lie to his doctor, or for an athlete to lie to his trainer about his physical condition.
> So philosophy is impossible among the common people.
> Quite impossible. (494)

The Justice for which Plato is searching belongs to the "real" world of unchanging objects, that is, it is an *ideal*. The quite different world of ordinary life is necessarily one of imperfection and change.

> Hard as it may be for a state so framed to be shaken, yet, since all that comes into being must decay, even a fabric like this will not endure for ever, but will suffer dissolution. In this manner: not only for plants that grow on earth, but also for creatures that move thereon, there are seasons of fruitfulness and unfruitfulness for soul and body alike, which come whenever a certain cycle is completed, in a period short or long according to the length of life of each species. (546)

Here is a problem which, as we shall see, recurs throughout the history of philosophy. If you can demonstrate that a way of life is necessarily the best possible one, then any change must necessarily mean decline. This is the subject of Books IX and X of *The Republic*. Here, Socrates successively examines four inferior forms of state. First we are given Thrasymachus' favorite, "timocracy," where ambition and greed hold sway, then oligarchy, democracy, and despotism. Plato shows how his best of states holds the possibility, even inevitability, that it will degenerate into one or other of these inferior forms.

Finally, Socrates, now concerned only with "the intelligent man," decides that, since such people are in short supply, his plan for the ideal *polis* is really unattainable.

> "Perhaps," I said, "it is laid up as a pattern in heaven, where those who wish can see it and found it in their own hearts. But it doesn't matter whether it exists or ever will exist; it's the only state in whose politics he can take part." (592)

Plato seeks the best form of community, and thinks he has found it in the propertyless, highly organized life of the specially selected, scientifically bred and philosophically trained Guardians. Everybody else lives at a lower level, busily making things and exchanging them to keep the *polis* going. Only the Guardians know the Forms, above all the Form of the Good, and this, Plato alleges, gives his ideal *polis* its objective foundation. Thus his solution to the contradiction between the individual and the common good is situated "in heaven," out of the reach of ordinary men and women. Indeed, the final section of the dialogue deals with the immortality of the soul and the structure and origin of the universe. The citizens, for whose well-being the Guardians were supposed to be responsible, seem to have been forgotten. While the Guardians philosophize, the ordinary people, *hoi polloi*, are left to make shoes or money, in Socrates' first city, the city "fit for pigs." This is the only way forward, Plato is certain, although without much optimism of success.

> The society we have described can never grow into a reality or see the light of day, and there will be no end to the troubles of states, or indeed, my dear Glaucon, of humanity itself, till philosophers become kings in this world, or till those we now call kings and rulers really and truly become philosophers. (473)

(b) Aristotle

Aristotle was Plato's most celebrated pupil, but his outlook differs in many ways from that of his great teacher. While Plato's celestial "Ideas" exist outside the existing world, only dimly and imperfectly reflected in it, Aristotle seeks the Forms in that world itself. His investigation of human life, which involves a great deal of empirical research, for example, classifying all the constitutions known to him, is based on the assumption that the human is "by nature" a city dweller, an "animal of the *polis*" (*zoon politikon*). "Man, when perfected, is the best of animals; but when isolated from law and justice, he is the worst of all."

> Hence it is evident that the state is a creation of nature, and that man is by nature a political animal. And he who by nature and not by mere accident is not a member of a state is either a bad man or above humanity; . . . he may be compared to an isolated piece at draughts. . . . He who is unable to live in society, or who has no need because he is sufficient for himself, must be either a beast or a god. (*Politics*, 1253a)[7]

This famous characterization has two sides, however. It not only stresses that human sociality is natural. It also applies this idea only to Greeks: "barbarians" don't qualify. The *polis* is part of the great organism of nature, so that justice has a natural basis. However, the way any particular *polis* functions must be decided by convention, and by the decision of rulers.

Aristotle's *Politics* seeks to understand the different kinds of "association" or "community," of which the *polis* is the highest form. "Every community is established with a view to some good; for everyone always acts in order to obtain that which they think good" (*Politics*, 1252a). The task Aristotle has set himself is to find the best way this may be achieved. "Our purpose is to consider what form of political community is best of all for those who are most able to realise their ideal of life" (*Politics*, 1260b). So *what* is best and *what* is ideal are the crucial questions. That is why the book must be taken together with the *Ethics*, which at its outset stresses the importance of studying politics as a science. To be a good man, you must live in a good *polis*. (Women don't count.) Studying politics, which aims to discover "the good for man," puts us in touch with something which stands above the individual.

> But, if all communities aim at some good, the state or political community (*polis*) which is the highest of all, and which embraces all the rest, aims at a good in a greater degree than all the rest.

But that does not tell us how the *polis* ought to be governed. Self-rule in society (*isonomia*) is a natural property of humanity. Aristotle believes in the importance of self-sufficiency (*autarkeia*), and argues that this is only possible within the *polis*, a "state which has a regard to the common interest," "a community of free men" (*Politics*, 1279a). Nonetheless, he does not regard Athenian democracy as the best way to organize. While not as violently opposed to it as Plato, Aristotle will classify it as one of the inferior forms of constitution. Power ought best to be in the hands of the "best people" (*aristoi*).

All of this assumes that the *polis* is a divided unity. What unites it? And what divides it? The *Ethics* devotes two whole books (Books VIII and IX), to the problem of friendship (*philia*). Aristotle quotes the old Greek saying: "Friends have all things in common," and believes, remarkably, that "where there is friendship, there is no need for justice." But this linking of community and friendship only applies where there is equality between the friends. If they are unequal—for example, where one is rich, the other poor—a way of measuring their respective rights has to be found.

So Aristotle must also examine those elements which make the inhabitants of the *polis* unequal. Aristotle thinks of the *polis* as made up of component associations, called households, within which a master rules his wife, his children, and his slaves. In each of the three pairs, man/woman; parent/child; master/slave, the first must govern the second.

That which can foresee by the exercise of mind is by nature lord and master, and that which can with its body give effect to such foresight is a subject, and by nature a slave; hence master and slave have the same interest.

There can be *philia*, he thinks, even between master and slave, although, he admits, this friendship is somewhat different from the friendship of equals:

Where the relation of master and slave between them is natural, they are friends and have a common interest, but where it rests merely on convention and force the reverse is true. (*Politics*, 1255b)

A little further on, Aristotle explains how this works:

The rule of a master, although the slave by nature and the master by nature have the same interests, is nevertheless exercised primarily with a view to the interest of the master, but accidentally considers the slave, since, if the slave perish, the rule of the master perishes with him. (*Politics*, 1278b)

(Two thousand years later, this idea finds an echo—implicitly critical of Aristotle, although he is not explicitly acknowledged—in the "Master and Slave" episode in Hegel's *Phenomenology of Spirit*.)

In the *Ethics*, Aristotle worries over the problem at some length. Somehow, he knows he must combine friendship with the relations of power. He seeks to escape from this difficulty through his conception that slavery in particular and social divisions in general are natural. "It is clear, then, that some men are by nature free, and others slaves, and that for these latter, slavery is both expedient and just" (*Politics*, 1255a).

Although this is obvious to Aristotle, he notes that others disagree with him. Moreover, he acknowledges, not all who are enslaved ought to be so.

For there is nothing common to the two parties; the slave is a living tool and a tool a lifeless slave. *Qua* slave, then, one cannot be friends with him. But *qua* man one can; for there seems to be some justice between any man and any other who can share in a system of law or be a party to an agreement; therefore there can also be friendship with him in so far as he is a man. Therefore while in tyrannies friendship and justice hardly exist, in democracies they exist more fully; for where the citizens are equal they have much in common. (*Ethics*, 1161b)

Occasionally, Aristotle gives us a glimpse of another way of living. Near the beginning of the *Politics*, he dreams of a world where labor is not drudgery:

For if every instrument could accomplish its own work, obeying or anticipating the will of others, like the statues of Daedelus, or the tripods of Hephaestus, which, says the poet, "of their own accord entered the assembly of the gods"; if in like manner, the shuttle would weave and the plectrum touch the lyre, chief workmen would not want servants, nor masters slaves. (1253–45)

And at the end of Book IX of the *Ethics*, we get a cameo picture of what a life of friendship is like:

> And so some drink together, others dice together, others join in athletic exercises and hunting, or in the study of philosophy, each class spending their days together in whatever they love the most in life; for since they wish to live with their friends, they do and share in those things as far as they can. (1172)

If friendship is a lynchpin holding Aristotle's *polis* together, the exchange of property forms the other essential aspect. But are these two things compatible? Can exchange be just? It is to answer this question that he tries to work out how there can be "just proportion" between exchangeable goods of different kinds. (We must not read into Aristotle's words meanings drawn from our own world. In the community he is meditating upon, *dike* means both *justice as legality* and also *justice as fairness*, *metadosis* means not only *barter* but also *sharing*, while *chreia* means not only *demand* for goods, but also *need*.) In the *Ethics* (1133), Aristotle explains how the link formed by the exchange is what holds the association together. And yet, without equality, exchange would be impossible, and this demands commensurability between goods of different kinds. Aristotle can't find an answer which satisfies him — nor does he pretend to — so money is brought into the story as a makeshift to fix the crucial break between exchange and justice.

Aristotle even derives a definition of justice from these exchange relationships: "We have now defined the just and the unjust," he says after his discussion of exchange (1133b). The fact that Aristotle is unable to reach the views of modern political economy is thus crucial for his attempt to resolve the fundamental contradiction between the individual and the common good. Particularly important — and much misunderstood — is Aristotle's distinction between *oikonomia* and *chrematistic*.[8] The former, the science of management of the household, aims at a balanced program of production and commercial exchange with the rest of the *polis*: this is the "natural" way to acquire wealth. The latter, the use of money to make money, is unnatural, growing beyond all bounds. Its very worst form is usury (*tokos*). "The most hated sort, and with the greatest reason, is usury, which makes a gain out of money itself, and not from the natural object of it. . . . Of all modes of getting wealth this is the most unnatural" (*Politics*, 1258b).

Though Aristotle was a little more moderate than his teacher in his criticism of democracy, he agrees that it has a major flaw: it might give poor people, who were in the majority, the chance to take the wealth away from rich ones, and this would never do. Toward the end of the *Politics*, after examining various forms of constitution, and always distinguishing "constitutions" from monarchies, he discusses the best form of state, spelling out some of his disagreements with Plato. Social ills do not arise from a reasonable level of self-interest, as Plato had said, but from "the depravity of human character" (1266b). The *polis* should be run by men of property. Production should be left to slaves, as well as free artisans, where the latter group, even though they may sometimes be quite well off, should not be accepted into citizenship. Even where they are citizens, says Aristotle, they should not be rulers, "for no man can practise excellence who is living the life of a mechanic or laborer." (*Politics*, 1278a).

> The citizens must not lead the life of artisans or tradesmen, for such a life is ignoble and inimical to excellence. Neither must they be farmers, since leisure is necessary both for the development of excellence and the performance of political duties. (*Politics*, 1328)

He is very practical on such matters, as always.

> The very best thing of all would be that the farmers should be slaves, taken from among men who are of the same race, but not spirited, for if they have no spirit, they will be better suited for their work, and there will be no danger of them making a revolution. (*Politics*, 1330)

The rulers should be soldiers when young and statesmen when older (*Politics*, 1328b–29a). However, he is aware that the inevitable conflicts resulting from the nature of property make an ideal state of affairs impossible. Instead, Aristotle puts forward a compromise solution, which he calls "polity" (*politeia*, which also means "constitution"). This turns out to be a mixture of oligarchy and democracy, best exemplified by Sparta (1295b).

Aristotle has no conception of a historical process. But, in Book V of the *Politics*, he is concerned with constitutional change, including revolutions, as well as the possibility of avoiding such instability. Aristotle does not accept Plato's arguments that the degeneration of the best form of rule always and necessarily occurs. "Why does Plato not talk about change affecting the other, lesser state-forms as well?" asks Aristotle. Plato thinks that the tendency of everything to deteriorate over time is the cause of social change. However, Aristotle's explanation of the "variety of different constitutions" is that, "while men are all agreed in doing homage to justice and to the principle of proportional equality" (1301a), they do not agree in their interpretation of the meaning of justice. So it is not only the best form of rule that is

subject to change, and Aristotle thinks that each form can turn into each of
the others.

In the end, despite all their disagreements, Aristotle's conclusions do not
differ so greatly from those of Plato. Near the end of the *Ethics*, he argues that
the highest happiness is to be found, not in practical activity of any kind, but
in contemplation. Making things (*poiesis*) is essentially servile, subordinate
to political practice (*praxis*), thinks Aristotle, and both are below the level of
intellectual contemplation (*theoria*—a word derived from that for a spectator
at the theater).

> For if the gods have any care for human affairs, as they are thought to have, it
> would be reasonable and best that they should delight in that which was best and
> most akin to them (ie intellect) and that should reward those who love and hon-
> our this the most, as caring for the things which that are dear to them and acting
> both rightly and nobly. And that all these attributes belong most of all to the wise
> man. (*Ethics*, 1179a)

Philosophy has begun as it would continue for the next couple of millennia.

(c) The Stoics[9]

With the collapse of the Athenian Empire, the Athenian philosophical tradition went into decline. The *polis* had ceased to be; philosophers no longer
thought about the "common good"; the divorce of ethics and politics was
complete. Epicurianism, Cynicism, and Stoicism, all turned to problems of
individual virtue and personal happiness, but it was Stoicism whose ideas re-
verberated down the centuries.

But which Stoicism? There seems to be a gulf between the founders of the
movement, their leader, Zeno of Tarsus (Citium) (334–262), and his pupil
Chrisippus (c. 280–206) on the one hand, and their later followers in Greece and
Rome on the other. They all believe that Nature includes "right reasoning"—
identified with virtue—within its structure. The wise man, the *phronimos*, who
is also the virtuous man, is impervious to "the passions" and acts in harmonious
accord with Nature. His life is his own affair, and nobody else's: if it turns out
badly, suicide is his own business too. There is a natural law, binding on all humans, independent of the laws of particular states. The course of natural development is predestined, and the sage is indifferent to external circumstances. The
only good is individual virtue and the only evil is individual vice.

But each of the founders of Stoicism, Zeno and Chrisippus, had written a
Republic, works known to us only through the loud denunciations of later
writers. Not only the enemies of Stoicism, but later Stoics, were scandalized
by Zeno's idea on the ideal *polis*, and his book was disowned, written off as

youthful excess and a reflection of his bad schooling by the Cynics. This reception might have been partly occasioned by his highly permissive views on sexual matters. But his scorn for social convention in general appears to have included radical ideas about property and political power. His *polis* was to have as citizens only wise men and women, who were therefore certain to be virtuous and to despise wealth and glory. Instead of ruling the fools, as in Plato's setup, the shared right reason of the wise would make money, laws and marriage unnecessary. However, all this was as unlikely of realization as Plato's ideal, for, as several Stoic texts admit, wise men are as rare "as the Egyptian Pheonix."

No wonder that the later Stoics try to distance themselves from such ideas. They come to consider society, if at all, only as a convenience for the individual. As we have seen, this was an argument Plato had combated, but it was to return in modern times as the basis for the ideas of political economy. While the Romans imitated a great deal of the culture of the Greeks, even in the days of the Republic, it was Sparta rather than Athens that provided the model for their political forms and theory. In the last days of the Roman Republic, three centuries after, its origin, Stoicism, found a sympathetic echo, influencing many of the writers of that troubled time, notably Cicero (106–43AD), the former slave Epictetus (55–135) and the Emperor Marcus Aurelius (121–180).

Amid the decadence and corruption of the Empire, where few voices spoke up for the old Republican virtues, Cicero transmitted the Stoic ideas of unchangeable, eternal, and universal natural law. These notions made possible a global view of society. "This whole universe must be considered a common city of gods and men" (*Laws*, I, 23). Roman jurists contrasted the natural law (*jus naturalis*) with the laws or statutes laid down by states, which they called *lex naturalis*. Later in our story, the Stoic idea of personal integrity, independent of society, will often reemerge in various guises, particularly because it was one of the influences feeding into the emergence of Christianity.

NOTES

1. G. E. McCarthy, *Marx and the Ancients: Classical Ethics, Social Justice and Nineteenth Century Political Economy* (Lanham, Md.: Rowman & Littlefield, 1990), has been very useful, especially on the relation between Marx and Aristotle. However, I part company with the author when he insists on regarding Marx as a maker of theories. Sean Sayers' *Plato's Republic: An Introduction* (Edinburgh: Edinburgh University Press, 1999) has also been very helpful. While I have only talked about Western philosophy, we ought really to consider also Indian and Chinese thinkers, too, and only ignorance has prevented me from doing this. It becomes increasingly clear that

communications between Europe, Asia, and parts of Africa were much closer than used to be supposed, so that all developments in the ancient world should be seen as an integrated whole.

2. The Minoan script disappeared, and writing had to be reinvented. So much for the account of Engels, uncritically taken from that of L. H. Morgan, of a once-for-all transition from "barbarism" to "civilization," in which clan society gave way to "slave society." Engels's work *The Origin of the Family, Private Property and the State* was a remarkable contribution in its time, but it does not represent the ideas of Marx, as publication of Marx's *Ethnological Notebooks* showed. The attempt to sustain Engels's authority in the face of the conclusions of modern research marred much work by would-be "Marxists."

3. See, for example, Ellen Meiskens Wood, *Peasant, Citizen and Slave* (London: Verso, 1989). See also Josiah Ober, *The Athenian Revolution: Essays on Ancient Greek Democracy and Political Theory* (Princeton, N. J.: Princeton University Press, 1996); James L. O'Neil, *The Origins and Development of Ancient Greek Democracy* (Lanham, Md.: Rowman & Littlefield, 1995), and Arlene W. Saxonhouse, *Athenian Democracy: Modern Mythmakers and Ancient Theorists* (Notre Dame, Ind.: University of Notre Dame Press, 1996).

4. C. L. R. James's "Every Cook Can Govern: A Study of Democracy in Ancient Greece in the Future and in the Present," in *Selected Writings* Alison and Busby, 1977, is an example of such idealization, although a beautifully written one.

5. Except for the word *polis*, I have used the translation by H. P. D. Lee (Penguin Classics, 1955).

6. Compare this remark with the passage on "the spiritual animal kingdom and deceit" in Hegel's *Phenomenology of Spirit*, where he satirizes civil society (Miller Translation, 237).

7. I have used the translations in Jonathan Barnes, *The Complete Works of Aristotle* (Princeton, N.J.: Princeton University Press, 1984), giving the traditional page numbers.

8. For a total misunderstanding and muddle, see Fowkes' Pelican translation of *Capital*, Vol. 1, pages 253–54 together with footnote 6, and 267. Marx himself had understood Aristotle perfectly, but Fowkes can't understand either of them.

9. J. M. Rist, *Stoic Philosophy* (Cambridge: Cambridge University Press, 1969), traces the connections of Stoicism to Plato and Aristotle. Andrew Erskine, *The Hellenistic Stoa: Political Thought and Action* (London: Duckworth, 1990) and Malcolm Schofield, *The Stoic Idea of the City* (Chicago: University of Chicago Press, 1999), reconstruct the ideas of Zeno's *Republic*.

Chapter Six

Toward the Modern State

SCHOLASTICISM

In the new Dark Ages, which followed the Christianization and collapse of the Roman Empire, the legacy of Athens was all but forgotten in Western Europe, kept alive largely through Islamic culture and scholarship. While a Stoicized version of Platonism was combined with Christianity by Augustine (354–430) and others in the early Church, Aristotle was only known in the Arabic translations and commentaries of Avicenna (980–1037) and Averroes (1126–1198). Only as Europe began to wake up from its Christian-feudal sleep did scholar-monks begin to translate Aristotle's works directly into Latin.

The *Politics* was one of the last of these works to be translated, in about 1260, and at first it encountered great opposition inside the Church. The idea that society exists "by nature" seemed to contradict Augustine's conviction that social life, "the City of Man," was spiritually lower than "the City of God." "Man is the image and resemblance of God on Earth," he wrote. Governments were needed, thought the devout theologians, only because of man's sinful character. Averroes' interpretation of Aristotle, which held that human consciousness was a unity, a single world intellect, opposed the idea of the individual soul, and Aristotelians who got into trouble were often accused of "Averroesism."

But, in the thirteenth century, some scholars, led by Albertus Magnus (1206–1280), began to synthesize Aristotle with Augustinian Christianity. It was Albertus's pupil, the Dominican monk Thomas Aquinas (1225–1274), who managed to construct a system of thought on this foundation, codifying everything from cosmology to contraception. Only after a struggle was

Thomas canonized and his ideas made into an established part of Catholic thinking for centuries to come.

Although he constantly employs the pagan Aristotle ("the Philosopher") in the service of the Church, Aquinas breaks away from his Greek master at crucial points in his work. Aristotle had a scale of forms of knowledge, with sense perception (*aisthesis*) at the bottom, followed by memory (*mneme*), experience (*empeiria*), art (*techne*), science (*episteme*), and at the very top, wisdom (*sophia*). Now, Aquinas finds a corresponding pecking order of sciences, but theology must occupy the highest level. He also requires a three-tier system of law: divine, natural, and positive.

So Aristotle's lively spirit of inquiry through discussion is replaced by a fixed structure, in which there is a correct answer to every question. (As is well known, if you weren't quite sure just what was "correct," the Church could help you to see the truth by methods which were not always entirely philosophical.) The complete system is enclosed within a hierarchical conception of reality, a cosmology deriving more from early Christian Neoplatonism than from Aristotle. In place of Aristotle's organic network of cause and effect, with the "unmoved mover" at its beginning, Aquinas places his three-in-one God firmly at the top, with angels in the next level, humans below that, and the rest of animate and inanimate creation down below. This entire outlook fits well, of course, with the feudal structure of medieval society. Aquinas thought this was because feudalism expressed the will of the Almighty, rather than his cosmology being the spiritual expression of feudalism.

Not surprisingly, Aquinas uses the *Politics* to formulate ideas about government which are welcome to the sacred and secular powers of his time. At the very start of his unfinished treatise "On Kingship" (commissioned by the King of Cyprus), Aquinas states that "men in society must be under rulers." "If it is natural for men to live in association with others, there must be some way for them to be governed," and "it is best for a human group to be ruled by one person." He wants this ruler to be "just," of course, but democracy is definitely ruled out.

An interesting question arises about what to do with an unjust ruler. In the equivalent of his doctoral dissertation in 1256, the young Aquinas argues that: "The Christian is obliged to obey authority that comes from God, but not that which is not from God." And, quoting Cicero, he declares that "someone who kills a tyrant to liberate his country is to be praised and rewarded." Ten years later, Aquinas has mellowed a bit: "However, if no human aid is possible against the tyrant, recourse is to be made to God, the king of all, who is the help of those in tribulation."[1]

Aquinas' discussion of slavery presents an interesting example of his differences with Aristotle. As we saw, Aristotle, himself an owner of household slaves, still believes that slavery is not always just. Only some people are "natural slaves," and the enslavement of others, even if it is necessary for the life of the *polis*, is a necessary evil. But Aquinas, in his commentary on the *Politics*, is less equivocal: enslavement through conquest is perfectly just, and good for both the conqueror and the conquered.

This is particularly important in relation to the concept of "natural law." As we have seen, Aristotle (*Ethics*, V, 8) uses the concept of natural justice, but always stresses that its implementation is determined by the decisions of the rulers. "While natural justice certainly exists, the rules under which justice is administered is everywhere being modified." Aquinas, on the contrary, believes that "positive law" (*lex*) is hemmed in by "natural law" (*jus*), while over both of them stands the "divine law." At the end of the day, the decisions of the just ruler are subject to God's power, and the teachings of the Church are left intact. While utilizing Aristotle's method of reasoning, Aquinas skillfully makes sure that the conclusions to which it leads are never out of line with Holy Scripture, which embodies divine revelation.

We must not forget that Aquinas was working at the time when the social order in Europe was already entering the centuries of its dissolution. As in Athens, philosophy comes on the scene when the reality it seeks to explain is coming to the end of its natural shelf life. Aquinas' understanding of the relation of individual and society points to the development of modern political thought. While Aristotle saw ethics and politics as studying inseparable aspects of the Good, Aquinas carefully distinguishes their respective spheres. Because each human has an individual, immortal soul, the city is not an organic unity. The goodness of each individual is a matter of his relation with God, quite distinct from the common good, which is in the hands of other, more mundane forces. For Aquinas, ethics and politics are quite independent sciences, and economic life is set apart from each of them.

MACHIAVELLI

As the feudal structures decay, and as market forces come to play an increasing part in the lives of West Europeans, and the modern state takes shape, thinkers begin more and more to see humans as individuals, as "selves," existing independently of political forms. Humanists like Erasmus (1466–1536), Rabelais (1493–1553), Pico della Mirandola (1463–1494), and Montaigne (1533–1592) challenge the powers that be. Despite the violent religious clashes going on around them, they write about how independent individuals could live freely and harmoniously. Moving in a different direction, Martin Luther (1483–1546), originally an Augustinian monk, took the development of individualism to the door of the Church, with uncompromising intolerance. John Calvin (1509–1564) and his followers describe a community of individuals, whose social organization and personal lives are prearranged by the Almighty. To clarify their philosophical disagreements, proponents of such views often find it helpful to burn each other.

In general, the thinkers of the seventeenth and eighteenth centuries reflect the growing dominance of market relations over the whole of social life. Humans are seen as independent, self-interested individuals, existing prior to society, but coming together in a social structure, where they are linked by money and governed by a state power. But this poses a huge problem: if God and His Holy Church are not available as the ultimate referees, how can these social atoms be united into a single social whole? Through what procedure could the mass of independent individuals be persuaded to accept an ordered structure?

Even today, the name of Nicolo Machiavelli (1469–1527) is a byword for the separation of ethics and politics. The brutal frankness of *The Prince*, with its rigorous and open analysis of the way that individual rulers could take and hold power, enraged the powers themselves, especially the Church. Apparently, this came as a surprise to this career civil servant and diplomat. When the Medicis took over Florence, his position as a servant of the previous regime was violently terminated. Apparently, he still hoped they would employ him, even after they had imprisoned and tortured him a bit. It was surely with misplaced optimism that he made *The Prince* part of his job application.

What this book ruthlessly demonstrates is that ethical politics has no place in the existing world of power. Moreover, this is a world where God's Will plays no part at all. Here, the resolute prince must seize each opportunity granted by Fortune (*fortuna*), using all his manly courage and skill (*virtú*) to press forward social and political change. In chapter XXV, "On Fortune's Role in Human Affairs and how she can be Dealt With," Machiavelli assesses the respective importance of Fortune and will:

> Nevertheless, in order that our free will be not extinguished, I judge it to be true that Fortune is the arbiter of one half of our actions, but that she leaves control of the other half, or almost that, to us. . . . She shows her force where there is no organized strength to resist her.

Machiavelli's understanding of Fortune is no way leads him to a passive conception of social action. *Fortuna* is a Roman goddess, not the Christian Providence, and she responds to forceful treatment, thinks this most politically incorrect thinker. Moral law has nothing to do with it. What so enraged Machiavelli's readers was his refusal to disguise this reality. For instance, in chapter VIII, "On Those who have become Princes through Wickedness," he advises anyone recognizing the applicability of this description how to be-have:

> In taking a state its conqueror should weigh all the harmful things he must do and do them all at once so as not to have to repeat them every day, and in not repeating them to be able to make men feel secure and win them over with the benefits he bestows upon them.

Welcome to the modern world! Chapter XVII, which has the title: "On Cru-elty and Mercy and Whether it is Better to be Loved or the Contrary," ex-plains that

> men are less hesitant about harming someone who makes himself loved than one who makes himself feared because love is held together by a chain of obliga-tion, which, since men are a sorry lot, is broken on every occasion on which their own self-interest is concerned; but fear is held together by a dread of pun-ishment which will never abandon you.

It is as if someone published a best seller called "How to be a spin doctor." Such a publication might not be welcomed by the politicians it was meant to benefit.

Machiavelli has little time for "writers who have imagined for themselves republics and principalities that have never been seen nor known to exist in reality." Drawing historical examples from classical history, as well as from his own time, including his own extensive personal experience, he wants to describe the world as it actually is. This refusal to conceal reality was what led many people to denounce his "immorality," falsely accusing him of mak-ing "the ends justify the means." In fact, it is in the penultimate chapter XVIII, "How a Prince should Keep his Word," that the much-mistranslated phrase occurs, in a passage showing Machiavelli's harsh realism.

> Everyone sees what you seem to be, few perceive what you are, and those few do not dare to contradict the opinion of the many who have the majesty of the state to defend them; and in the actions of all men, and especially of princes, where there is no impartial arbiter, one must consider the final result. Let a prince therefore act to seize and to maintain the state; his methods will be judged honorable and will be praised by all.

Christian authors had, of course, always explained how honesty was the best policy, in the face of all evidence to the contrary. Expediency would al-ways be moral and vice versa, they assured their readers. Machiavelli pre-tends to be sad to tell us that this doesn't really work at all. (The pious ones knew this too, of course, but didn't like to say so.) "A man who wishes to make a vocation of being good at all times will come to ruin among so many who are not good." (It would be worthwhile pondering the relation between this idea and the theme of another important work of ethical theory: Heller's *Catch 22*. Yossarian's argument is very close to that of Machiavelli.) Finally, Machiavelli exhorts the Prince "to Liberate Italy from the Barbarians," founding a unity of free city-states.

When Machiavelli wrote *The Prince* in 1513, he had to interrupt work on a longer book, the *Discourses on the First Ten Books of Titus Livius*. This is a detailed comparison of the contemporary condition of Italy with Machiavelli's ideal model: the Roman Republic. In it, he presents his own preferences for republicanism in a manner which would have been quite inappropriate in *The Prince*. However, a republic must be founded by a great single figure, and if this involves violent acts, they may be justified. "For one should reproach a man who is violent in order to destroy, not one who is violent in order to mend things." (Book 1, chapter IX.) Most people, he thinks, will give their backing to tyranny, instead of earning "fame, glory, honor, tranquillity and peace of mind" by fighting against it.

And yet the title of chapter LV tells us that "where equality exists, no principality can be established, and where equality does not exist, a republic cannot be established." For "the masses are wiser and more constant than a prince" (chapter LVIII). Whereas in *The Prince*, *virtú* was a requirement for princes, here it is important for ordinary people. From the history of the ancient Romans he learns how stubbornly a free people will fight for their liberty. "For it is the common good and not private gain that makes cities great" (Book 2, chapter II). A citizens' militia is better than relying on mercenary troops, he is certain, not just because they will fight better, but also because it will help the avoidance of tyranny after military victory.

But this raises a central problem, unique to this writer: how is *virtú* to be spread among a whole body of citizens? This is the angle from which Machiavelli examines the question of the best form of state. Like Aristotle and others, he accepts the traditional three-way division of monarchy or principality, aristocracy, and democracy. None of these is stable: monarchy degenerates into tyranny, aristocracy into oligarchy and democracy into anarchy. For stability a mixture of the three is required. But Machiavelli's use of this scheme is quite new. For him, the forms make up a cycle, driven round by the conflicts between rich and poor.

But he does not merely seek to avoid such conflict. Instead, he seeks a way to harness it, and believes that this was how the Roman Republic lasted for three centuries. It was precisely "the division between the plebeians and the Roman Senate that made the Republic rich and powerful" (Book 1, chapter IV). If we can balance out the "rich men's arrogance" and the "people's licence," then liberty might remain uncorrupted. This startling idea makes Machiavelli one of the most modern of writers.

HOBBES

At least two seventeenth-century thinkers, far from sharing the general horror of Machiavelli, openly proclaimed their admiration for him. However, while they each lived through an age of political upheaval, their views on many questions are very different. One is the Englishman Thomas Hobbes, the other the Dutch-Portuguese Jew Benedict de Spinoza.

Many writers of their times explicitly and directly oppose Aristotle's conception of the *zoon politikon*, but Thomas Hobbes (1588–1679) is, as usual, more forthright than most. In his *De Cive* he says that anyone who thinks man is social by nature is stupid. In general, he accepts the picture of Aristotle presented to him by the Scholastics, as may be seen in chapter 44 of *Leviathan*, "Of Darkness from Vain Philosophy, and Fabulous Traditions." He revels in putting the metaphysical boot in, writing about Aristotle as

> an example of the errors which are brought into the Church, from the *entities* and *essences* of Aristotle: which it may be he knew to be false philosophy; but writ as a thing consonant to, and collaborative of their religion; and fearing the fate of Socrates.

In seventeenth-century England, the issue of sovereignty, which caused such enormous upheaval in practice, naturally brought great confusion in theory. The Stuarts asserted that they were monarchs by divine right, but this no longer carried enough weight to save them. Their Royalist supporters had to combine this with a claim that Charles I also based his kingship on the original consent of the people of England. Their Parliamentary opponents, on the other hand, almost to the time they had their monarch's head cut off, tried to deny that they were disloyal to the monarchy as such. Even members of the court which sentenced to death "Charles Stuart, that man of blood," wavered in the face of his insistence that God Almighty had appointed him for life— or even longer.

In his time, Hobbes' name was almost as hated as that of his hero Machiavelli had been. He sought a way to achieve stability and peace through a rigorously scientific investigation of the nature of social life, one which ruthlessly cut through all confusion. Hobbes' infamous book, *Leviathan*—its brutality still shocks us—attempted to explain the nature of power, as part of a scientific view of Nature. Each component of a vast clockwork operated externally to the rest, pushing and pulling each other into motion. Hobbes starts his introduction with a confident declaration on the mechanisms of nature and man (women rarely enter into Hobbes' argument!):

> Nature (the Art whereby God hath made and governs the World) is by the *art* of man, as in many other things, so in this also imitated, that it can make an artificial animal. For seeing life is but a motion of limbs, the beginning whereof is in some principal part within; why may we not say, that all *automata* (engines that move themselves by springs and wheels as doth a watch) have an artificial life? For what is the *heart*, but a *spring*; and the *nerves*, but so many *strings*; and the *joints*, but so many *wheels*, giving motion to the whole Body, such as was intended by the artificer? *Art* goes yet further, imitating that rational and most excellent work of nature, *man*. For by art is created by that great LEVIATHAN, called a COMMONWEALTH, or STATE, in Latin Civitas, which is but an artificial man.

As Cromwell's "Long Parliament" began its revolutionary work, Hobbes, who thought the Cromwellians would open the way to anarchy, went to live in Paris. But by 1651 he had fallen out with the Royalists who were his fellow exiles. They were not at all pleased by his open and totally unromantic way of justifying monarchical power. At the same time, his attack on the Papacy enraged his French Catholic hosts. He returned to England, and made his peace with Cromwell, now Lord Protector of a republic who had defeated the Levellers and other radicals.

The cover of the first edition of *Leviathan* depicts a great, crowned figure, seen on inspection to be made up of many small men. How and why is this artificial machine made of humans constructed? What makes it tick? Hobbes derives its properties from those of the individual components of the mechanism. Men, he tells us, are pushed by "appetite or desire" and pulled by "aversion," especially fear of death. "For there is no such thing as perpetual tranquillity of mind while we live here; because life itself is but motion, and can never be without desire, nor without fear." Man must seek power, and "shuns . . . the chiefest of natural evils, which is death."

From these two assumptions springs the whole of Hobbes' argument. "The POWER of a man (to take it universally), is present means, to obtain some future good." Men will differ in their natural powers, which mean "the eminence of the faculties of body or of mind." Note that such powers are measured competitively, relative to other men. With their aid, "or by fortune," certain other powers, may be acquired. These "are means and instruments to acquire more: as riches, reputation, friends, and the secret working of God, which men call good luck." Thus the nature of human society is such that individuals must inevitably clash. By their human nature they must continually seek power over each other.

I put for a general inclination of all mankind, a perpetual and restless desire of power after power that ceaseth only in death. And the cause of this, is not always that a man hopes for more delight, than he has already attained to; or that he cannot be content with a moderate power: but because he cannot assure the power and means to live well, which he hath present, without the acquisition of more.

It is "in the nature of man" to fight his neighbors, and unless a power over them prevent it, they will kill each other. "During the time men live without a common Power to keep them all in awe, they are in a condition which is called war; and such a war, as is of every man, against every man."

Only if all men put themselves under the absolute control of a central power can they avoid what Hobbes regards as their natural state. As he explains in his most famous passage:

Whatsoever therefore is consequent to a time of war, where every man is enemy to every man; the same is consequent to the time, wherein men live without other security, than what their own strength, and their own invention shall furnish them withal. In such condition, there is no place for Industry; because the fruit thereof is uncertain; no culture of the earth; no navigation, nor use of the commodities that may be imported by sea; no commodious building; no instruments of moving, and removing such things as require much force; no knowledge of the face of the earth; no account of time; no arts; no letters; no society; and, which is worst of all, continual fear, and danger of violent death; and the life of man, solitary, poor, nasty, brutish and short.

In the state of nature, there can be no such thing as justice. "For where no Covenant hath preceded, there hath no Right been transferred, and every man has right to every thing; and consequently, no action can be Unjust."

There are natural laws, but no way to enforce them. Hobbes uses the terms *jus naturale* and *lex naturalis*, but gives them entirely new meanings.

THE RIGHT OF NATURE, which writers commonly call *jus naturale*, is the liberty each man hath, to use his own power, as he will himself, for the preservation of his own Nature. . . . By LIBERTY, is understood, according to the proper signification of the word, the absence of external impediments; . . . A LAW OF NATURE, (*lex naturalis,*) is a precept, or general rule, found out by reason, by which a man is forbidden to do that which is destructive of his life, or taketh away the means of preserving the same. (chapter 14)

Any reasonable being living under the state of nature can only try to get out of it, and there is only one way of escape: each man has to give up part of his freedom to a central, absolute coercive, sovereign power. Only when this social contract has been entered into, can men live in peace. The power of the

Sovereign has to be absolute. "The validity of covenants begins not but with the constitution of a civil power, sufficient to compel men to keep them; and then it is also that propriety begins." So there can be no "propriety" (property) without state power, for then "there is no visible power to keep them in awe, and tie them by fear of punishment to the performance of their Covenants and observation of those law of nature."

Hobbes does not think that either the state of nature or the social contract were actual historical events. They are rather logical postulates which must be assumed in a society of atoms. From these axioms his plan for a peaceful and stable monarchy can be logically derived. The consequence is ethics—of a special kind. Each man is obliged to give up some of his rights to a sovereign, and obliged to obey him. Accepting this obedience, fulfilling this obligation, each individual will strive for his own good. The result will be the common good—of a special kind. The "Covenant" is between the individuals, who give up their rights to the sovereign. There is no contract with the sovereign, whose power is absolute.

The sovereign may grant some liberties to his subjects, making rules to govern its exercise. Among these are the rules of property,

> Whereby every man may know, what goods he may enjoy, and what actions he may do, without being molested by any of his fellow-subjects; and this is it men call *propriety*. For before constitution of sovereign power…all men had the right to all things; which necessarily causeth war; and therefore this propriety, being necessary to peace, and depending on sovereign power, is the act of that power, in order to the public peace. (chapter 18)

In his summing up of the whole book, Hobbes gives his picture of how a society of such atoms must function: "I think a toleration of a professed hatred of tyranny is a toleration of hatred to commonwealth in general."

Society *is* tyranny.

SPINOZA

Spinoza (1632–1677) appears to be continuing the work of Machiavelli and Hobbes, and, in a way, so he is. Like them, he seeks to understand the problems of a collection of independent individuals trying to organize its political life. But actually he transforms these problems completely. Instead of questions of power, rights, and responsibilities, Spinoza investigates the notion of the self-governing community, and for this he develops an entirely new view of humanity. He is the only figure in the tradition of political philosophy to defend the idea of democracy. But in the end, even his democracy is limited by the historical conditions of his turbulent time and by the barrier of property.

Baruch de Espinosa was born into a leading family—though commercially a not very successful one—among those wealthy Jews who came from Portugal to Amsterdam to escape from Catholic persecution. The Amsterdam Portuguese Sephardic Synagogue was dominated by some of the most influential merchants of the Netherlands, and its leaders were supporters of the Orange cause. The young Espinosa was educated in its Rabbinical School. On the death of his father and elder brother, he became the head of the family business. But in 1656 he broke with the world of commerce forever and was ritually excommunicated, cursed, and expelled from the Synagogue.

A bit of the history of the Netherlands is needed here. In the previous century, after decades of struggle, under the leadership of William of Orange (the Silent), the Netherlanders had liberated themselves from Catholic Hapsburg Spanish rule. In the new Dutch Republic, a federation of seven provinces, the majority of the people were fervent Calvinists who wanted to install the House of Orange as a monarchy. At the same time, a powerful and enlightened oligarchy of "Regents," representing the prosperity of the new Republic, was politically influential, especially in the leading Province, Holland.

In 1650, William II was poised to set himself up as king, but died just before this move was completed. Holland then experienced its "golden age," under the twenty-two-year rule of the "Regent" Jan de Witt. Based upon its leading role in international trade, Holland enjoyed a religious and intellectual toleration unknown elsewhere in Europe. That is why the Frenchman Descartes (1696–1749) chose to live in the Netherlands for much of his life, and religious radicals came there from England after the retreat of the Revolution. Philosophy, music, the arts, and the sciences flourished.

In Amsterdam, the young Baruch was able to discuss the most advanced ideas in religion, natural science, and philosophy. An important influence on him was Franciscus Van den Enden (1602–74), who taught him Latin, the language in which Spinoza"s works were to be written, and in whose house he lived for a time. Van den Enden was a democrat and an opponent of private property. He later went to France and took part in a conspiracy to overthrow Louis XIV. When it was betrayed, Van den Enden was hanged.

In 1660, Baruch, henceforth called Benedict de Spinoza, went to live in Rijnsburg, near Leiden. This was the center of the Collegiant sect, the most extreme of a multitude of anti-Trinitarian groups. Derived from the Anabaptists, the Collegiants were also antipolitical and millenarian, like some of the English groups with whom they were in close contact. Although Spinoza did not join them, nor any other sect, they always remained his friends and defenders.

While in Rijnsburg, he learned to be a grinder of lenses, and supported himself for the rest of his life by manufacturing microscopes and telescopes.

This is how he summed up that life in one of his many letters: "So far as in me lies, I value, above all other things out of my control, the joining of hands of friendship with men who are lovers of truth." Throughout his short life, he never compromised his complete independence of philosophical, political, and religious thought. He demonstrated this when, in 1673, not long before he died, he politely and firmly declined a plum job as professor at Heidelberg when it was offered to him.

In Rijnsburg he completed and published his *Principles of Cartesianism* (1660), and worked on, but never completed, the *Shorter Treatise on God, Man and His Well-being*, and the *Treatise on the Correction of the Understanding*. At the beginning of this latter work, Spinoza explains how he came to study philosophy. He found, he says, that riches, fame, and honor distracted him from his main inquiry, which concerned "whether I might discover and acquire the faculty of enjoying throughout eternity continual supreme happiness."

> This then is the end to attain which I am striving, namely, to acquire such a nature and to endeavour that many also should acquire it with me . . . and moreover to form such a society as is essential for the purpose of enabling most people to acquire this nature with the greatest ease and security.

Spinoza's aims were always entirely individual and, simultaneously, entirely social in character.

In 1663, he moved to Voorburg, near the Hague, where he wrote the *Tractatus Theologico-Politicus* (TT-P). It was published anonymously in Latin in 1670, but its authorship was soon obvious to the Calvinist authorities. A Dutch translation was made of this work but Spinoza stopped it being printed. Even the Latin original was banned and assailed by a storm of criticism. For example, a Calvinist pamphlet describes the book as the work of "the renegade Jew in collaboration with the devil and the connivance of Mr. Jan and his accomplice."

The following year, Spinoza moved to the Hague itself, just before the political situation was violently transformed. In 1672 De Witt was first forced to resign, and then, together with his brother Cornelius, murdered by a Calvinist-Orangist mob which also hacked their bodies to pieces.

All this time, Spinoza had been working on his chief work, the *Ethics* (E). He completed it in 1675, but it was not published until after his death. For the next two years, he worked on his last work, the *Tractatus Politicus*. Spinoza died of what today would be called silicosis, the result of his glass grinding, before it was completed.

Spinoza's work, political, theological, ethical, psychological, and metaphysical, forms a totally unified whole. At its foundation is a conception of the world, humanity, and God, which challenges all the basic conceptions of both Judaism and Christianity. He sets out from Aristotle's concept of Substance, "the cause of itself," but identifies it with both God and Nature. Instead of being Lord of the World, freely willing the course of His Creation, God's power is identified with the laws of Nature.

"God or Nature" is the one and only substance, but humanity is necessarily made up of a multitude of individual subjects. Humans are parts of Nature, and Spinoza is scornful of any other view.

> They seem to have conceived man in nature as a kingdom within a kingdom. For they believe that man disturbs rather than follows the course of nature, and that he has absolute power in his actions, and is not determined in them by anything other than himself. (*E*, part 3 preface)

Each of these humans is at the same time body and soul, which are not two opposites, but two aspects of one entity. Each individual subject has both reason and emotion. If an emotion is governed by reason, it is active and free, something which *we do*. Otherwise it is a passion, to which the individual is enslaved, something *done to us*. "Human lack of power in moderating and checking the emotions I call servitude" (*E*, part 4). Thus power is freedom and lack of power is slavery. It is the nature of reason to perceive things under a certain species of eternity (*sub quadam aeternitatis species*)" (*E*, part 2, proposition XLIV, corollary 2). However, only "God or Nature" knows the whole story.

Spinoza has much in common with the Stoics, but unlike them he is not concerned only with "wise men" but with humans as they are. In part 2 of the *Ethics*, in the Corollary to Proposition XLIX, Spinoza proves that "will and intellect are one and the same thing." Any truth about the world is either self-evident to all men of reason, or reason can derive it with the certainty of geometry. He never imagines that all humans are totally governed by reason: if that were the case, there would be no need for government at all. (As the crisis of 1672 confirmed only too sharply, some people are undoubtedly more reasonable than others.)

> Now if men were so constituted by nature to desire nothing but what is prescribed by true reason, society would stand in no need of any laws. Nothing would be required except to teach men true moral doctrine, and they would then act to their true advantage of their own accord, whole-heartedly and freely. (*TT-P*, chapter 5)

Reason pertains to the intellect of "God or Nature." Reasonable action unites humans, while passion divides them. Spinoza stresses many times "the difference between a man who is led by emotion and one who is led by reason."

The former whether he wills it or not performs things of which he is entirely ignorant; the latter is subordinate to noone, and only does those things which he
knows to be of primary importance in his life, and which on that account he desires the most. (*E*. part 4, proposition LXVI, Note)

He ridicules those who hold any other idea of freedom. "This, therefore, is
their idea of liberty, that they should know no cause of their actions" (*E*, part
2, proposition XXXV, Note).

Like Hobbes, Spinoza explains all human action in terms of self-preservation,
but the conclusions he draws about the nature of social life could not be more
different, because Spinoza's understanding of "self" is always social. In part 4,
Proposition XVIII, Note, he writes:

Nothing, I say, can be desired by men more excellent for their self-preservation
than that all with all should so agree that they compose the minds of all into one
mind, and the bodies of all into one body, and all endeavour at the same time as
much as possible to preserve their being, and all seek at the same time what is
useful to them as a body. From which it follows that men who are governed by
reason, that is, men who under the guidance of reason seek what is useful to
them, desire nothing for themselves which they do not also desire for the rest of
mankind, and therefore they are just, faithful and honorable.

Having disposed of the idea of free will, problems of good and evil are easily dealt with.

By good I understand here all kind of pleasure and whatever may conduce to it,
and more especially that which satisfies our fervent desires, what ever they may
be; by bad all kind of pain, and especially that which frustrates our desires. (*E*,
part 4, proposition XXXIX, note 1)

So in Spinoza's ethics there is no room for "ought." Humans, like God, operate under the laws of nature, laws which humans can increasingly grasp as
knowledge grows. His theology, psychology, and politics all flow from this
understanding, as clearly as Euclid's geometry. This is how he describes a human community founded on reason:

Without any infringement of natural right, a community can be formed and a
contract be always preserved in its entirety in absolute good faith on these terms,
that everyone transfers all the power that he possesses to the community, which
will therefore alone retain the sovereign natural right over everything, that is, the
supreme rule which everyone will have to obey either of free choice or through
fear of the ultimate penalty. Such a community's right is called a democracy,
which can therefore be defined as a united body of men which corporately possesses sovereign right over everything within its power. (*TT-P*, chapter 16)

Democracy, he believes, is "the most natural form of state, approaching most closely to that freedom which nature grants to every man" (*TT-P*, chapter 16). Spinoza is totally hostile to all forms of superstition and to any infringement of freedom of thought.

> The supreme mystery of despotism, its prop and stay, is to keep men in a state of deception, and with the specious title of religion to cloak the fear by which they may be kept in check, so that they fight for servitude as if for salvation. (*TT-P*, preface)

In fact the main point of the *Tractatus Theologico-Politicus* is to free philosophy from clerical control: "Our object has been to separate philosophy from theology and to show that the latter allows freedom to philosophize for every individual" (*TT-P*, chapter 16), and Spinoza never misses a chance to hit back at his Calvinist persecutors. "Nothing . . . save gloomy and mirthless superstition prohibits laughter" (*E*, part 4, proposition XLV, note 2). And later (proposition LXIII, note 1) he lashes out again.

> The superstitious, who know better how to reprovate vice than to teach virtue, and who do not endeavour to lead men by reason, but to so inspire them with fear that they avoid evil rather than love virtue, have no other intention than to make the rest as miserable as themselves; and therefore it is not wonderful that for the most part they are a nuisance and hateful to men.

So Spinoza's advocacy of democracy is essentially a matter of finding the best way of promoting the power of reason.

> Thus when I say that the best state is one in which men live in harmony, I am speaking of a truly human existence [*vitam humanum intelligo*], which is characterized, not by the mere circulation of blood and other vital processes common to all animals, but primarily by reason, the true virtue and life of the mind. (*TP*, chapter V, para 5)

Democracy is the best such form of state.

> All men have one and the same nature: it is power and culture which mislead us. . . . If men are puffed up by appointment for a year, what can we expect of nobles, who hold office without end? (*TP*, chapter VII, para 27)

But Spinoza does not question property as an institution. He only wants to keep it within the bounds of reason.

> Now this vice is only theirs who seek to acquire money, not from need or reasons of necessity, but because they have learned the arts of gain wherewith to

raise themselves to a splendid estate. . . . But those who know the true use of money and moderate their desire of money to their requirements alone are content with very little. (*E*, part 4, appendix, XXIX)

The section of the *Tractatus Politicus* which Spinoza leaves unfinished is chapter XI, on democracy, the "completely absolute state." The only passage he left was an explanation of why women cannot be citizens of such a state, "proving" that they must be subject to men "due to their weakness." Nor can he allow citizenship to aliens or servants, who will not be independent. His "argument" for all this is not much better than an appeal to history. So even Spinoza's calm and profound reflection cannot go far beyond the bounds of traditional forms of oppression.

However, Spinoza's conception of the role philosophy itself is quite unique. The philosophical investigation of political life could never be for him merely a commentary on an external object. Since true humanity means collective freedom, and freedom means the power of reason over passion, the work of philosophy in clearing the intellectual path for reason is central to the life both of humanity and of the philosopher himself.

LOCKE

John Locke (1632–1704) was fifty-six when the Stuart James II was deposed and the throne given to William III and his wife Mary. (William, of course, was the Dutchman William of Orange and Mary was the daughter of Charles I.) Locke was the philosopher of the Whig victory in this "Glorious Revolution." His philosophy is, above all, the theory of this compromise between the aristocratic landed interest and the rising power of the City of London. The conception of the independent individual, existing in splendid isolation, a conception now fully developed and widely accepted, formed the foundation of both his metaphysics and his political philosophy. In the *Essay Concerning Human Understanding*, published in 1690, he explains all knowledge as the outcome of the processing by the mind of data received through the senses: there were no "innate ideas," and the whole operation was entirely a private matter. In the *Two Treatises on Government*, published anonymously in the same year, he explains the character of society as a collection of private property owners.

Locke had been a schoolboy when Charles I was executed, and his father fought in the Royalist armies. When he was young, he was conservative in outlook, but grew more radical as he got older. In the 1660s he was employed by Lord Shaftesbury, the founder of the Whigs. He also worked at Christ Church, Oxford, until he was sacked, under pressure from King

James, in 1684. He went to live in Holland, and returned with William and Mary in 1689.

Locke takes it for granted that some people must have power over others. But he denies that this is a divine right, inherited from Adam, and investigates the question which most exercised the ruling classes of Britain at the time: Who was destined to hold this power? As he explains in the *First Treatise* (chapter 11):

> The great question which in all ages has disturbed mankind, and brought on them the greatest part of those mischiefs which have ruined cities, depopulated countries and disordered the peace of the world, has been, not whether there be power in the world, nor whence it came, but who shall have it.

In chapter 1 of the *Second Treatise*, he defines political power. It is

> the right of making laws with penalties of death, and consequently all less penalties, for the regulating and preserving of property, and of employing the force of the community, in the execution of such laws, and in the defence of the commonwealth from foreign injury, and all this only for the public good.

Clearly, this is a power quite different from that of Hobbes' absolute sovereign. To expound his conception, Locke also starts with a state of nature, but it is a very different setup from that war-torn battlefield surveyed by Hobbes. Locke's state of nature is a peaceful, fairly comfortable place:

> a state of perfect freedom to order their actions and dispose of their possessions, and persons, as they think fit, within the bounds of the law of nature, without asking leave, or depending upon the will, of any other man.

Men live outside society as equals, but they own private property—or at least, some of them do. "God . . . hath given the world to men in common," and "hath also given them reason to make use of it to the best advantage of life, and convenience." Property arises because things are produced by labor, and "every man has a property in his own person." Property in land and the invention of money follow logically. Despite the resulting inequality, men in the state of nature are still free and independent. All of this before there is a system of government.

Why should men leave this idyllic state of affairs? Only, thinks Locke, because a government is necessary to protect private property. Men need a system of justice to settle disputes over property, a legislative to enact the laws, and an executive to keep the whole business going. These three functions of government—legislative, executive, and judicial—are distinct, but depend on each other. There is also a Federative function, concerned with foreign defense and conquest. But the government had no right to encroach on the private affairs of any citizen, including his religious opinion. Absolute monarchy was thus definitely ruled out. "Absolute monarchy, which by some men is counted the only government in the world, is indeed inconsistent with civil society, and so can be no form of civil government at all."

The particular form of government might be, as for Aristotle, monarchic, oligarchic, or democratic, or some mixture of these. But in any case, it was to be chosen by the majority of free citizens, that is, men of property. Unlike Hobbes, Locke believes that there is a contract between government and the people. Political power means, as with Hobbes, that there is an agreement by individuals to give up power to a central authority, but it is no longer to an all-powerful sovereign. Instead, Locke explains, "whosoever therefore out of a state of nature unite into a community, must be understood to give up all the power, necessary for the ends for which they unite into society, to the majority of the community."

However, slavery is justified. In fact, Locke manages to make the slave responsible for his or her own enslavement. It is quite simple: you can always choose to die instead.

> Whenever he finds the hardship of his slavery outweigh the value of his life, 'tis in his power, by resisting the will of his master, to draw on himself the death he desires. . . . These men, having, as I say, forfeited their lives, and with it their liberties, and lost their estates, and being in the state of slavery, not capable of property, cannot in that state be considered as any part of civil society; the chief end thereof is the preservation of property.

Thus, the founder of liberalism had no trouble reconciling his conception of liberty with his ownership of shares in Jamaican slave plantations. He was also happy to serve for a time as the Secretary to the Council of Trade and Plantations, and in 1669, he had written a Constitution for Carolina, whose "democratic" character involved giving more votes to those who owned more slaves. (And, of course, no votes to those who had no slaves.)

Locke has no problem about the conflict between property owners and those without property. If some people are poor, it is their own fault, anyway, and they are not to be thought of as fully human. Chapter 3 of the *Second Treatise*, entitled "Of the State of War," makes it quite plain.

> For by the fundamental law of nature, man being to be preserved, as much as possible, when all cannot be preserved, the safety of the innocent is to be preferred: and one may destroy a man who makes war on him, or has discovered an enmity to his being, for the same reason that he may kill a wolf or a lion; because such men are not under the ties of the common law of reason.

So we should not be surprised to hear that Locke was an enthusiastic advocate of workhouses for the poor, starting, he advised, from the age of three.

The last chapter of the *Second Treatise*, called "Of the Dissolution of Government," tells us what it has all been about. If governments are the outcome of popular decision, so must be the replacement of one form of government by another. He sets out the possible situations in which a government may be dissolved. The fifth and last of these is

> when he who has the supreme executive power, neglects and abandons that charge, so that the laws already made can no longer be put in execution. This is demonstratively to reduce all to anarchy, and so effectually to dissolve the government.

Of course, this was precisely the Whig argument for getting rid of James II and for establishing the joint monarchy of William and Mary. The political problem was to explain why this was right, without at the same time seeming to justify the execution of Charles I forty years earlier. Locke was showing them how this could be done: if the government broke its side of the contract with the people, the people had the right and duty to get a new government.

In the century following the appearance of Locke's book, his conception of the independent property owner tacitly formed the basis of that science which, more than any other, characterized the social order which came to dominate the planet: political economy. In the American and French revolutions, its political meaning was revealed. Some individual citizens might be allowed to express dissenting opinion now and then, religious differences might be tolerated, but interference with the rights of private property was out of the question. In the American Declaration of Independence, and then in the French Rights of Man, the individualism inherent in private property is made explicit. The "freedom" the revolutions produced was the freedom of private property. Thus they led to bourgeois society and to the bourgeois state.

Against only a small amount of opposition, the American Constitution was tailored to justify the continuation of slavery and the theft of the land of the native Americans. In Britain, France, and the United States, parliamentary forms of government developed as the way that the bourgeoisie would exercise power in a state which, increasingly obviously, belonged to them.

In the eighteenth century, the philosophers of the Enlightenment founded their complete world outlook on the conception that society was a collection of free and independent individuals. When Locke's American disciples fought the English King, they were firm in the knowledge that "all men are created equal, and endowed with certain inalienable rights." Reason, the universal property of each individual human being, could investigate the working of both nature and society, but for this it had to be freed from the authority of tradition, especially that of Plato and Aristotle. If superstition could be eradicated from the minds of men, the flourishing of science and industry would bring about the mastery of nature, for systematic knowledge would inevitably be coupled with benevolence toward all humankind. Political economy was victorious, that is, political and economic life were totally distinct.

MONTESQUIEU

Charles Louis de Secondat, Baron de Montesquieu (1689–1755) was one of the grandest noblemen of Bordeaux, and a great landowner, but he was also keenly engaged in making money in the domestic and international wine trade. His ideals were close to those of the bourgeois settlement of Locke's "Glorious Revolution," and regard for English political forms permeates his life's work, *The Spirit of the Laws*. This book is famously obscure in its overall argument, which sometimes seems to be overloaded with a thousand historical examples, but this appearance is deceptive. Much of the obscurity is deliberate, aiming to protect some strikingly modern notions from reprisal by the Church and the Bourbon Court.

While he is not afraid to disagree with Aristotle, Montesquieu treats him with rather more respect than Hobbes had done. Like Hobbes, he also starts with a "state of nature." However, "Hobbes gives men first the idea to subjugate one another, but this is not reasonable" (*The Spirit of the Laws*, Book 1, chapter 2). Thus the first of four "natural laws" that govern man "before the establishment of societies," is the desire for peace. Second and third come biological laws, hunger, and the need for sex. Men naturally have the faculty of gaining knowledge, but each feels his own weakness and his own needs. And so "the desire to live in society is a fourth natural law."

Laws of nature form the framework for all of Montesquieu's account of society and its political forms. This is how Book 1 of the entire work begins:

> Laws, taken in the broadest meaning, are the necessary relations deriving from the nature of things; and in this sense, all beings have their laws, the divinity has its laws, the material world has its laws, the intelligences superior to man have their laws, the beasts have their laws, man has his laws.

Man, as a physical being, is governed by invariable laws like other bodies, but there is a difference between humans and everything else in the world: "As an intelligent being, he constantly violates the laws god has established and changes those he himself establishes; he must guide himself, and yet he is a limited being."

Montesquieu does not believe that there is some universally "best" form of government, appropriate for all nations. Each nation has its own specific conditions, for which it must find the optimum form.

> The government most in conformity with nature is the one whose particular arrangement best relates to the disposition of the people for whom it is established. . . Law in general is human reason insofar as it governs all the peoples of the earth; and the political and civil laws of each nation should be only the particular cases to which human reason is applied.

Different climates and other geographical features, and especially different histories, lead to different ways of organizing social life. By examining these particular relations, Montesquieu aims to discover what he calls "the Spirit of the Laws," a unifying principle standing above individuals. "Many things govern men: climate, religion, laws, the maxims of the government, examples of past things, mores, and manners; a general spirit is formed as a result" (Book 19, chapter 4).

While carefully denying that he is condemning any form of state, Montesquieu divides political states into "despotic" and "moderate." The principle of despotic government is fear of the despot. Moderate government he classifies as monarchy or republic, and republics, in turn, are either democratic or aristocratic.

> Republican government is that in which the people as a body, or only a part of the people, have sovereign power; monarchical government is that in which one alone governs, but by fixed and established laws; whereas, in despotic government, one alone, without law and without rule, draws everything along, by his will, and his caprice. (Book 2, chapter 1).

But Montesquieu's democracy is not government by *all* the people, either, for the poor are excluded.

> In choosing a representative, all citizens in the various districts should have the right to vote, except those whose estate is so humble that they are deemed to have no will of their own. (Book 11, chapter 6)

In any case, democracy is only suitable to small states (Book 11, chapter 6). The principle of a republic, especially of democracy, is political virtue, while the principle of monarchy is "honor." Monarchy does not know political virtue, and despotism does not even have a word for honor.

One of Montesquieu's chief advances on Aristotle is his concept of Liberty, for which he offers a precise definition.

It is true that in democracies the people seem to do what they want, but political liberty in no way consists in doing what one wants. In a state, that is, in a society where there are laws, liberty can consist only in having the power to do what one should want to do and in no way being constrained to do what one does not want to do. One must put oneself in mind of what independence is and what liberty is. Liberty is the right to do everything the laws permit; and if one citizen could do what they forbid, he would no longer have liberty, because the others would likewise have this same power. (Book 11, chapter 3)

Political liberty in a citizen is that tranquillity of spirit which comes from the opinion each one has of his security, and in order for him to have this liberty the government must be such that one citizen cannot fear another citizen. (Book 11, chapter 6)

Of course, this sets him against Aristotle on the question of slavery, which "is not good by its nature" (Book 15, chapter 1). And yet he seems to go on to give examples of situations where slavery might be appropriate, even in "moderate governments." Some of the remainder of this book might well be intended ironically. And this is the only kind of ownership he even questions. Land ownership and money are discussed but their existence taken for granted.

Each of the forms of government, however, is subject to corruption of its principle. In the case of despotism, little needs to be said, because "it is corrupt by its own nature" (Book 8, chapter 10). "A monarchy is ruined when the prince, referring everything to himself exclusively, reduces the state to its capital, the capital to the court, and the court to his person alone" (Book 8, chapter 6). The principle of democracy too, however, can be corrupted, "not only when the spirit of equality is lost but also when the spirit of extreme equality is taken up and each one wants to be the equal of those chosen to command" (Book 8, chapter 2).

It is in the course of his discussion of the constitution of England that Montesquieu sets out his theory of the three powers within the state.

In each state there are three sorts of powers: legislative power, executive power over the things depending on the right of nations, and executive power over the things depending on civil right. By the first, the prince or magistrate makes laws for a time or for always, and corrects or abrogates those that have been made. But the second, he makes peace or war, sends and receives embassies, establishes security and prevents invasions. By the third, he punishes crimes or judges disputes between individuals. The last will be called the power of judging and the former simply the executive power of the state. (Book 11, chapter 6)

The conflicts between these separate powers are the way Montesquieu thinks corruption can be avoided.

In his autobiography, Montesquieu gives summaries of the Enlightenment and its conception of humanity which are worth quoting: "I wake up in the morning with a secret joy in the light of day. I behold that light with a kind of rapture." And

> If I knew of something which would be of benefit to me personally, but which would harm my family, then I would dismiss it from my mind. If I knew of something that would benefit my family, but not my country, then I would try to forget it. If I knew of some thing that would benefit my country but harm Europe, or benefit Europe but be harmful to mankind, then I would consider it a crime.[2]

ROUSSEAU

Now we are in the eighteenth century: the market has come to dominate social forms, even though political relations have some way to go before they catch up. These forms imply the imposition of wage labor on masses of people and the breakup of all the older ways of making a living and all older relations. During the seventeenth and eighteenth centuries, there were massive struggles against these changes, as against the enslavement of Africans forced to work for capital in the Americas, but political philosophy never reflects these directly. Even their history has only begun to emerge fairly recently.[3]

Although Jean-Jacques Rousseau (1712–1788) was a major contributor to the *Encyclopédie* and friend of its editor, Diderot, he was remarkable for being directly opposed to many of the basic notions of the Enlightenment. For Rousseau, reason was not the natural characteristic of humans, as it was for most of his fellow Enlighteners. The "arts and sciences," far from leading to an improvement in moral life, he thought would promote the corruption, inequality and injustice which he believed characterized modern society. His thought contains many paradoxes—he often points to them himself—but these are his most important contribution, since they express openly some of the most deep-seated contradictions of society.

At the heart of all Rousseau's inconsistencies is the certainty that nature and society are not merely unconnected. They are actually incompatible. Civilization itself had been a huge step back from man's "natural state." In his state of nature, Rousseau sees

> an animal, less strong than some, less agile than others, but taken as a whole, the most advantageously organized of all. I see him satisfying his hunger under an oak, quenching his thirst at the first stream, finding his bed under the same tree which provided his meal, and, behold, his needs are furnished. (*Discourse on Inequality*, Part I)

But there is no going back to this idyllic condition of freedom, independence, and equality.

While hating inequality of all kinds, Rousseau thinks that property is both natural to human beings, and the source of all their misery and corruption.

> It is certain that the right of property is the most sacred of all citizens' rights, and in some respects more important than freedom itself, whether it is more closely connected with the preservation of life; or because, a man's property being easier to appropriate and harder to defend than his person, the thing that is more readily taken should be the more respected; or finally because property is the true foundation of civil society and the true pledge of the citizens' fidelity in fulfilling their obligations. (*Political Economy*.)
>
> The first man who, having enclosed a piece of land, thought of saying "This is mine" and found people simple enough to believe him, was the true founder of civil society. How many crimes, wars, murders; how much misery and horror the human race would have been spared if someone had pulled up the stakes and filled in the ditch and cried out to his fellow men: "Beware of listening to this impostor! You are lost if you forget that the fruits of the earth belong to everyone and that the earth belongs to no one!" (*Discourse on Inequality*, Part II)

Passing through a stage of "nascent society," humans had no choice but to develop social forms which led inevitably to all the ills of civilization. However, despite the inevitability of these features of human enslavement, in no way is Rousseau ever reconciled with them. Unlike Locke and his American followers, Rousseau knows that slavery is totally inhuman: humanity, the entire human population of the world, is by nature free.

> To renounce our freedom is to renounce our character as men, the rights, and even the duties, of humanity. . . . It is incompatible with the nature of man; to remove the will's freedom is to remove all morality from our actions. (*Social Contract*, Book I, chapter iv)

Rousseau describes the necessity for a social contract like this:

> Find a form of association which will defend and protect, with the whole of its joint strength, the person and property of each associate, and under which each of them, uniting himself to all, will obey himself alone, and remain as free as before. This is the fundamental problem to which the social contract gives the answer. (*Social Contract*, Book I chapter vi)

In a way, Rousseau's work as a whole may be regarded as the proof that this problem has no answer. His knowledge of this is precisely how he shows his immense superiority over Hobbes and Locke.

He sees the question as centering on the formation of a "general will," which is not the will of all the "associates." They must make a contract, in which they agree to the complete transfer of each associate, with all his rights, to the whole community. . . . Each, in giving himself to all gives himself to none, and since there are no associates over whom he does not acquire the same rights as he cedes, he gains the equivalent of all that he loses, and greater strength for the conservation of what he possesses. . . . Each of us puts his person and all his power in common under the supreme direction of the general will; and we as a body receive each member as an indivisible part of the whole. (Social Contract, Book I, chapter vi)

How can this work? There can be no sovereign, except the people as a whole. Rousseau tries as carefully as he can to distinguish this whole from its separate parts, the individual citizens.

The public person that is formed in this way by the union of all the others once bore the name *city,* and now bears that of *republic,* or *body politic*; its members call it *the state* when it is passive, *the sovereign* when it is active, and a *power* when comparing it to its like. As regards the associates, they collectively take the name of the *people*, and are individually called *citizens* as being participants in sovereign authority, and *subjects* as being bound by its laws. (Social Contract, Book I, chapter vi)

Rousseau is often regarded as a major democratic thinker. However, while insisting that all sovereignty springs from the people as a whole, he also declares that

a people that always governed well, would not need to be governed. True democracy has never existed and never will. . . . If there were a nation of gods it would be governed democratically. So perfect a government is not suitable for men. (*Social Contract*, Book I chapter iv)

His ideal republic is modeled, not on Athens, but on Sparta and Rome. "Athens was not really a democracy, but an extremely tyrranical aristocracy, controlled by philosophers and orators" (Article in the *Encyclopédie* on *Political Economy*) (Here he expresses his debt to Machiavelli, whom he regarded as a great democrat.) The social contract was binding on those, and only those, who had accepted it, and from this, Rousseau thought, followed his attitude to majority voting. This is remarkable for its emphasis on the contradictions in the very system he is advocating for the way that the people must exercise its sovereignty.

For civil association is the most completely voluntary of acts; each man having been born free and master of himself, no one, under any pretext at all, may enslave him without his consent. . . . But the question is how a man can be free and forced to conform to the will of others than himself. How can those who are in opposition be free and subject to the laws to which they have not consented? My reply is that the question is wrongly put. The citizen consents to every law, even those which punish him when he dares to violate one of them. The constant will of all the citizens of the state is the general will; it is through the general will that they are citizens and have freedom. (*Social Contract*, Book IV, chapter ii)

Related to this is the distinction Rousseau makes between legislative power, which belongs solely to the people, and government, the executive power. The latter is an intermediate, between the people as sovereign and the citizens, as subjects. There is no contract by which subjects agree to obey a government, Rousseau insists. "The government receives commands from the sovereign, and gives them to the people" (*Social Contract*, Book III, chapter 1). This is related to his famous formula about freedom: "If anyone refuses to obey the general will, he will be compelled to do so by the whole body; which means nothing else than that he will be forced to be free" (*Social Contract*, Book I, chapter vii).

Here we see what has been called Rousseau's totalitarian democracy. It explains his love of Sparta and Rome. He therefore can say that there is a gap between the individual as human and as citizen. Discussing education for citizenship, he says, you are forced to combat either nature or society, you must make your choice between the man and the citizen.

You cannot train for both. . . . The natural man lives for himself; he is the unit, the whole, dependent only on himself and his like. The citizen is but the numerator of a fraction, whose value depends on its denominator; his value depends on the whole, that is, on the community. Good social institutions are those best fitted to make a man unnatural, to exchange his independence for dependence, to merge the unit in the group, so that he no longer regards himself as one, but as a part of the whole, and is only conscious of the common life. (*Emile*, Book I)

Later in the same book, Rousseau appears to make explicit the impossibility of such a common life. Repeating that the state of nature contains "an actual and indestructible equality," Rousseau contrasts this with civil society.

In the civil state, there is a vain and chimerical equality of right; the means intended for its maintenance, themselves serve to destroy it; and the power of the community, added to the power of the strongest for the oppression of the weak, disturbs the sort of equilibrium which nature has established between the two. (*Emile*, Book IV)

In a footnote to this passage he hammers the point home, with an allusion to Montesquieu:

The universal spirit of the laws of every country is always to take the part of the strong against the weak, and of him who has against him who has not; this defect is inevitable and there is no exception to it.

No wonder that this book was burned by the censor when it was first published in 1762, while its author had to creep out of Paris in the middle of the night!

KANT

For Immanuel Kant (1724–1804), Rousseau was "the Newton of the moral world." (Rousseau's portrait was the only one to adorn Kant's house.) Like his French hero, Kant was both part of the Enlightenment and not part of it. In his critical writings, beginning with the *Critique of Pure Reason*, he seeks a way out of the contradictions encountered by enlightened Reason, limiting its field of action in relation to knowledge of nature. But on moral issues, he opposes all such limitation. At the head of his essay: "What Is Enlightenment?" he gives the famous quotation from Horace: "*Sapere aude!*," "Dare to be wise!" to which he gives the explanation: "Dare to use your *own* understanding!"

Like Hobbes, Kant had a conception of a warlike "state of nature," but had a very different conception of its relation to civil society. Only in a "civil state" with a legal structure could peace be found, he believed. The social contract, which Kant thought was the basis for such a state,

can oblige every legislator to frame his laws in such a way that they could have been produced by the united will of a whole nation, and to regard each subject, in so far as he can claim citizenship, as if he had consented to within the general will. This is the test of the rightfulness of every public law. (*Theory and Practice*)

Kant enunciates a "universal principle of right," which makes this political state and its legal structure the basis for all morality:

Every action which by itself or by its maxim enables the freedom of each individual's will to co-exist with the freedom of everyone else in accordance with a universal law is *right*. (*Metaphysic of Morals*, Introduction)

Here, Kant's understanding of freedom, of the individual subject and of law are all involved. Freedom for him means that each individual acts as his will decrees, without restriction and independently of everyone else's will. But each individual's freedom must—that means, "must reasonably"—be limited so that it does not interfere with that of fellow citizens. That is why morality is impossible without laws which apply universally, and provide rules to sort out the inevitable clashes between individual wills. At the same time, he sees the difficulties of ever achieving such a condition.

> The greatest problem for the human species, the solution of which nature compels him to seek, is that of attaining a civil society which can administer justice universally. . . . This problem is both the most difficult and the last to be solved by the human race. (*Idea for a Universal History*)

The trouble with humans is that "man is an animal who needs a master," he believes. And yet a civil state must by definition be one where the people rule themselves.

> The civil state, regarded purely as a lawful state, is based on the following *a priori* principles: 1. The *freedom* of every member of society as a *human being*; 2. The *equality* of each with the others as a *subject*; 3. The *independence* of each member of the commonwealth as a *citizen*. (*Theory and Practice*)

There is an inevitable clash between the freedom of the wills of individuals, and yet, somehow, this conflict must be regulated. "A civil state . . . is characterized by equality in the effects and counter-effects of freely-willed actions which limit one another in accordance with the general law of freedom." There has to be a state, with powers of coercion and punishment. And yet, at the same time, "people too have inalienable rights against the head of state, even if these are not rights of coercion." Kant tells us that he aims this last remark against Hobbes.

The contradictions of these requirements for the civil state are clearly expressed in Kant's attitude to the French Revolution. Republicanism is central to his political theory, which precludes as irrational any form of autocracy. He supports the Jacobins from the start, and, unlike many of their supporters, he never changes this opinion, nor does he hide it. But he is certainly no revolutionary, nor is he a democrat: any democracy, he thinks, is necessarily despotic.

Kant's approach reunifies ethics and politics—but only in a way which also keeps them apart. Each citizen has his own property, his own rights, and his own experiences. Towering over him is the modern state and the law, a logical necessity. Morality is reduced to the free activity of the independent individual will, but what is moral is inseparable from the universal good of society as a whole, embodied in laws and the constitutions under which they are enacted and enforced. Kant keeps the individuals and the universals in quite separate compartments. A passage from the *Critique of Pure Reason*, at the beginning of the "Transcendental Dialectic," connects Kant's thinking with Plato and his *Republic*.

> The Platonic Republic has been supposed to be a striking example of purely imaginary perfection. . . . We should do better, however, to follow up this thought and endeavour (where that excellent philosopher leaves us without his guidance) to place it in a clearer light by our own efforts, rather than to throw it aside as useless, under the useless and very dangerous pretext of its impracticability. A constitution founded on the greatest possible human freedom, according to laws which enable the freedom of each individual to exist by the side of freedom of others . . . is . . . a necessary idea.

Kant refuses to discard such a "necessary idea" merely because experience has shown that it hasn't worked. "It is altogether reprehensible to derive or limit the laws of what we ought to do according to our experience of what has been done." So is there no hope of achieving such a constitution? In his later writings, Kant struggled to answer this objection. "Nature"—Kant's pseudonym for Divine Providence—has some tricks up her sleeve, which might possibly move human history in the right direction, precisely by means of those unattractive features of humanity which appear to stand in the way.

> The means which nature employs to bring about the development of innate capacities is that of antagonism with society, in so far as this antagonism becomes in the long run the cause of a law-governed social order. By antagonism I mean in this context the unsocial sociability of man. . . . Man wishes to live comfortably and pleasantly, but nature intends that he should abandon idleness and inactive self-sufficiency and plunge instead into labor and hardships, so that he may, by his own adroitness find means of liberating himself from them in turn. The natural impulses which make this possible, the sources of the very unsociableness and resistance which cause so many evils, at the same time encourage man towards exertions of his powers and thus towards further development of his natural capacities. (*Idea for a Universal History*, Fourth Proposition)

ADAM SMITH

The work of Adam Smith (1723–1790)—a near contemporary of Kant—bears on many of the themes we are discussing. Although, of course, he is mainly known as the father of economics, the chair he held at Glasgow University was that of Moral Philosophy. If we pay attention to *The Theory of Moral Sentiments* (1759) (*TMS*), we can see *The Wealth of Nations* (1776) as a detailed working out of the main ideas of the other work.

Smith often openly identifies himself with the Stoics. He has some disagreement with them—for instance, he doesn't share their feelings about suicide. But like them, he sees morality as lying in the sphere of the independent
individual, while social and political life are a framework within which this
operates. Of course, he reinterprets their outlook in terms of the world of
eighteenth-century Britain.

Thus their fundamental notion that the wise man is able to command himself, appears in the shape of Smith's "prudence," embodying qualities like
"steadiness of industry and frugality." The prudent man "lives within his in-
come, is naturally contented with his situation, which, by continual, though
small accumulations, is growing better and better every day." His passions
are "restrained by the sense of propriety." To back up this modern, somewhat unheroic, version of the virtue of late Stoicism, Smith introduces his
main innovation, the "impartial spectator, the man within the breast." This
is the "higher tribunal" of conscience, "the great judge and arbiter of their
conduct."

At the same time, Smith's account of social life is founded upon his belief
in social order, underwritten by a Supreme Being.

> All the inhabitants of the universe, the meanest as well as the greatest, are un-
> der the immediate care and protection of that great, benevolent, and all-wise be-
> ing, who directs all the movements of nature; and who is determined by his own
> unalterable perfections, to maintain in it, at all times, the greatest possible quan-
> tity of happiness. (*TMS*, part VI, section ii, chapter 3)

In the very first sentences of the *Theory of Moral Sentiment*, he introduces
us to the two aspects of humankind which have been arranged by Providence,
and whose balancing relationship he has to outline: selfishness and sympathy.

> How selfish soever man may be supposed, there are evidently some principles in
> his nature, which interest him in the fortune of others, and render their happiness
> necessary to him, though he derives nothing from it except the pleasure of seeing
> it. Of this kind is pity or compassion, the emotion we feel for the misery of oth-
> ers, when we either see it or are made to conceive it in a very lively manner.

Some sentiments he calls "social passions," and others "unsocial." In the first
group are "generosity, humanity, kindness, compassion, mutual friendship
and esteem, all the social and benevolent affections." In the second kind he
includes "hatred and resentment, with all their different modifications." Between these two sets lies a third, called the "selfish passions," which "is never
either so graceful as sometimes the one set, nor is ever so odious as is sometimes the other." "Grief and joy, when conceived upon account of our own
private good or bad fortune, constitute this third set."

Smith knows that the society in which he lives needs both sympathy and selfishness to work. It is a machine, whose working parts are individual humans, their passions driving them to behave in ways whose interaction determines the course of social development. Smith discusses the ideas of Mandeville (1670–1733), whose *Fable of the Bees*, subtitled *Private Vices, Public Benefits*, so incensed his contemporaries. For Mandeville, all human actions are motivated by selfishness, even when we pretend otherwise. There is no real difference between vice and virtue, and only self-love drives society along. Smith makes a lot of noise about rejecting such notions, but has to agree with Mandeville that, without selfishness, the economic machine would not function. The progress of humanity would be impossible without its darker sides.

> The ancient stoics were of opinion, that as the world was governed by the all-ruling providence of a wise, powerful, and good God, every single event ought to be regarded as making a necessary part of the plan of the universe, and as tending to promote the general order and happiness of the whole: that the vices and follies of mankind, therefore, made as necessary a part of this plan, as their wisdom or their virtue; and by that eternal art which educes good from ill, were made to tend equally to the prosperity and perfection of the great system of nature. (*TMS*, part I, section I, chapter 2)

Smith updates this Stoic view of God's wisdom and the harmony of the universe into a form fit for the modern world. Although people aim only to pursue their self-interest, the social machine is so beautifully constructed that they nonetheless promote the well-being of society as a whole. In the *Theory of Moral Sentiments*, this is explained in terms of the drive for the "pleasures of wealth and greatness," resulting from a deception practised on them by nature. The outcome, however, is that wealth is eventually spread throughout society. The rich

> are led by an invisible hand to make nearly the same distribution of the necessaries of life, which would have been made, had the earth been divided into equal portions among all its inhabitants, and thus, without intending it, without knowing it, advance the interest of the society.

The *Wealth of Nations*, of course, develops this idea in much greater detail. As it famously explains:

> It is not from the benevolence of the butcher, the brewer or the baker, that we expect our dinner, but from their regard to their own interest. We address ourselves, not to their humanity, but to their self-love, and talk to them, not of our own necessities, but of their advantages. (*Wealth of Nations*, I, ii)

And every individual, Smith later explains,

> generally, indeed, neither intends to promote the publick interest, nor knows
> how much he is promoting it. . . . He intends only his own gain, and he is in this,
> as in many other cases, led by an invisible hand to promote an end which was
> no part of his intention. (IV, ii)
>   Without any intervention of law, therefore, the private interests and passions
> of men naturally lead them to divide and distribute the stock of every society,
> among all the different employments carried on in it, as nearly as possible in
> the proportion which is most agreeable to the interests of the whole society. (IV,
> vii, c)

However, contrary to some of his latter-day devotees, Adam Smith was by
no means content to leave the running of society completely to the blind
workings of the market. The important final section of the *Wealth of Nations*,
Book V, is devoted to the problems of the State and its relations with commerce, and its final pages investigate in great detail how taxation would af-
fect the market.

But Smith is in no doubt as to the ultimate purpose of all government: the
protection of property and the enforcement of labor.

> But avarice and ambition in the rich, in the poor the hatred of labour and the love
> of present ease and enjoyment, are the passions which prompt to invade prop-
> erty, passions much more steady in their operation, more universal in their in-
> fluence. Wherever there is great property, there is great inequality. For one very
> rich man, there must be at least five hundred poor, and the affluence of the rich
> excites the indignation of the poor, who are often driven by want, and prompted
> by envy, to invade his possessions. (*WN*, V, I, 2)

And more succinctly, and more brutally:

> Civil government, so far as it is instituted for the security of property, is in real-
> ity instituted for the defence of the rich against the poor, or of those who have
> some property against those who have none at all. [*WN*, V, I, 12.]

What could be clearer?

NOTES

1. Thomas Acquinas, *On Kingship* (Westport, Conn.: Hyperion Press, 1979), chapter 11. See also *Summa* II ii, Qu 42.
2. Quoted in Ulrich Im Hof, *The Enlightenment* (Oxford: Oxford University Press,
1994).

3. For the recovered history of such movements, see, for example, the work of Edward Thompson (*The Making of the English Working Class*), the later work of Christopher Hill and two marvelous more recent books: Peter Linebaugh, *The London Hanged* (Cambridge: Cambridge University Press, 1991) and Peter Linebaugh and Marcus Rediker, *The Many-Headed Hydra Sailors, Slaves, Commoners and the Hidden History of the Revolutionary Atlantic* (Boston: Beacon Press 2000).

Chapter Seven

Hegel's Contradictory Summary of the Tradition

In the German-speaking countries at the end of the eighteenth century, modern forms of economic and political life still largely lay in the future. Thinkers like Schiller, Goethe, and Hölderlin looked back to ancient Athens for a criterion against which they could criticize the kind of society that they saw developing in England and France. In ancient Greece, they believed, life, politics, and art had been united. Now, they were torn apart. They measured the horrors of the industrialism, individualism, and fragmented labor of their own time against "the glory that was Greece."

Hegel's conception of society, in fact, his entire philosophical work, including his unique notion of logic, centered on the attempt to bring these opposites together, without ignoring their conflict or trying to wish it away. Seen through the eyes of science (*Wissenschaft* = the craft of knowing), he believed, the interests of the community as a collective entity could be harmonized with the rights of private individuals and in this way philosophy could transcend the fragmentation of social life. The democratic *polis* of ancient Athens was, he thought, the "living work of art," but when the French Revolution had failed to fulfill its promise, he knew that it was impossible for that life to be recalled. It was clear to him that, in modern times, economic and political life were separated from each other, and that, in "civil society"—"the battlefield of private interests"—the wills of individual property owners clashed with the social organism as a whole. But, Hegel argued, the modern state, if it could be philosophically comprehended, would transcend these conflicts. An organic whole revealed itself to science, in which individual freedom was actualised in the life of the state. Following Hölderlin, he took as his motto the Greek notion of "*hen kai pan*," the One and the All.

But we ought to be clear about what "actuality" means here. For this, first of all, Hegel's work must be taken as a unity, not piecemeal. "The True is the Whole," he wrote. If you cut any piece—for instance the *Logic*—out of the entire system, you falsify both whole and part. This is not merely a matter of logical exposition, the order in which he deals with the categories, for each aspect ("moment") of his philosophy, each category, represents at the same time a stage in the history of philosophy. His *History of Philosophy* is the other side of the coin to his *Philosophy of History*, which traces the unfolding of Spirit, that is, the entire way of life of the species. Each philosopher's work is "its own time expressed in thought," the most clear reflection of a stage of development of society and of society's consciousness of itself. Each outlook is a valid part of this entire historical process. (The relation of Hegel's "Spirit" to Montesquieu's "spirit of the laws" is worth noting.)

Hegel has summarized the whole of this history to date, not as a random sequence of opinions, nor as a linear development which excludes the conflicts between successive stages, but as it unfolded precisely through their opposition, and the resolution of opposition in a higher stage. The truth was not a simple correspondence between a thought and its particular object, but a process in which both thought and object developed. This is the basis for his identification of philosophy with science, and for his claim that his philosophy is absolute. Every one of the thinkers we have briefly discussed finds a place in Hegel's contradictory summary of the development of history, as expressed in the development of knowledge.

In particular, Hegel wanted to bring together what he recognized as two opposites: the universal conceptions of Aristotle, and Kant's summation of the Enlightenment. But this implied a sharp criticism of the Enlightenment view of society as the combination of clashing private wills, which were somehow transcended by the universal needs of the community. Hegel condemned this conception as a "mere ought." Reason was not the private property of each individual, but the purposive activity of the whole of humanity. Like Aristotle's Forms, but unlike Plato's Ideas, Reason *worked in the world*. It was the task of philosophy to find out about it, after its work was done.

This joint movement of history and self-consciousness is the coming to be of Freedom, in Hegel's special meaning of this word. This is not the "negative freedom" of the Enlightenment, which declared that individuals ought not to be prevented from doing whatever they happened to feel like. Hegel denounces this as "arbitrariness" (*Willkur*). Instead, freedom is the self-creation of Spirit (*Geist*). Spirit finds itself in its objects, uniting what we are with what we can be through their mutual contradiction.

"To be unfree simply consists in our being involved with something else and not at home with ourselves." The history of philosophy, on the contrary, "is the history of untrammelled thinking, or of reason. Thinking of that kind is concerned solely with itself" (*History of Philosophy,* Introduction). Now we can see Hegel's answer to the question "What is actuality?" It is what exists, but only when the reasonableness of existence has revealed itself to science. This is the "work" which actuality (*Wirklichkeit*) must accomplish, transforming existence from the inside into what it actually is. The objects of nature simply *exist* as separate, discrete things. Ethical life, however, is *actual* and forms an organic unity. This is not the life of independent individuals, each equipped with Reason, that the Enlightenment had expected, but the movement of the whole of humanity as an organism, only grasped through science and otherwise unknown to the individuals.

> Reason is as cunning as it is *mighty*. Its cunning consists in the mediating activity which, while it lets objects act upon one another according to their own nature, and wear each other out, executes only *its* purpose without itself mingling in the process. (*Encylopaedia Logic*, para 209, Addition)

One way to look at Hegel's career is as a series of disappointments. Hegel, Schelling, and Hölderlin, that remarkable trio of theological students in Tübingen, were highly enthusiastic about the storming of the Bastille. The Revolution, they were sure, was bringing about a revival of the virtues of the Ancient Athenian *polis*. All such dreams were shattered by the Terror. This was the background to Schelling's later defection to reaction and, perhaps, to Hölderlin's mental breakdown. Hegel, however, turned to philosophy ("unwillingly," as he writes in a letter to Schelling).

Here, he believes, in the development of Spirit, Reason finds the way to reconcile the contradictory features of modern Europe. He wants the outcome of the Revolution, but without the revolution, precisely what could be summed up in the name: Napoleon Bonaparte. With such an outlook, Hegel could not but be a highly political man, greatly involved with attempts to reform the German state, that at that time did not exist as a unity. Early in the century, Hegel looked forward to a Germany united by Napoleon. After the defeat of Prussia at Jena in 1807, the hope of reforms from above inspired many thinkers and officials. So the final defeat of Napoleon, the last echo of the Revolution, came as a second great shock to Hegel.

But, with high hopes of success, he joined those seeking reform. In 1815, Kaiser Wilhelm Friedrich III of Prussia promised his loving subjects a written constitution. His reforming Chancellor, Prince von Hardenberg, drew up a draft for such a constitution early in 1819, and its proposals for a constitutional monarchy were close to those Hegel was about to publish in the *Philosophy of Right*. In 1816, Hegel got his first university job, in Heidelberg, founded less than a decade before. (Look at the powerful optimism of Hegel's inaugural lecture on the History of Philosophy, delivered in Heidelberg in 1816.) A couple of years later, Hegel was offered an even better post, Fichte's old chair of philosophy in the University of Berlin, being personally invited by Altenstein (in full, Karl Sigmund Franz Freiherr vom Stein zum Altenstein), the reforming Prussian Minister for Education.

Precisely at this moment of triumph, in the summer of 1819, the reactionaries struck back. The King withdrew his promise of a constitution, the censorship was intensified, all the reformers were dismissed and all their hopes dashed. From the time Hegel arrived in Berlin, his position was continually under attack from many quarters. But, just before he died, yet one more blow struck the Hegelian system. In 1830, the restored Bourbon monarchy was overthrown. Hegel's fellow reformers were overjoyed, but Hegel himself was not. One reason was that a completely new force entered the European political arena: the organized proletariat of Paris. In many parts of Germany, the movement in France found an echo among the nascent working class. This was quite outside anything Hegel's outlook could handle. He was conscious of poverty as a major problem of the modern world, and he also knew that he had no complete answer to it. But he could never have expected the poor themselves, the "rabble" (*"Pöbel"*), to take a hand in the game, and to emerge as rivals to his favored "estate," the educated and enlightened state bureaucracy. The following year, Hegel was dead.

In every part of his vast system, Hegel is keenly aware of the atomized relations between isolated individuals in bourgeois society. His first book, the *Phenomenology of Spirit*, claims to investigate every form through which self-consciousness examines itself, from mere individual sensation to the Absolute Knowledge available only to scientific cognition.

Studying the way that individual self-consciousness grasps itself as a concept, Hegel entitles a section expounding and criticising Kant: "Individuality which takes itself to be real in and for itself." The first of its three parts has the satirical title: "The Spiritual Animal Kingdom and Deceit." A little later, he discusses the idea of the abolition of private property, and shows how Kant's analytical method is incapable of deciding on whether such an idea is either true or false.

Suppose the question is: Ought it to be an absolute law that there should be property? Absolute, and not on grounds of utility for other ends: the essence of ethics consists just in law being identical with itself and through this self-identity, ie having its ground in itself, it is unconditioned. Property, simply as such, does not contradict itself; it is an *isolated* determinateness, or is posited as merely self-identical. Non-property, the non-ownership of things, or a common ownership of goods, is just as little self-contradictory. That something belongs to nobody, or to the first comer who takes possession of it, or to all together, to each according to his need or in equal portions—that is simple determinateness, a *formal* thought, like its opposite, property. (*Phenomenology of Spirit*, Miller translation, 258)

(The whole of this section should be compared and contrasted with Marx's *Critique of the Gotha Program*, written seventy years later.)

To place Hegel in the context of our brief account of the history of political thought, we shall examine his last book, the *Philosophy of Right*.[1] It will also be useful to refer to the *Lectures* on this topic, delivered in Heidelberg in 1817–18.[2] He had used these as a first draft for the *Philosophy of Right*, but they have a greater significance in understanding Hegel's political thought than a mere draft. For, just when this manuscript had been prepared for publication, the Carlsbad Decrees sent all notions of reform scuttling for cover, and Hegel had to rewrite it completely to get it past the censors. Even with these amendments, the publication of the *Philosophy of Right* was in itself an act of defiance.[3] So we might expect Hegel to have revealed more of what he believed in the *Lectures* than in the book. (In the end, I don't think the *Lectures* add a great deal.) As Hegel explains in his preface to the *Philosophy of Right*, the book gives the philosophical background to the Section on "Objective Mind" in his *Encyclopedia*, paras 483–546.

In the Preface, Hegel explains the political role of philosophical science:

> The *truth* concerning *right, ethics, and the state* is at any rate as *old* as its *exposition and promulgation* in *public laws and in public morality and religion*. What more does this truth require, inasmuch as the thinking spirit (*Geist*) is not content to possess it in this proximate manner? What it needs is to be *comprehended* as well, so that the content which is already rational in itself may also gain a rational form and thereby appear justified to free thinking. (*Philosophy of Right*, 11)

Hegel's famous dictum, "What is reasonable is actual; what is actual is reasonable," must be read carefully in this light. He is not justifying whatever happens to exist. Only what has revealed itself to pass the test of Reason is actual, and when Reason has done its work, reality will either show itself to have been necessary, or it will cease to exist, although patience is necessary. His book, he explains, is "an attempt *to comprehend and portray the state as inherently rational*." Hegel is consistently hostile to any kind of Utopian dreaming, the kind of thing of which he accuses the Enlightenment. There must be no pretence at "issuing instructions on how the world ought to be." Philosophy, he insists, "always comes too late to perform this task."

> Since philosophy is *exploration of the rational*, it is for that very reason the *comprehension of the present and the actual*, not the setting up of a *world beyond*,

which exists God only knows where—or rather, of which we can very well say
that we know where it exists, namely in the errors of a one-sided and empty ra-
tiocination. (*Philosophy of Right*, 20)

But this means that it would be quite wrong to think of Hegel's last book
as being about his "theory of the state," or a justification of some political
views. Here is the embodiment of the whole of the Hegelian system.
Thought reconciles itself to the world, by recognizing that social forms are
the product of thought itself. So the task of philosophical science, reflecting
upon and comprehending this development, can only be accomplished after
the event whose essential meaning it reveals is over and done with. The science of right, then, could only be a part of the whole of philosophy and its
history, from which the will and freedom could be deduced. We have seen
that philosophy has throughout its history sought to perform two different
tasks. On the one hand, it tried to give an account of the way things were,
and to explain why they were just so. On the other hand, it tried to find out
how they ought to be, and to discover how they could be made to conform
to this ideal pattern. The task Hegel is attempting to accomplish is both and
neither of these. The Idea, to which philosophy has to find its way, also
guides the movement of history, through which it actualizes itself. Philosophical science has to find the unifying principles which underlie this entire development.

In the preface, Hegel makes an important reference to Plato's *Republic*. On
the one hand, he sees this work as "a proverbial example of *an empty ideal*"
(*Philosophy of Right*, 20), describing the world as it "ought" to be. However,
Hegel's historical understanding enables him to do more than merely reject
Plato's conceptions. The *Republic* is "essentially the embodiment of nothing
other than the nature of Greek ethics," which Plato can see being undermined
by a "destructive force" which was penetrating the life of the *polis*. Elsewhere, Hegel identifies this force with the coming of Christianity, and in the
preface, he describes it as expressing "the free infinite personality." Hegel's
philosophy of reconciliation seeks to overcome the conflict between ethics
and this principle of individuality. He sees philosophy originating in Greece
precisely as an expression of the breakup of community.

It may be said that philosophy only commences when a people has left its concrete life in general, when separation into different estates has begun, and the
people approach their fall (*Untergang*), where a gulf has arisen between inner
striving and external actuality, when the hitherto existing form of religion etc. is
no longer satisfying, when spirit manifests indifference towards its living existence or dwells unsatisfied therein, when ethical life dissolves. Then spirit takes
refuge in the space of thought and forms for itself a realm of thought standing

against the actual world. Philosophy, then, is reconciliation of ruin, which was begun by thought. (*History of Philosophy,* Introduction*)*

One interesting aspect of the *Philosophy of Right* is the paucity of references to Aristotle. This tends to obscure the fact that Hegel is really engaged here in a continual debate with the Aristotle of the *Ethics* and the *Politics*. In general, in exploring the distinctions between ancient Athens and modern Europe, above all the disappearance of slavery, Hegel stresses the importance of free individuality in the modern world. This element, he points out, was unknown to his Greek forerunners.

Early in the book, Hegel tells us explicitly where his account of sociopolitical life begins.

> The basis (*Boden*) of right is the *realm of spirit* in general and its precise location and point of departure is the *will*; the will is *free*, so that freedom constitutes its substance and destiny (*Bestimmung*) and the system of right is the realm of actualised freedom, the world of spirit produced from within itself as a second nature. (*Philosophy of Right*, para 4, 35)

This is his starting point: the will, which cannot and must not be deduced from anything else. From the will, he must unfold the entire structure of society, economy, and politics. (He spells out this unifying principle in the *Philosophy of Right*, addition to para 279, 317.) At first, the will is abstract, the single individual. "Freedom is here the freedom of the abstract will *in general*, or . . . the freedom *of an individual person* who relates only to himself."

In beginning his work in this way, Hegel has separated himself from his Greek predecessors. Will is a concept hardly known to Plato and Aristotle, while for Hegel will and freedom are the characteristics of the modern world. The two great Ancients knew freedom only as the distinguishing mark separating the citizen from the slave, while for Hegel, modernity means that "all are free." Nonetheless, they agree across the millennia that philosophical comprehension is crucial for social life.

But the immediate abstract shape of will is only a starting point. In the *Lectures*, he explains that "Right expresses in general a relationship constituted by the freedom of the will and its realisation" (56). This individual abstraction uncovers its meaning explicitly only in the forms of social life, in the economic structure, in the State and in the international system of states. "Merely formal right" has to unfold its more concrete stages of development.

Hegel explains how "the concept of the absolute free will is the finite free being. We begin with the individual free being, and then consider how it frees itself from this finitude" (*Lectures*, 61). "Freedom from finitude" is only possible in society where the abstract individual becomes a *person*, and this in turn is inseparable from the possession of things, for only in possession does personality show its objective character. Will is "the abstract basis for abstract and hence formal right. The commandment of right is therefore: *be a person and respect others as persons.*"

> A person, in distinguishing himself from himself, relates himself to *another person*, and indeed it is only as owners of property that the two have existence (*Dasein*) for each other. Their identity *in themselves* acquires existence (*Existenz*) through the transference of the property of one to the other by common will and with due respect to the rights of both – that is by *contract*. (*Philosophy of Right*, para 40, 70)

In opposition to Plato, Hegel thinks he can prove the necessity for private ownership.

> As a person I am a free being; in the sphere of universality I am wholly an individual; in the thing I own I must be for myself in all my individuality, and so I must own it fully, freely; and it follows that there must be private ownership. (*Lectures*, 75)

The abstract individual, Hegel believes, is merely a natural being with a natural will. Persons, on the contrary, live in society. None of Hegel's categories thereafter is to be found within the "natural realm." At this abstract level, freedom is merely something negative. As the *Lectures* put it, in a critical allusion to Kant: "'Respect human beings as persons' is the imperative of abstract right; thus all imperatives of right (other than the command 'Be a person') are merely prohibitions" (62).

Hegel analyzes what is meant by "taking possession." He distinguishes three aspects: physically seizing something, giving it form (*formierung*), and designating its ownership. Of these, the second is the most important. Every human activity produces an objective result outside itself, something which exists independently in the world and necessarily stands opposed to the actor. Hegel not only sees the act of forming something as one of the ways of taking possession of it: he is unable to consider forming anything, that is, any act of human creativity, *except* as a way of possessing it. Hegel's other works contain some wonderful insights into fine art and its history; but in the *Philosophy of Right* the only mention of art is in a sentence about the commercial value of an art object (para 68).

Hegel goes on to develop three aspects of abstract right: property, contract, and wrong (*das Unrecht*). Simple possession becomes *property*, when society as a whole recognizes the right of each individual. Hegel takes the word "alienation" (*Entaüsserung*), meaning the transfer of property to someone else, and gives it a universal spiritual significance. Particularly interesting is his belief that you can sell the use of your "physical and mental powers," but only for a limited time. This is "because they have they have the aspect of an external relationship to my personality" (*Lectures*, 79).

When he talks about contract, Hegel reveals a significant disagreement with Aristotle. We saw in the *Politics* that lending money at interest was classified as the most hateful way to get a living. For Hegel, on the contrary, it is quite acceptable. His classification of contracts (in para 80), following that of Kant as well as the Roman jurists, includes rent, money lending, and wages, all, of course, under the overall heading: "Morality."

Like Aristotle, Hegel must describe the exchange of commodities and this leads him to attempt to expound the relationship between the exchangeability of a thing and its usefulness in satisfying a need.

> A thing (*Sache*) in use is an individual thing, determined in quantity and quality and related to a specific need. But its specific utility, as *quantitatively* determined, is at the same time *comparable* with other things of the same utility, just as the specific need which it serves is at the same time *need in general* and thus likewise comparable in its particularity with other needs. Consequently, the thing is also comparable with things which serve other needs. (*Philosophy of Right*, para 63, 92)

This "consequently" is astounding in so profound and subtle a thinker. Throughout its entire history, economics has struggled—and totally failed—to carry out the task which Hegel thinks he has polished off in a couple of sentences: to derive quantitative proportions of exchange from the utilities of commodities. (We have seen how Aristotle stubbed his toe on the very same obstacle.) And yet this error reveals the deepest truth, as Marx was to demonstrate. For it contains Hegel's understanding that human needs and forms of exchange are not something merely "natural," but are themselves produced through social activity.

Paragraph 66, in the section headed "The Alienation of Property," is interesting for containing, in the accompanying remark, a reference to Spinoza. Hegel identifies Spirit with self-caused substance, whose concept involves its existence. Hegel ties together the necessary existence of property with Spirit and the inalienability of personality. Hegel seeks to distinguish between the slave, whose personality is alienated, and the modern wage earner, who is free because he can own property.

The transition from property to contract is the next step in the development toward concreteness in Hegel's conception of social relations.

> Contract presupposes that the contracting parties *recognise* each other as persons and owners of property. . . . In a contract, I have property by virtue of a

common will; for it is the interest of reason that the subjective will should become more universal. (*Philosophy of Right*, para 71, 103)

By considering the possibility of wrong and its punishment, Hegel shows how the abstract person is not yet a conscious moral *subject*. From here, Hegel arrives at the idea of morality (*Moralität*), where will is subjective. The individual, standing opposed to the universal, expresses itself in action.

> Action contains the following determinations: (a) it must be known by me in its externality as mine; (b) its essential relation to the concept is one of obligation; and (c) it has an essential relation to the will of others. (*Philosophy of Right*, para 113, 140)

Hegel is not satisfied with Kant's exposition of the contrast between individual decision and the Good as "a mere ought." The will

> first posits itself in the opposition between the universal will which has being *for itself*; then, by superseding this opposition—the negation of the negation – it determines itself as will *in its existence* (*Dasein*). . . . Thus it now has its *personality* . . . as its *object* (*Gegenstand*); the infinite subjectivity of freedom, which now has being *for itself*, constitutes the principle of the *moral point of view*. (*Philosophy of Right*, para 104, 131–32)

The subjective action has purpose and the subject is responsible for it. Hegel discerns two opposed totalities: good in the abstract and conscience. How are these two to be reconciled? Hegel considers the unity, "the reconciliation," of abstract right with morality, in which we reach the level of ethical life (*Sittlichkeit*), the final destination of Hegel's journey.

Hegel sees that morality is limited by its individualist character, and he associates this limited point of view with Kant. In contrast, he explains,

> the determinations of ethics constitute the concept of freedom. They are the substantiality or universal essence of individuals who are related to them merely as accidents. Whether the individual exists or not is a matter of indifference to objective ethical life, which alone has permanence, and is the power by which the lives of the individuals are governed. (*Philosophy of Right*, para 145, Addition, 190)

We have reached a new level in Hegel's attempt to reconcile the individual and society. "Ethical life is the unity of the will in its concept with the will of the individual" (*Philosophy of Right*, para 33, 64). "Ethical life is the interpenetration of the subjective and the objective" (*Lectures*, 129). In relation to this "ethical substance," individuals are merely accidental. Unlike Aristotle,

Hegel does not see Ethics as a science to be studied by the citizens, helping them to make choices about the best way to live. Instead, he regards Ethical Life as an objective process of development, which philosophy has the task of raising to the level of consciousness.

This, the third part of his book, deals with the sociohistorical form within which the "ethical substance" unfolds. It contains three sections: Family, Civil Society, and the State. The family, in turn, is divided into marriage, family property, and the bringing up of children. At the heart of Hegel's notion of marriage is the status he gives to women: they are "passive and subjective." On this question, at least, Hegel insists on being more backward than Plato. "Woman has her substantial vocation in the family, and her ethical disposition consists in family piety." "Women may well be educated, but they are not made for the higher sciences, for philosophy and certain artistic productions which require a universal element" (*Philosophy of Right*, para 166, 206–207).

And so on.

The position of the family in Hegel's scheme is determined by its being a foundation for the holding of property. Hegel thinks it obvious that "the family as a legal person in relation to others must be represented by the husband as its head." Children, while they are not things to be owned, like slaves, have to be subject to parental discipline, "the purpose of which is to break their self-will." All of this is to prepare them to belong to civil society. While the family, Hegel says, is founded upon relationships of love, civil society is governed purely by selfishness.

> The selfish end in its actualisation, conditioned . . . by universality, establishes a system of all-round interdependence, so that the subsistence and welfare of the individual and his rightful existence are interwoven with, and grounded on, the subsistence, welfare and rights of all, and have actuality and security only in this context. (*Philosophy of Right*, para 183, 207)

Civil society was the term used by the eighteenth-century Scots, Steuart, Ferguson and Adam Smith, to denote the social relations between independent property owners. From his study of political economy, Hegel sees civil society (*bürgerliche Gesellschaft*) as a combination of two "principles." One is "the concrete person who, as a particular person, as a totality of needs and a mixture of natural necessity and arbitrariness, is his own end." The other is the universal mediation between each such individual and the rest. "Their relation is such that each asserts itself and gains satisfaction through the others."

> In civil society, each individual is his own end, and all else means nothing to him. But he cannot accomplish the full extent of his ends without reference to

others; these others are therefore means to the end of the particular person. But through its reference to others, the particular end takes on the form of universality, and gains satisfaction by simultaneously satisfying the welfare of others. (*Philosophy of Right*, para 182, 220)

Thus the universal needs of society are satisfied through the actions of individuals who are not conscious of these needs, who only see and only act upon their own individual needs. This development of needs and their satisfaction forms a system of needs.

The account of civil society in the *Lectures* begins like this:

The more precise concrete characteristic of universality in civil society is that the subsistence and welfare of individuals is conditioned by and interwoven with the subsistence of all other individuals. This communal system provides individuals with the framework of their existence and with security, both externally and with regard to right. So civil society is in the first place the *external state* or *the state as the understanding envisages it*. . . . because the main purpose is to secure the needs of individuals. (*Lectures*, 161–62)

Alluding to Rousseau, Hegel adds,

Here the burghers are *bourgeois*, not *citoyens*. . . . Here is the sphere of the mediation involved in the fact that the individual's purpose also has universality as one of its aspects. But here we do not yet have life within the universal for the universal.

Hegel's interpretation of Adam Smith's "invisible hand" is central to his entire outlook.

Individuals, as citizens of this state, are *private persons* who have their own interest as their end. Since this end is mediated through the universal, which thus *appears* to the individuals as a *means*, they can attain their end only in so far as they themselves determine their knowledge, volition and action in a universal way and make themselves *links* in the chain of this *continuum* (*Zusammenhang* = connection). (*Philosophy of Right*, para 187, 224)

Hegel has many criticisms of civil society and its fragmentary character, but they are subordinate to his belief that, precisely through the collisions between the particular individual interests, the universal is being furthered. Reason governs the world, but only via unreason.

Particularity, in its primary determination as that which is opposed to the universal of the will in general, is *subjective need*, which attains its objectivity, ie its satisfaction, by means of (a) external things, which are likewise the *property* and product of the needs and *wills* of others and of (b) activity and work, as the mediation between the two aspects. The end of subjective need is the satisfaction of subjective *particularity*, but in the relation between this and the needs and free arbitrary will of others, *universality* asserts itself, and the resultant manifestation of rationality in the sphere of finitude is *the understanding*. This is the chief aspect which must be considered here, and which itself constitutes the conciliatory element within this sphere. (*Philosophy of Right*, para 189, 227)

This is where Hegel pays tribute to the achievements of political economy, mentioning specifically Smith, Say, and Ricardo. However, his task is not merely to praise them, but to uncover the inner meaning of their work. The path to freedom passes through the civil society they studied, and only here, in the form of social needs, do the needs of the individual develop and find their satisfaction. Hegel dismisses Rousseau's notion that freedom existed in a "state of nature," which he has already identified with abstract individuality.

For a condition in which natural needs as such were immediately satisfied would merely be one in which spirituality was immersed in nature, and hence a condition of savagery and unfreedom; whereas freedom consists solely in the reflection of the spiritual into itself, its distinction from the natural and its reflection upon the latter.

The system of production that underlies civil society gives rise to a division of labor, through which

the work of the individual becomes simpler, so that his skill at his abstract work becomes greater, as does the volume of his output. at the same time this abstraction of skill and means makes the dependence and reciprocity of human beings in the satisfaction of their other needs complete and entirely necessary. Furthermore, the abstraction of production makes work increasingly mechanical, so that the human being is eventually able to step aside and let a machine take his place. (*Philosophy of Right*, para 198, 232–33)

Hegel's picture of the modern economic system never depicts it as an ideal state of affairs. "In these opposites and their complexity, civil society affords a spectacle of extravagance and misery as well as of the physical and ethical corruption common to both." As he had learned from Adam Smith, and as he stated more clearly in his early (1801–1802) lectures in Jena, the division of labor has a devastating effect on the individual laborer. "Through the work of the machine, the human being becomes more and more machine-like, dull, spiritless." Twenty years later, in the *Philosophy of Right*, he says that the differentiation between individuals brought about by the system "does not cancel out the inequality of human beings."

As we shall see, he is also well aware of the wide disparity of wealth which is engendered by the system. In the *Lectures*, Hegel was more forthright in his criticism of the way that market society functions, than he was in the book in which he had to tailor his criticisms to the censors. For instance, his account of the factory is quite startling:

> Factory workers become deadened (*stumpf*) and tied to their factory and dependent on it, since with this single aptitude they cannot earn a living anywhere else. A factory presents a sad picture of the deadening of human beings, which is also why on Sundays factory workers lose no time in spending and squandering their entire weekly wages. (*Lectures*, 177)

However, because the machine makes it possible to replace workers, "human beings are . . . first sacrificed, after which they emerge through the more highly mechanised condition as free once more." The overall development which is the outcome of all this inequality, misery and oppression makes it all worth while, Hegel believes, as did Adam Smith. (Neither of them asked the factory workers what *they* thought!)

Up to this point in Hegel's argument, he has effectively been uncovering the rational meaning of the type of social life which throughout Europe was either already in existence, or coming into being. Now his account moves into a new gear. He must explain more and more what he thinks ought to be, what a rational sociopolitical order would be like. This is by no means a kind of utopian scheme, because he has to try to present each element of his account as taking its place as part of a single, rational whole.

In Hegel's picture, each individual has to belong to one of three estates (*Stände*). This word does not mean classes. Like the "corporations," which we shall meet in a moment, they look like an attempt by Hegel to call into play some aspects of medieval society, in order to sort out the problems of modernity. However, they are actually part of his preparation for the transition to the state. The concept "estate" is essential for Hegel's task of reconciling individual subjectivity with the state: it is only through membership of an estate that each individual's activity becomes a contribution to the universal development of society.

The *substantial* or immediate estate includes all those engaged in agriculture, lumping together the wealthy landowner and the agricultural laborer. The reflecting or *formal* estate covers everybody involved in trade and industry, so that factory workers are thrown together with the owner of the factory. "It relies for its livelihood on its *work*, on *reflection* and the understanding, and essentially on its mediation of the needs and work of others." Notice, above all, that there is no space left vacant for the modern wage earner, so the modern form of class struggle cannot appear in the picture. Over the substantial and formal estates stands that section which has "*the universal interests* of society as its business." These are the bureaucrats who run the state. They are thus to live in conditions which contrast strongly with those of Plato's Guardians: while the Guardians were to be kept free of all entanglement with family and property, Hegel makes sure that his bureaucrats are part of a comfortable middle class.

> It must therefore be exempted from work for the direct satisfaction of its needs, either by private resources or by receiving an indemnity from the state which calls upon its resources. (*Philosophy of Right*, para 205, 237)

Hegel also dislikes Plato's notion that the rulers should assign each individual his particular place. He believes that each individual must decide what he will do for a living. (A woman's place is another matter. That's fixed biologically, he thinks!) In the *Philosophy of Right* (para 207, 239), this leads him to a deprecatory remark about the caste system in India. However, in the corresponding place in the *Lectures*, Hegel had inserted this comment:

> For privileges accorded to one class in regard to communal tasks are very oppressive. For instance the Prussian nobility used to have the sole right to be commissioned officers. This class distinction based on privilege, where one class participates to a greater extent in communal tasks, is one of the most repugnant forms of distinction. (*Lectures*, 185–86)

He thought it prudent to miss this idea out of the work as published, as he did another reference to privilege (*Lectures*, 224–26).

Now he describes the administration of justice and the role of law in society, if it is to function as the realisation of freedom. For this, the automatism of civil society, governed unaided by the market, must be tempered by conscious decision, by Reason. "The development of law founded on right . . . is an affair of the understanding" (*Lectures*, 190). What is right has to be recognized by all.

For the system of needs to operate, Hegel requires the intervention of a set of institutions which he calls the police (*Polizei*). (Maybe "polity" would be a better translation: Aristotle's *politeia*, though not mentioned, is never far away.) This does not just refer to the forces of law and order. Hegel means public authority in general, which also includes the provision of welfare for those who need help. Not only "the undisturbed security of persons and property should be guaranteed, but also . . . the livelihood and welfare of individuals should be secured." It is in this context that Hegel considers the existence of widespread poverty in modern society.

When a large mass of people sinks below the level of a certain standard of living
   . . . that feeling of right, integrity and honour which comes from supporting
oneself
   by one's own activity and work is lost. This leads to the creation of a rabble
(*Pöbel*), which in turn makes it much easier for disproportionate wealth to be
concentrated in a few hands. (*Philosophy of Right*, para 244, 266)

Hegel makes no pretence of having a solution to this "problem." As possible ways to combat unemployment, he considers attempts to expand markets through what we would nowadays call advertising, and by international expansion and colonization. But he goes no further than saying: "The important question of how poverty can be remedied is one which agitates and torments modern societies especially." In a lecture delivered toward the end of his life, Hegel declares: "These two sides, poverty and wealth, thus constitute the corruption of civil society." So Hegel has more than an inkling that civil society is already showing its limits. In the *Lectures*, Hegel goes into more detail about the problem of poverty. "The whole community (*das Allgemeine*) must therefore make provision for the poor, in regard both to what they lack and to the idle, malevolent disposition that may result from their situation and the wrong they have suffered" (*Lectures*, 209).

The final category of Hegel's account of civil society is what he calls "Corporations." Something like the medieval guilds, each corporation should coordinate the activities of people engaged in a particular economic activity, and thus overcome the isolation of individuals. They thus come between the estates and the state. Hegel needs this structure of estates and corporations to mediate between the state and the mass of individual citizens, and to confront the problem with which all the political thinkers had been trying to answer: the relation between individuals and the universal.

Only now is Hegel ready to discuss the political arrangements of the modern social order. For the first time, we encounter the State as a political entity. For Hegel, the individual finds his freedom only within the community as a whole, which he identifies with the political state, and that is why membership in the state as a political form is for him the highest freedom. "The state is the actuality of concrete freedom." Hegel stresses that the economic structure of modern society, which works through each individual striving to satisfy their own desires, had become distinct from the state, which is needed as the universal political power and the highest expression of reason.

The state is the actuality of the substantial will, an actuality which it possesses
in the particular self-consciousness when this has been raised to its universality;
as such, it is the rational, in and for itself. This substantial unity is an absolute
and unmoved end in itself, and in it, freedom enters into its highest right, just as

this ultimate end possesses the highest right in relation to individuals whose *highest duty* is to be members of the state. (*Philosophy of Right*, para 258, 275)

(There is an echo here of Aristotle's "unmoved mover.") This is the cornerstone of Hegel's entire account modern social life. The state exists with absolute necessity. Hegel enters into a discussion of Rousseau's conceptions of social contract and of "the general will," and this is the occasion for a clear reference to the French Revolution, and the dangers inherent in revolution in general.[4]

When these abstractions were invested with power, they afforded the tremendous spectacle, for the first time we know of in human history, of the overthrow of all existing and given conditions within an actual major state and the revision of its constitution from first principles and purely in terms of *thought*; the *intention* behind this was to give it what was *supposed* to be a purely *rational* basis. On the other hand, since these were abstractions divorced from the Idea, they turned the attempt into the most terrible and drastic event. (*Philosophy of Right*, para 258, 277)

In the *Lectures*, he gives a useful pointer to his concept of the state. The family, he explains, "is marked by the tie of love," while civil society has instead "the tie of necessity, where people behave to one another as independent beings." The state, the third moment of Ethical Life, is "the unity of the two, which appears as consciousness of freedom" (*Lectures*, 220). Individuals can choose whether to "enter the state . . . of their own free will." If they choose otherwise, they "place themselves in a state of nature, where their right is not recognised" (*Lectures*, 223).

The state, he argues, shows itself in three aspects. It is a particular, internal, constitution; it is an individual entity in international law; and, in combination with other states, it takes its place in world history, chiefly through war. What is the relation of the constitution to the "spheres of family and civil society"? Hegel poses the problem of their unity like this:

The state is one the one hand an *external* necessity and the higher power to whose nature their laws and interests are subordinate and on which they depend. But on the other hand, it is their *immanent* end, and its strength consists in the unity of its universal and ultimate ends with the particular interest of individuals, in the fact they have *duties* towards the state to the same extent as they also have rights. (*Philosophy of Right*, para 261, 283)

What matters most is that the law of reason should merge with the law of particular freedom, and that my particular end should become identical with the universal; otherwise, the state must hang in the air. It is the self-awareness of individuals which constitutes the actuality of the state, and its stability consists in the identity of the two aspects in question. (*Philosophy of Right*, para 265, 287)

Here is that organic unity of individual and universal which runs through every part of Hegel's work. It is also his answer to the problems which broke up the Athenian *polis* and which he believes could restore its harmony in the only form he believed to be possible for modernity: a system of philosophical science. His criticism of Plato, who also sees the *polis* as an organism, is that he leaves no room for individual subjectivity. His Idea stands outside the world, while Hegel's Idea lives and develops in the world.

But *how is this unity to be realized*? Hegel struggles with this question in great detail in order to construct his constitution. He never "holds these truths to be self-evident," as the Enlightened authors of the American Constitution did! If such important knowledge about society were directly available to anyone, there would be no need for philosophy. Only through the action of Spirit can sociopolitical life have any meaning, and uncovering the springs of that action demands hard philosophical work. "Opinion" is no use here.

> The political *disposition*, i.e. *patriotism* in general, is certainty based on *truth* (whereas merely subjective certainty does not originate in *truth*, but is only opinion) and a volition which had become *habitual*. . . . This disposition is in general one of *trust* . . . or the consciousness that my substantial and particular interest is preserved and contained in the interest and end of another (in this case the state), and in the latter's relation to me as an individual. As a result, this other ceases to be an other for me, and in my consciousness of this, I am free. (*Philosophy of Right*, para 268, 288)

Here we see the importance of Hegel's claim that his philosophy is Absolute Knowledge. But now he has to carry out a still more difficult task: he must produce a rational constitution and show that it is the only one possible. It turns out to be a constitutional monarchy. Far from upholding the existing Prussian state, as some people still insist on repeating, what he aims for is closer to the character of the British monarchy of William IV. Hegel is quite certain that

> for a people that has developed to civil society, or in general to consciousness of the free ego in its determinate existence, in its needs, its freedom of choice and its conscience, *constitutional monarchy* alone is possible. (*Lectures*, 249)

The constitution of the state is rational. It divides itself into legislative, executive and sovereign powers (*fürstliche Gewalt*). This is "in accordance with the nature of the concept" and its three "moments," universality, particularity, and singularity. On the basis of this logical framework, he "proves" the necessity for an individual monarch.

> Sovereignty, which is initially only the *universal* thought of this ideality, can *exist* only as *subjectivity* which is certain of itself. . . . But subjectivity attains its truth only as a *subject*, only as a *person*, and in a constitution which has progressed to real rationality, each of the three moments of the concept has its distinctive shape which is *actual for itself*. This absolutely decisive moment of the whole, therefore, is not individuality in general, but *one* individual, the *monarch*. (*Philosophy of Right*, para 279, 317)

In the *Lectures*, Hegel is more outspoken about the restrictions which his constitution would place upon the monarch, but the main substance of his argument is the same. The monarch does not have a contract with the people, even though he is their "supreme representative." He has a "body of counsellors," but they only advise him. Ministers of State are responsible for executing decisions, but they must be chosen by the monarch, who deposes them when he thinks it necessary.

Hegel regards democracy as quite unworkable in a modern state. "Without its monarch and that articulation of the whole which is necessarily and immediately associated with monarchy, the people is a formless mass." That is why Hegel thinks that monarchy, kept within constitutional bounds, is superior to democracy as a political form. "The people" are no more than a collection of individual atoms and therefore a threat to the unity and harmony of the state.

> Popular sovereignty is one of those confused thoughts which are based on a garbled notion of the people. Without its monarch and that articulation of the whole which is necessarily and immediately associated with monarchy, the people is a formless mass. (*Philosophy of Right*, para 279, 319)

And later,

> To know what one wills, and even more, to know what the will which has being in and for itself—i.e. reason—wills, is the fruit of profound cognition and insight, and this is the very thing which "the people" lack. (*Philosophy of Right*, para 301, 340)

Hegel's bureaucracy, as we have already seen, is drawn from the educated middle class. It is prevented from using its position to dominate society by (a) the monarch and (b) the corporations. Hegel's legislative power is based upon the three estates (*Stände*), which we have already encountered. These resemble the *trois états* of prerevolutionary France.

Viewed as a *mediating organ*, the Estates stand between the government at large on the one hand and the people in their division in particular spheres and individuals on the other. Their determination requires that they should embody in equal measure both the *sense* and *disposition* of the *state* and *government* and the *interests* of particular circles and *individuals*. . . . They ensure that individuals do not present themselves as a *crowd* or *aggregate*, unorganized in their opinions and volition, and do not become a massive power in opposition to the organic state. (*Philosophy of Right*, para 302, 342)

Hegel "proves" that the Legislature has to be divided into two Houses, and that the Upper House has to consist of the "estate of natural life"—in practice, the land-owning nobility.

The first house contains the universal class, the land-owning class. Members of the agricultural class who wish to enter the estates assembly must not only belong to this immediate class, but must also be wealthy landowners. (*Lectures*)

The second estate—in practice, the business class—will choose their representativesto the Lower House, but that in no case implies democratic elections.

As for mass elections, it may also be noted that, in large states, the electorate inevitably becomes indifferent in view of the fact that a single vote has little effect when numbers are so large; and however highly they are urged to value the right to vote, those who enjoy this right will simply fail to make use of it. (*Philosophy of Right*, para 311, 350)

All the previous work, the movement from morality to ethical life, the discussion of family and civil society, the structure of a rational state, leads to the discussion of the monarchy. This is the climax of Hegel's argument. As he puts it at the end of the *Lectures*,

Rationality is to be found in the middle class, which is the intellectual estate. The people are a material extreme; to say that the people will what is good means that they do not want to be oppressed, and that they want to give as little as possible and get as much enjoyment as possible. It is through the middle class that the wishes of the people are laid before the sovereign. (*Lectures*, 315)

The subsequent sections of the *Philosophy of Right* seek to place the modern state as an individual entity in the world community of states and in the process of world history. In international relations, there is no place for ethical life. The individual states relate to each other in a way analogous to the individuals in Hobbes "state of nature." Rejecting with contempt Kant's efforts to find the way to "perpetual peace" between the warring nations, Hegel sees war between states as the concomitant of harmony within states. At the end of the century following Hegel's, we have a rather different perspective on what this means for the life of humanity! Hegel thinks war "should not be regarded as an absolute evil."

> Through its agency (as I have put it on another occasion), "the ethical health of nations is preserved in their indifference towards the permanence of finite determinacies, just as the movement of the winds preserves the sea from that stagnation which a lasting calm would produce—a stagnation which a lasting, not to say perpetual, peace would also produce among nations." (*Philosophy of Right*, 361)

Finally, Hegel sets the State in the context of world history, recapitulating some of the ideas to be found in his *Lectures on the Philosophy of History*. History is "the exposition and the *actualisation of the universal spirit*" (*Philosophy of Right*, para 342, 372). The very last sentences of the book declare:

> The present has cast off its barbarism and unjust arbitrariness, and truth has cast off its otherworldliness and contingent force, so that true reconciliation, which reveals the *state* as the image and actuality of reason, has become objective. In the *state*, self-consciousness finds the actuality of its substantial knowledge and volition in organic development; in *religion*, it finds its feeling and representation, of this truth as ideal essentiality; but in *science*, it finds the free and comprehended cognition of this truth as one and the same in all its complementary manifestations, i.e., in the *state*, in *nature*, and in the *ideal world*. (*Philosophy of Right*, para 360, 380)

Hegel has given the most complete attempt possible to make sense of the modern world, the world of money, capital, wealth, and poverty, bureaucratic power and war. Within a decade of his death, his powerful philosophical influence had faded, and later revivals of interest in his ideas have usually tended to downplay the significance of this particular book. After the succeeding nightmare century, the question whether this world does indeed "make sense" raises itself with ever-greater force.

NOTES

1. Hegel, *Elements of the Philosophy of Right, or Natural Law and Political Science in Outline*, ed. Allen W. Wood (Cambridge: Cambridge University Press, 1991).
2. A student's notes of these, discovered and published in Germany in the 1970s, have recently been translated into English: *Hegel's Lectures on Natural Right and*

Political Science: The First Philosophy of Right, trans. Michael Stewart and Peter J. Hodgson (Berkeley: University of California Press, 1995). The same ground is covered, more schematically, in the third part of the *Encyclopedia, the Philosophy of Mind*, paras 483–552.

3. So much for the nonsense about Hegel in his last book being "a conservative upholder of the Prussian state." This rubbish is still repeated in textbooks. Its currency in "Marxist" circles dates back at least to 1870. See Engels's letter to Marx, May 8, 1870, protesting against its ignorant repetition by Wilhelm Liebknecht.

4. See also the section of the *Phenomenology of Spirit*, trans. H. Kainz (University Park, Pa.: Pennsylvania State University Press, 1999) headed "Absolute Freedom and Terror."

Chapter Eight

Karl Marx's Critique of Politics

From the very beginning of Marx's work to the very end of his life, he is engaged in a struggle with and against Hegel. Referring to Hegel as "our great teacher," he never ceases to criticize his teachings. Marx's thesis for a doctorate, on the philosophy of Democritus and Epicurus, was itself part of this struggle, taking as its standpoint the direct opposite opinion to Hegel's on these two great materialists. But when Marx decides to make a "critical examination" of Hegel's *Philosophy of Right*, he is confronting, not just Hegel, but the entire tradition of political thought, critically embodied in that book. His work thus opens the way to tackle the problem with which that tradition has battled since the Athenians, the highest expression of the contradiction between individual and universal, between privately owned property and the self-governing community. The philosophers, culminating in Hegel, had attempted to reconcile these opposites in various ways, but Marx declares for community and against private property.

But how is it possible to "confront" an entire tradition?[1] From what standpoint could we begin such a task? It was heroic for Socrates to upset his fellow citizens with his unsettling questions, or for Kant to pose his critical riddles about the conditions which made knowledge possible. But they, at least, remained within the general arena in which such matters had been grappled with before them. Marx's work, which was just getting started in 1843, implicitly poses questions about the very nature of humanity and its knowledge of itself, and these questions transcend the philosophical tradition as a whole.

Marx worked on his *Contribution to the Critique of Hegel's Philosophy of Law* between May and August 1843.[2] The extant manuscript consists of

131

a detailed discussion of paragraphs 261–312 of the *Philosophy of Right*. (There is evidently a missing first page, so the commentary probably started at paragraph 260.) Thus his study covers most of the section "Constitutional Law," with which Hegel begins his concluding chapter, "The State." By the time he reaches paragraph 313, Marx has lost patience with Hegel's account, and just breaks off this study. He has now discovered those questions to which he has to devote the rest of his life.

Marx's comments operate on two levels. On the one hand he targets Hegel's attempt at the reconciliation of civil society—the Hobbesian "battle-field of private interest"—with communal, ethical life. On the other, he attacks the method with which Hegel tries to demonstrate that this reconciliation is a logical necessity. Many commentators have concentrated on this second aspect, stressing Marx's repeated allegation that Hegel has inverted the relationship between subject and predicate. It is often stated—usually without the slightest attempt at proof—that Marx gets this idea from Feuerbach. In fact, the charge that an opponent has inverted subject and predicate is an old one in the history of philosophy, and both Feuerbach and Marx would have been well aware of this. Marx himself discusses this issue in the preparatory material for his doctoral thesis, and thus at least a year before Feuerbach's book was published.[3]

Much more important is the close connection Marx reveals between (i) Hegel's logical method, (ii) his reconciliatory project, and (iii) his conception of human social life. This relationship is not only found in the *Philosophy of Right*, but runs right through the entire Hegelian system.

Hegel's paragraphs 260 and 261, Marx points out, argue that "concrete freedom consists in the identity (as an ought, a dual identity) of the system of particular interest (the family and civil society) with the system of general interest (the state)" (*C*, 5). (*C = MECW*, volume 3)

When Hegel asserts that "the state is on the one hand an external necessity" and "on the other hand . . . their immanent end," Marx attacks this as an "unresolved antinomy," and accuses Hegel of "logical, pantheistic mysticism" (*C*, 7).

> The unity of the ultimate general purpose of the state with the particular interest of individuals is supposed to consist in the fact that their duties to the state and their rights in the state are identical. (Thus, for example, the duty to respect property is supposed to coincide with the right to property.) (*C*, 6)
>
> The fact is that the state issues from the multitude in their existence as members of families and as members of civil society. Speculative philosophy expresses this fact as the idea's deed, not as the idea of the multitude, but as the deed of a subjective idea different from the fact itself. . . . Empirical actuality is thus accepted as it is. (*C*, 9)

Marx remarks that "the entire mystery of the philosophy of law and of Hegel's philosophy as a whole is set out" here. Giving the first of many examples of Hegel's upside-down logic, Marx comments:

> It is important that Hegel everywhere makes the idea the subject and turns the proper, the actual subject, such as "political conviction," into a predicate. It is always on the side of the predicate, however, that development takes place. (*C*, 11)

When Hegel refers to the state as an "organism," Marx notes that

> The organic is just *the idea of the distinct aspects*, their ideal definition. Here, however, the *idea* is spoken of as a subject, which develops itself into its distinct aspects. (*C*, 12)

Marx accepts Hegel's metaphor of the state as an organism, but challenges the way that he uses this to turn the idea into the subject, as the power which determines the individuals. This is his first step toward challenging Hegel's conception of human freedom. "Their fate is predetermined by 'the nature of the concept,' sealed in "the sacred registers of the Santa Casa", of logic. . . . 'Idea' and 'Concept' are here hypostasised abstractions" (*C*, 15). (The Santa Casa was the prison of the Spanish Inquisition.)

> *The general interest and, therein, the conservation of particular interests*, constitutes the general purpose and content of this mind — the enduring substance of the state, the political aspect of self-knowing and self-willing mind. (*C*, 16)

And here is Marx summing up his view on the work of Hegel and philosophy in general:

> The concrete content, the actual definition, appears as something formal; the wholly abstract formal definition appears as the concrete content. The essence of the definitions of the state is not that they are definitions of the state but that they in their most abstract form can be regarded as logical-metaphysical definitions. Not the philosophy of law but logic is the real centre of interest. Philosophical work does not consist in embodying thinking in political definitions, but in evaporating the existing political definitions into abstract thoughts. Not the logic of the matter, but the matter of logic is the philosophical element. The logic does not serve to prove the state, but the state to prove the logic. (*C*, 17–18)

A little later, where Hegel has declared that the constitution depends on the "character and development of the self-consciousness" of a people, Marx accuses him of not drawing the logical conclusion from this remark:

> What would really follow would be simply the demand for a constitution which contains within itself the designation and the principle to advance along with

consciousness, to advance as actual men advance; this is only possible when "man" has become the principle of the constitution. Here, Hegel is a *sophist*. (*C*, 19)

Marx has no difficulty with Hegel's huffing and puffing to "prove" that an individual hereditary monarch must embody sovereignty. Hegel says that, while the concept of the monarch is most difficult for "the standpoint of isolated categories," he knows that "this concept is not derivative, *but originates purely in itself*." Marx answers: "In a certain sense every necessary being "originates purely in itself"—in this respect, the monarch's louse is as good as the monarch" (*C*, 21).

Marx does more than justify republicanism here. He gets to the heart of Hegel's entire system. The will, says Hegel, "gives itself the form of *individuality*." Marx comments:

> He forgets, though, that the particular individual is human and that the functions and activities of the state are human functions. He forgets that the essence of a "particular personality" is not its beard, its blood, its abstract physical character, but its *social quality*, and that state functions, etc., are nothing but modes of being and modes of action of the social qualities of men. (*C*, 21–2)

Marx accuses Hegel of using mystical language, and tries to produce a man-in-the-street paraphrase of some passages from Hegel. Marx comments:

> If Hegel had set out from real subjects as the bases of the state he would not have found it necessary to transform the state in a mystical fashion into a subject. "In its truth, however," says Hegel, "subjectivity exists only as *subject*, personality only as *person*." This too is a piece of mystification. Subjectivity is a characteristic of the subject, personality a characteristic of the person. Hegel gives the predicates an independent existence and subsequently transforms them in mystical fashion into their subjects. . . . This subject then appears, however, as a self-incarnation of sovereignty; whereas sovereignty is nothing but the objectified mind of the subjects of the state. (*C*, 23–24)

Hegel writes that "the sovereignty of the state is *the* monarch," and that sovereignty is "the will's abstract and to that extent unfounded *self-determination*." Here, Marx presents the way that "the common man" would understand the same notion: simply that "the monarch has sovereign power, sovereignty," and that "sovereignty does what it wills." Marx describes the way that Hegel gives priority to the abstract notion of monarchy, over the concrete entity, the people.

> As if the actual state were not the people. The state is an abstraction. The people alone is what is concrete. And it is remarkable that Hegel, who without hes-

itation attributes a living quality like sovereignty to the abstraction, attributes it only with hesitation and reservations to something concrete. (C, 28)

Where Hegel attacks talk about "the sovereignty of the people" in opposition to the monarchy as "one of those confused notions which are rooted in the wild idea of the people," Marx makes the comment:

It is not a question of the same sovereignty which has arisen on two sides, but *two entirely contradictory concepts of sovereignty*, the one a sovereignty such as can come to exist in a *monarch*, the other such as can come to exist only in a *people*. It is the same with the question: "Is God sovereign or is man?" One of the two is an untruth, even if an existing untruth.

Marx is certain, right from the start, that to be human means to be at once a social being and a self-determining individual, that is, to be a subject. Thus self-rule, which Marx at this time called "true democracy," is essential to any way of life worthy of humanity. Not for nothing had Marx two years earlier made copious excerpts from Spinoza's *Tractatus Logico-Theologicus* and several of his letters.[4]

Democracy is the solved riddle of all constitutions. Here, not merely implicitly and in essence, but existing in reality the constitution is constantly brought back to its actual basis, the actual human being, the actual people, and established as the people's own work . . . a free product of man. . . . Hegel starts from the state and makes man the subjectified state; democracy starts from man and makes the state objectified man. . . . Democracy is the essence of all state constitutions— socialised man [*sozialisierte Mensch* = human] as a particular state constitution. (C, 29–31)

With the notion of socialized humanity, Marx is groping for the idea that he will shortly call first "true democracy," and then "communism." True de-mocracy cannot be just a kind of political constitution, a form of rule. If it is restricted to politics, and coexists with the rights of antagonistic classes and of individual property, it must be a lie.

In democracy the abstract state has ceased to be the dominant factor. The strug-gle between monarchy and republic is itself still a struggle within the abstract state. The political republic is democratic within the abstract state form. The ab-stract state form of democracy is therefore the republic; but here it ceases to be the merely political constitution. (C, 31)

Marx probes the problem of the separation of political life from others spheres of social activity.

Up till now the *political constitution* has been the *religious sphere*, the *religion* of national life, the heaven of its generality over against the *earthly existence* of its actuality. The political sphere has been the only state sphere in the state, the only sphere in which the content as well as the form has been species-content, the truly general; but in such a way that at the same time, because this sphere has confronted the others, its content has become formal and particular. . . . *Monarchy* is the perfect expression of this estrangement. (*C*, 31)

Marx is thus approaching a partial conclusion: politics represents one side of social life in general, but as such it stands in irreconcilable opposition to the fragmentation of the rest of social being, and in particular to civil society. In his investigation of Hegel's elaborate structure of monarchy, bureaucracy, estates and corporations, Marx emphasizes the formal, hierarchical, machine-like character of the bureaucracy. (His many clashes with the Prussian censorship as a newspaper editor are still fresh in his memory.)

The "bureaucracy" is the "*state formalism*" of civil society. It is the "state consciousness," the "state will," the "state power," as *one corporation*—and thus a particular, closed society within the state . . . The bureaucracy must therefore protect the *imaginary* generality of the particular interest. (*C*, 45–56)

What for Hegel was the "universal class" is for Marx the protector of an illusion, an "imaginary generality." He attacks Hegel's conception that the bureaucracy must be entrusted with all general thinking.

Its hierarchy is a *hierarchy of knowledge*. The top entrusts the understanding of detail to the lower levels, whilst the lower levels credit the top with understanding of the general, and so all are mutually deceived. (*C*, 47)

Now he can pose the question of the abolition of the bureaucracy, and then grasp the essential relation between the state and private property. "The abolition of the bureaucracy is only possible by the general interest *actually*— and not, as with Hegel, merely in thought, in *abstraction*—becoming the particular interest" (*C*, 48). When Marx considers Hegel's corporations, he makes another major advance:

The administration of the corporation therefore has this antithesis: *Private property and the interest of the particular spheres against the higher interest of the state; antithesis between private property and the state.* . . . The antithesis of state and civil society is thus fixed: the state does not reside in, but stands outside civil society. (*C*, 49)

Now he can explain his earlier remark that "the abstraction of the political state is a modern product" (*C*, 32). Hegel has asserted that civil society and the state are organically united. But, says Marx,

> The identity which he has constructed between civil society and the state is the identity of *two hostile armies*, where "every soldier" has the "opportunity" to become, by "desertion," a member of the "hostile" army; and indeed Hegel herewith correctly describes the present empirical position. (*C*, 51)

Hegel's legislature is given the function of making laws, but is denied the opportunity of changing the constitution. Marx comments: "Certainly, entire state constitutions have changed in such a way that gradually new needs arose, the old broke down, etc.; but for a *new* constitution a real revolution has always been required" (*C*, 56).

> Posed correctly, the question is simply this: has the people the right to give itself a new constitution? The answer must be an unqualified "Yes," because once it has ceased to be an actual expression of the will of the people the constitution has become a practical illusion. (*C*, 57)

Marx points out that Hegel is reluctant to allow the constitution any historical origin, or to change in any major respect once it is in being. Any change has to be so gradual that no one will notice.

When Hegel tries to "prove" that the state is a logical consequence of private property, he is disguising the actual nature of the modern—bourgeois—state. Marx is sure Hegel has got to the essence of the modern state form, but denies his claim to have shown that this form is logically necessary. He accuses Hegel of indulging himself in "the pleasure of having demonstrated the irrational as absolutely rational" (*C*, 33).

> Precisely because he does not establish objective freedom as the realisation, the practical manifestation of subjective freedom, subjective freedom appears in Hegel as formal freedom. (*C*, 62)

"Hegel is not to be blamed for depicting the nature of the modern state as it is, but for presenting that which is as the nature of the state" (*C*, 63). Hegel is to be praised for grasping that the separation of civil society and the "political state" is a contradiction, but blamed for trying to prove that this contradiction has a rational resolution. "He has presupposed the *separation* of civil society and the political state (a modern condition), and expounded it as a *necessary element of the idea*, as absolute rational truth" (*C*, 73).

Hegel has achieved the feat of deriving the born peers, the hereditary landed property, etc., etc.—this "pillar both of the throne and of society"—from the absolute idea. . . . It shows Hegel's profundity that he feels the separation of civil from political society as a *contradiction*. He is wrong, however, to be content with the appearance of this resolution and to pretend it is the substance, whereas the "*so-called theories*" he despises demand the "*separation*" of the civil from the political estates. (*C*, 75)

Following Rousseau, Marx discovers the human meaning of the opposition within modernity between political and human social life.

The *general law* here appears in the individual. Civil society and state are separated. Hence the citizen of the state is also separated from the citizen as the member of civil society. He must therefore effect a *fundamental division* within himself. As an *actual citizen* he finds himself in a twofold organisation: the *bureaucratic* organisation, which is an external, formal feature of the distant state, the executive, which does not touch him or his independent reality, and the *social* organisation, the organisation of civil society. But in the latter he stands as a *private person* outside the state. (*C*, 77)

What is divided and distorted by the nature of civil society and its political expression is the individual human being. Here are the germs of many ideas which Marx developed over the next four decades. At this point, of course, what he has found is only the key to this life work—his critiques of dialectic, of political economy and of socialism—but it is the true key. "Marxism" believed that Hegel's idealism was a "mistake," an incorrect "theory of knowledge." The answer, it thought, was to hitch up Hegel's "dialectic" to "materialism." Marx does not think this at all. Hegel tries hard to exhibit the reconciliatory work of the Idea, and that is precisely how he points to the deepest contradictions of modern life.

The powers of money, of capital, of the "political state," are first of all spiritual powers, which deny the essentially free potential of humanity. They are indeed abstractions, but abstractions which govern our lives. But, because they have been fabricated, not by God Almighty, but through our own human actions, they can be grasped and overthrown by human action. The entire history of philosophy, as can be seen in its Hegelian culmination, has negatively made this clear. The critique of that tradition is thus the prelude to finding the solution to the riddles of history, not in science, but in revolutionary practice guided by the contradictions in that science. Demolishing Hegel's carefully constructed edifice of reconciliation can only be the beginning, merely clearing the ground for what Marx now has to undertake:

The atomism into which civil society plunges in its *political act* follows necessarily from the fact that the community (*Gemeinwesen*), the communal being (*Kommunistiche Wesen*) in which the individual exists, is civil society separated from the state, or that the *political state* is an *abstraction* from it. (*C*, 79)

The French Revolution, Marx says, marks the completion of this separation (*C*, 80). Since property is the key to the fragmentation of human life, the negation of property which is the germ of Marx's conception of the proletariat, points the way to its transcendence.

> Only one thing is characteristic, namely, that *lack of property* and the *estate of direct labour*, of concrete labour, form not so much an estate of civil society as the ground upon which its circles rest and move. (*C*, 80)

Marx can now see the conflict between the modern world and "humanity":

> Present-day civil society is the realised principle of *individualism*; the individual existence is the final goal; activity, work, content, etc., are *mere* means. . . . The modern era, civilisation . . . separates the objective essence of the human being from him as merely something *external*, material. It does not accept the content of the human being as his true reality. (*C*, 81)

Marx has got to the heart of Hegel's account of the modern state, or rather, to the place where the heart ought to be. In mercilessly dissecting Hegel's intricate construction, purported to be the rational state, Marx has uncovered some new questions: "What is it to be human?" and "Why do we live inhumanly?" At the same time, he has attacked the central core of Hegel's logical doctrine, his conception of contradiction, and his reconciliatory understanding of mediation. "Abstract *spiritualism* is abstract *materialism*; abstract materialism is the *abstract spiritualism of matter*" (*C*, 88).

Later, Marx will show how social mediations can come to dominate the individuals they link, and in fact to build barriers between them. Here, he criticizes Hegel's attempt to make the legislative and the monarchy two sides of a unity.

> Hegel's chief error is to conceive the *contradiction of appearances* as *unity in essence, in the idea*, while in fact it has something more profound for its essence, namely, an *essential contradiction*, just as this contradiction of the legislative authority within itself, for example, is merely the contradiction of the political state, and therefore also of civil society itself. (C, 91)

Marx goes into great detail to refute Hegel's attempt to justify the special position he gives to landed property. He concludes:

> The political constitution at its highest point is therefore the *constitution of private property*. The supreme *political conviction* is the *conviction of private property*. *Primogeniture* is merely the *external* appearance of the *inner* nature of *landed property*. (*C*, 98)
>
>   The *"inalienability" of private property* is one with the *"alienability" of the general freedom of will and morality*. . . . My will does not possess, it is possessed. (*C*, 101)

When he condemns Hegel's opposition to "the idea that all should individually participate in deliberating and deciding the general affairs of the state," Marx clarifies what he understands by democracy.

> If they are a part of the state, then their social *being* is already *their real participation* in it. . . . To be a conscious part of it means consciously to acquire a part of it, to take a conscious interest in it. Without this consciousness the member of the state would be an *animal*. (*C*, 117)

To repeat the point: what Marx sees as "true democracy" is not at all what we know today as democracy, but something much more like Athenian democracy. "It is precisely the participation of civil society in the political state through *delegates* that is the *expression* of their separation and of their merely dualistic unity" (*C*, 119). "*Electoral reform* within the *abstract political state* is therefore the demand for its *dissolution*, but also for the *dissolution of civil society*" (*C*, 121).

Overcoming the contradiction between civil society and political life is possible only through the negation of them both, a negation which at the same time preserves their human, communal content. For this, the atomization of society which keeps people apart from each other, and the relations of political power which abstractly hold the structure together, must be transcended, not in just thought but in practice. When private property ceases to dominate the lives of humans, when it no longer joins them together while keeping them apart, the division between private and public life will vanish.

Marx abandoned the *Critique* at this point, but proceeded to write an introduction, published in the *Deutsch-Französische Jahrbücher* early in 1844, as *A Contribution to the Critique of Hegel's Philosophy of Law: Introduction*. Concerned with the character of the coming revolution in Germany, the introduction embodies all the lessons Marx has learned from his unpublished study of Hegel's book. It is remarkable how far Marx's political thought has traveled in the few weeks since he abandoned his manuscript. He starts with the critique of religion, drawing from it a paradigm of his conception of critique. "The critique of religion turns into the critique of law and the critique of theology into the critique of politics" (*C*, 176). Moreover, "the weapon of critique cannot, of course, replace the critique by weapons, material force must be overthrown by material force."

> The critique of religion ends with the teaching that *man is the highest being for man*, hence with the *categorical imperative to overthrow all relations* in which man is a debased, enslaved, forsaken, despicable being. (*C*, 182)
> It is not the *radical* revolution, not the *general* human emancipation which is a utopian dream for Germany, but rather the partial, the *merely* political revolution. (*C*, 184)

What class of German civil society can carry out such a revolution, fighting to achieve "general human emancipation"?

> Where, then, is the *positive* possibility of a German emancipation? *Answer*: In the formation of a class with *radical chains*, a class of civil society which is not a class of civil society, an estate which is the dissolution of all estates, a sphere which has a universal character by its universal suffering . . . which can no longer invoke a *historical* but only a *human* title. . . . This dissolution of society as a particular estate is the *proletariat*. (*C*, 186)

Marx has inverted the relation between two extremes of Hegel's constitution: the bureaucracy and "the rabble." Once Marx has understood the revolutionary role of the proletariat, he can reply to the split between the modern "political state" and the fragmented society from which it springs. Equipped with his comprehension that the task facing humanity now was nothing less than "universal human emancipation," Marx can see that the state is not the real, but the "illusory community." That is why "political emancipation itself is not human emancipation" (*C*, 160).

He can also get to grips with the limitations of socialist and communist theories. Seeing only the maldistributive form of property, they were unable to grasp the inhuman content of private property as such. Marx has found the standpoint from which to understand all these problems: the standpoint of "human society and social humanity."[5] For the next four decades, he devoted himself to the task of working out the implications of these ideas in his critique of political economy. He has arrived at the threshold of his notion of communism and communist revolution, whose aim is the fusion of political and individual life in a single human life.

NOTES

1. For an important critical discussion of many philosophical ideas that bear on this question, see Ute Bublitz, *Beyond Philosophy: Three Essays on Aristotle and Hegel*, 1998.

2. Riazanov first discovered this work and published it in 1927. There have been several English translations of parts of it, and a full translation, by O'Malley, appeared in 1970. I have used the version given in *Marx-Engels Collected Works* (*MECW*), Vol. 3.

3. *MECW*, Vol.1, 458.

4. See *Marx-Engels Gesamtausgabe*, Abt. 4, Bd. 1.

5. Tenth Thesis on Feuerbach.

Chapter Nine

Marx, Communism, and Revolution

As the twenty-first century gets going, a widespread opinion holds that, whether you like it or not, the world is going to be run by the global market forever. Many people don't like this and see clearly its terrible effects on the way we all live, but the vast majority are convinced that nothing can be done about it, shrugging their shoulders at the absurdity of the very idea. Meanwhile, the market is destroying, not just the environment in which humans can live, but their humanity.

Over the past eighty years or so, the notion of a revolution which would transform social and economic relations was largely absorbed into the idea that a bureaucratic state would take the place of privately owned industry. The Russian Revolution was supposed to provide the model of how such a change would come about. Marx's understanding of revolution was totally obscured by the iron-clad dogmas of "Marxism."

In this book, we have been trying to uncover the ideas of Marx and rescue them from all such dogma. For him, the social revolution had to be the work of the immense majority. The idea that "the masses" were to be used as muscle to overthrow the old order, then handing over power to their "leaders" was quite alien to him. The new world had to be founded upon a transformation of humanity itself, by itself, its universal emancipation. That is why we have concentrated on Marx's critique of the tradition of systematic notions which explained why the world was like it is. Without dealing fundamentally with all such ideas a free association of humans is not possible.

According to the traditional "Marxist" account of the ideas of Karl Marx, Marx and Engels started off as "revolutionary democrats" and "Left Hegelians," who, some time in 1844, turned into "dialectical and historical materialists" and communists. A causal model to explain social development worked like this: changes in production methods led to changes in social relations, which were accompanied by changes in forms of consciousness; social and political struggles at each stage of history were "really" the conflicts between economic classes. When they reached boiling point, these struggles spilled over into revolutions and a new set of social relations were established.

"Marxism" also identified the state as an instrument with which the ruling class oppressed the exploited class, so that they could go on exploiting them. "Marxists" often quoted Engels about the state being "bodies of armed men." In the socialist revolution, according to this scheme, a new, "workers' state" had to be established, to replace the old bourgeois state, just as the bourgeois had replaced the feudal state in the bourgeois revolution. The communists would use this new form of power as an instrument to transform the economic and social landscape. Eventually, society would be ready to do without the state. In the meantime, the "workers' state" had to get tough with those who got in the way, whether the remnants of the old ruling classes, or those sections of the masses who were misguided enough to oppose what their own state was doing for their own good.

Our analysis of the 1843 *Critique* helps to show that none of this represents the thought of Karl Marx. Consider, in particular, just where freedom fits into this picture: it doesn't, as the history of communism demonstrates only too graphically. In the 'Marxist' tradition, "freedom" could only be mentioned in the same breath as "necessity," regarded purely as its opposite. The class struggle, private property and the state were not seen as aspects of estrangement. Marx showed that they were the outcome of the activities of humans, but of humans living inhumanly. However each partial and local struggle might appear to the participants, any movement of the working class actually "represents man's protest against a dehumanised life, because. . . man's true community (is) human nature."[1] Of course the activities of the state apparatus are, indeed, frequently violently coercive. But this does not explain what the state *is*, its essence, and how it relates to communal "human nature."

Is a free, united, self-governing association only possible for gods, as Rousseau thought? Is the task of emancipation too hard for mere mortals? Marx's conception of history is the key to an answer to these questions: "Communism is the riddle of history solved, and it knows itself to be this solution."[2] Humans have themselves unconsciously made this inhuman world, and have now reached the stage where, on the basis of past conquests, they can and must consciously remake it. That is how freedom, which is the essence of humanity, emerges into the open and the nightmare of our prehistory gives way to our real, conscious, human history.

The real Marx is engaged precisely with the problem of how human freedom in society is possible, how the individuals can freely associate. As we have seen, this same problem lies at the heart of the entire history of political thought, and Hegel's attempt to reconcile private property with free communal life was the last and most advanced step along that road. Indeed, Hegel's great contribution was to pinpoint the contradiction between these two sides of society. So when Marx demonstrates that Hegel's attempt at their reconciliation has failed, this is not just another station along the philosophical path, but the beginning of the search for a different kind of answer. Before he could conceive of the transcendence of both private property and political power, Marx had to subvert the opinion which philosophy had of itself. Then, the universal emancipation of humanity, which could only be *self*-emancipation, could be seen as a conscious practical task for the whole of humanity.

Marx was always simultaneously an admiring follower of Hegel and one of his sharpest critics. He upheld Hegel's break with the Enlightenment's view of society as a collection of independently existing individuals, each armed with individual rationality, and with the corresponding logic, as summarized by Kant. But, against Hegel, Marx fought throughout his life for his conception of "true democracy," a free association. When he had completed the 1843 *Critique*, he discovered that he could give this political conception the name "communism," not in the shape of an addition to an already long list of enlightened utopian "doctrines," but as the "real movement." Having dismantled Hegel's intricate constitutional devices for reconciling community with private property, Marx had now to ask new questions about how the transcendence of this contradiction was to be understood and achieved in practice. The answers to these questions were no longer contained within a framework which accepted the existence of private property, but soon revealed themselves to center on the very nature of what already in the 1843 *Critique* he had called "socialized humanity."

When Marx discovered that his "true democracy" was really communism, he could begin to criticise existing communist and socialist ideas. In the main, the socialist heirs of the Enlightenment had accepted the notion that society was a collection of individuals, whose defects might be attributed to their "material circumstances." Once the socialists had got control of these circumstances, and changed them for the better, they could educate people to be better, too, and communal life could be harmonized. But, as Marx explains, this Enlightenment view (a) ignores the fact that we also make the circumstances, and (b) leaves unanswered the question: "Who will educate the educators?"[3] Only when these linked paradoxes had been resolved were either communist revolution or communism possible. Revolutionary practice did not just mean change, but *self*-change, and, as Hegel understood, critical consciousness must also be *self*-consciousness. For utopianism in general, the communist revolution was something to be imposed on society—for its own good, of course—by enlightened leaders. In many ways, the history of socialism is about its failure to understand this break with the Enlightenment. Like the Utopians, the "Marxists" regarded the revolutionary overthrow of the old order as quite unrelated to the characteristics of a communist society.

Marx continually deepened his conception of what humanity was, and showed that it was essentially a process of social self-creation. So when he considered social revolution, he insisted that what was needed was

> the alteration of men [*Menschen* = humans] on a mass scale, an alteration which can only take place in a practical movement, a *revolution*; the revolution is needed, not only because the *ruling* class cannot be overthrown in any other way, but also because the class *overthrowing* it can only in a revolution succeed in ridding itself of all the muck of ages and become fitted to found society anew.[4]

These words, written two or three years after the *Critique*, show how, after that work, Marx's conception of revolution is quite foreign to the idea of a mere transfer of state power. The proletarian revolution is not a more radical rerun of the French Revolution. The problem is not to "take power" into enlightened hands, but to transcend power and to learn to live without it. This is still our problem today.

Through the clarification of his relationship with Hegel, Marx has also got to grips with the entire philosophical tradition. He has settled accounts with Plato's Guardians and with Aristotle's understanding of "association," not by throwing them away, but by drawing out of them their human meaning. At the same time, his critical analysis of the notions of individuality and community enable him to answer the attempts of Hobbes, Rousseau, and Kant to confront the problems of the modern state. Now he has to move further in understanding the nature of property in general and its modern form, capital, on which the modern state was founded.

Early in 1844, strongly influenced by Engels' 1843 article, *Outlines of a Critique of Political Economy*, Marx began his study of the great political economists. This task, never completed, continued for the rest of his life. Hegel had accepted the work of political economy, which tried to explain the unity of society in terms of the exchange of property. He then attempted to transcend the contradictions inherent in such an explanation, with his notion of the state as a spiritual entity. That is why he could not engage in a critique of political economy: its one-sided view of humanity was built into the foundation of Hegel's system. In 1844, Marx could state: "The standpoint of Hegel is that of modern political economy."[5]

Right at the beginning of his work, in some "Comments on James Mill's *Elements of Political Economy*," Marx tells himself what this science signified for him. Examining the elder Mill's conception of money, Marx says:

Mill very well expresses the essence of the matter in the form of a concept by characterising *money* as the *medium* of exchange. The essence of money is not, in the first place, that property is alienated in it, but that the *mediating activity* or movement, the *human*, social act by which man's products mutually complement one another, is estranged from man and becomes the attribute of money, a *material thing* outside man. Since man alienates this mediating activity itself, he is active here only as a man who has lost himself and is dehumanised; the *relation* itself between things, man's operations with them, becomes operation with them, becomes the operation of an entity outside of man and above man.[6]

Relations between individuals, in this case in the shape of money, have come to dominate the individuals related, isolating them from each other. To grasp the inhuman nature of these atomized relations was to reveal the true, human, communal relations which they concealed and distorted.

The *community of men*, or the manifestation of the nature of *men*, their mutual complementing the result of which is species-life, truly human life—this community is conceived by political economy in the form of *exchange* and *trade*.[7]

Exchange or *barter*, is therefore the social act, the species-act, the community, the social intercourse and integration of man within *private ownership*, and therefore the external, *alienated* species-act. . . . For this reason . . . it is the opposite of the social relationship.[8]

Political economy, as well as political philosophy, took the exchange of private property for granted as the typically human activity, as the foundation of all social connection and as necessary for the organization of social labor. Hegel's discussion of civil society takes the same starting point. Marx declares that it is "the opposite of the social relationship," and thus *in*human. He shows how political economy enshrines the *inhuman* character of bourgeois economic and political relations and their mutual separation.

Society, as it appears to the political economist, is *civil society*, in which every individual is a totality of needs, and only exists for the other person, as the other exists for him, insofar as each becomes a means for the other. The political economist reduces everything (just as does politics in its *Rights of Man*) to man, i.e., to the individual whom he strips of all determinateness so as to class him as capitalist or worker.[9]

Political philosophy had striven to resolve the contradiction between private property and community. Hegel, in summing up this work, had tried to show how the modern state, emerging from the French Revolution provided this resolution. But none of these thinkers had come anywhere near an explanation of the origin of private property, apart from some pseudo-psychological "just-so stories," set in a mythical "state of nature."

Through his critiques of Hegel, political economy and socialism, Marx can now find the central importance of labor which was "alienated," that is, whose product became a power over the producer. Political economy had made labor the foundation for its analysis. But it took the estranged form of labor as the natural social form. Marx's new discovery is that alienated or estranged labor is the basis for property. Once he has overthrown Hegel's conception of *needs*, Marx can see the foundation for the entire character of a fragmented society. "The object which labour produces—labour's product—confronts it as *something alien*, as a *power independent* of the producer."[10] Both Hegel and political economy had identified the *objectification* (*Vergegenständlichkeit*) of labor, its embodiment in a product, with its *alienation* or estrangement (*Entfremdung*).

Marx must now face the problem of the relation of private property to "*truly human* and *social property*."[11] Alienation is not to be seen as a matter of "economics." It is "self-alienation," involving the very life of the worker as a human being, and thus the very nature of humanity. In the Paris Manuscripts, Marx combined political economy's crudely material conception of labor with Hegel's spiritualized understanding. Humanity creates itself by socially producing its own life. Today, this is only in opposition to itself.

> For labour, *life activity*, *productive life* itself, appears to man in the first place merely as a means of satisfying a need—the need to maintain physical existence. Yet the productive life is the life of the species. It is life-engendering life. The whole character of a species—its species-character—is contained in the character of its life-activity; and free, conscious activity is man's species-character. Life itself appears only as a *means to life*.[12]

The understanding that labour is alienated reveals the human content of labor, and the possibility of its liberation from its estranged, inhuman form.

> The animal is immediately one with its life activity. . . . Man makes his life activity itself the object of his will and of his consciousness. He has conscious life activity. . . . Only because of this is his activity free activity. . . . An animal forms [things] in accordance with the standard and need of the species to which it belongs, whilst man knows how to produce in accordance with the standard of every species, and know how to apply everywhere the inherent standard to the object. Man therefore also forms [things] in accordance with the laws of beauty.[13]

"Forms (things)" is here the translation of the single word "*formieren*." But Marx employs it in an unusual way. In a deliberate allusion to the *Philosophy of Right*, he uses it as if it were an intransitive verb, just as Hegel had done. Marx's conclusion, however, is quite opposed to that of Hegel, and gets to the heart of bourgeois society. For Hegel, as we saw, *"formieren"* is always bound up with individual possession, while Marx is talking about the true but hidden human meaning of social labor. This is the relation between humanity and nature, a social relation distorted and perverted by the fragmenting effect of private property.

In tearing away from man the object of his production, therefore, estranged labour tears from him his *species-life*, his real objectivity as a member of the species, and transforms his advantage over animals into the disadvantage that his inorganic body, nature, is taken away from him.[14]

But, if we all live within social forms which are estranged from us, and dominate us as alien forces, a very simple question arises: how is it possible for anyone to know this? How can Marx or any of us have knowledge of *non-alienated* life? Neither political economy nor Hegel had this knowledge, and it is not usually available to the ordinary citizen of civil society, so why does Marx think he has discovered it? There seem to be two answers to these questions. On the one hand, Marx criticizes Hegel's remarks about that mass of people without property which grows within modern society. Marx—and not Hegel—is led to see this mass of *laborers*, of alienated producers, growing into a class of inhumanly treated humans, and becoming conscious of that inhumanity. This is the key to universal emancipation.

From the relation of estranged labour to private property it follows further that the emancipation of society from private property, etc., from servitude, is expressed in the political form of the *emancipation of the workers*; not that *their* emancipation alone is at stake, but because the emancipation of the workers contains universal human emancipation—and it contains this, because the whole of human servitude is expressed in the relation of the worker to production, and all relations of servitude are but modifications of this relation.[15]

On the other hand, Marx knows that truly human production can exist. He knows about the work of art, for instance, and scientific work. Like Hegel, he knows about the life of the ancient Greek *polis*, and can contrast it with production for private need, mere "working for a living." So he can begin to ask: What would a truly human relation and a truly human life activity look like? Here is Marx's critical reworking of Hegel's "mutual recognition." If humans lived truly humanly, they would mutually recognize, not each other's rights to own property, excluding everybody else, not their relative positions in a power structure, but their common humanity. And what is that humanity? It is not a property of each individual in isolation from all the others, as the Enlightenment had taught. Each of us is directly an embodiment of the whole of society and its history. The human essence is "the ensemble of social relations," so that what each of us recognizes in the other turns out to comprise the social whole, and includes ourselves.

Let us suppose that we had carried out production as human beings. Each of us would have *in two ways affirmed* himself and the other person. 1) In my *production* I would have objectified my *individuality*, its *specific character*, and therefore enjoyed not only an individual; *manifestation of my life* during the activity, but also when looking at the object I would have the individual pleasure of knowing my personality to be *objective, visible to the senses* and hence a power *beyond all doubt*. 2) In your enjoyment or use of my product I would have the *direct* enjoyment both of being conscious of having satisfied a *human* need by my work, that is, of having objectified man's essential nature, and of having thus created an object corresponding to the need of another man's essential nature. 3) I would have been for you the *mediator* between you and the species, and therefore would become recognised and felt by you yourself as a completion of your essential nature and as a necessary part of yourself, and consequently would know myself to be confirmed both in your thought and your love. 4) In the individual expression of my life, I would have directly created your expression of my life, and therefore in my individual activity I would have directly *confirmed* and *realised* my true nature, my *human* nature, my *communal nature*. Our products would be so many mirrors in which we saw reflected our essential nature. This relationship would moreover be reciprocal; what occurs on my side has also to occur on yours.[16]

Plato and Aristotle, together with all their successors, right down to Hegel, had accepted, and thought they had demonstrated, the necessity of rule by the intellect over material labor. All of them knew that this demonstration raised powerful difficulties, and tried, in different ways, to indicate how they might be overcome. Marx, for the first time, finds the possibility for revolutionary practice in which humanity could liberate itself from them, and finds it *within these difficulties*. Here is the essence of Marx's critique of political economy and of politics, which emerged from his critique of the political philosophy of over two millennia. For the first time, a scientific account of alienated social life is possible, which is at the same time imbued with hatred for oppression and exploitation. Ethics and human science have been united.

Marx never ceased to believe that the state as an institution was an aspect of an inhuman way of living. Already in 1843, in yet another reference to Hegel, Marx knew that "the philistine world is a *political world of animals*," and that "centuries of barbarism engendered and shaped it, and now it confronts us as a consistent system, the principle of which is the *dehumanised world*."[17] The communist revolution, with all its difficulties, was the transcendence of all such "barbarism," which was summed up in the division be-

tween civil society and politics. Despite all their talk about individual freedom, bourgeois thinkers had accepted without question the subordination of
individuals to the economic and political forms in which they lived. Revolution for Marx now centers on the self-change of humans though their revolutionary practice. Such practice breaks through what appear to be necessary,
immutable historical laws, laws imposed on individuals. This is how Marx
himself understood the communist revolution:

> It can only be effected through a union, which by the character of the proletariat
> can only be a universal one, and through a revolution, in which, on the one
> hand, the power of the earlier mode of production and intercourse is over-
> thrown, and, on the other hand, there develops the universal character and the
> energy of the proletariat, which are required to accomplish the appropriation,
> and the proletariat moreover rids itself of everything that still clings to it from
> its previous position in society. Only at this stage does self-activity coincide
> with material life, which corresponds to the development of individuals into
> complete individuals and the casting off of all natural limitations. The trans-
> formation of labour into self-activity corresponds to the transformation of the
> previously limited intercourse into the intercourse of individuals as such. With
> the appropriation of the total productive forces by the united individuals, pri-
> vate property comes to an end.[18]
>
> The first step in the revolution by the working class is to raise the proletariat
> to the position of ruling class, to win the battle of democracy. The proletariat
> will use its political supremacy to wrest, by degrees, all capital from the bour-
> geoisie, to centralise all instruments of production in the hands of the State, i.e.
> of the proletariat organised as the ruling class; and to increase the total of pro-
> duction as rapidly as possible. . . . If the proletariat during its contest with the
> bourgeoisie is compelled, by the force of circumstances, to organise itself as a
> class, if, by means of a revolution, it makes itself the ruling class, and, as such,
> sweeps away by force the old conditions of production, then it will, along with
> these conditions, have swept away the conditions for class antagonisms and of
> classes generally, and will thereby have abolished its own supremacy as a class.
> In place of the old bourgeois society, with its classes and class antagonisms, we
> shall have an association, in which the free development of each is the condition
> for the free development of all.[19]

Marx's communism is in no way separated from his conception of the path
to its achievement. It implies the practical task of removing all those institutions which divided and fragmented community. The communist revolution
itself, while centered on the movement of the proletariat, implies the flowering of the joint activity of the whole of society in governing its own affairs.

Instead of a special caste of Guardians, as in Plato's *Republic*, the entire
community had to find the way to rule itself and to live without property or

state power. Here is Aristotle's *autarkeia*, without slavery or any other form of class division or gender oppression. It requires the search for the Good, not as a contemplative task for a leisured few but as a practical task for all. The Stoic understanding of individual virtue and self-sufficiency, as continued by political economy, is not simply rejected by Marx, but is now shown to be essentially bound up with its opposite, community. Adam's Smith's "Providence" cannot be relied upon to balance "self-interest" and "sympathy," as unavoidable opposites: we ourselves have consciously to accomplish their unification. Hegel's bureaucracy is not the "universal class," but the proletariat, which will find the way to its own abolition, along with all class division and struggle.

A crucially important passage from his 1846 book, *The Poverty of Philosophy* indicates what this implied for the role of science as such:

> Just as the economists are the scientific representatives of the bourgeois class, so the socialists and the communists are the theoreticians of the proletarian class. . . . In the measure that history moves forward, and with it the struggle of the proletariat assumes clearer outlines, they no longer need to seek science in their minds; they have only to take note of what is happening before their eyes and to become its mouthpiece.[20]

The community of property is the only way that true democracy—self-rule without rulers—can exist. Throughout his life, Marx maintained this understanding and fought for it. In the opening chapter of his most important work he foresaw

> an association of free men, working with the means of production held in common, and expending their many different forms of labour-power in full self-awareness a one single social labour force.[21]

Near the end of Volume 3, he is as certain as ever that only such a way of life will be "worthy of and appropriate for their human nature."[22]

Nowadays, it is often loudly argued that "Marxism is irrelevant." Yes, but the ideas of Karl Marx are desperately relevant, not as a finished doctrine, but as a starting point to guide future work, in thought, and in practice comprehended in thought. He never wrote his projected book about the state. But if we draw out the implications of his early attack on this problem, we find it startlingly contemporary, as vast, corrupt and brutal bureaucratic machines oppress billions of us, on behalf of the transnational corporations, or on their own account. It is precisely Marx's conception of freedom which must illuminate the struggles for a truly human society in the new millennium, and show the way to a human future.

NOTES

1. *Marx-Engels Collected Works* (*MECW*), Vol. 5 (Moscow: Progress Publishers), 205.
2. *MECW*, Vol. 3, 296–97.
3. Theses on Feuerbach.
4. *MECW*, Vol. 5, 53.
5. *MECW*, Vol. 3, 333.
6. *MECW*, Vol. 3, 212.
7. *MECW*, 217.
8. *MECW*, 219.
9. *MECW*, 317.
10. *MECW*, 272.
11. *MECW*, 281.
12. *MECW*, 276.
13. *MECW*, 276–77. Compare and contrast this with *PR*, para 190.
14. *MECW*, 277.
15. *MECW*, 280.
16. *MECW*, 227–28.
17. *MECW*, 137.
18. *MECW*, Vol. 6, 88.
19. Communist Manifesto.
20. *The Poverty of Philosophy. MECW*, Vol. 6, 177.
21. *Capital*, Vol. 1, 171.
22. *Capital*, Vol. 3, 949.

Part Three

MARX AND MYSTICISM

Both for the production on a mass scale of this communist consciousness, and for the success of the cause itself, the alteration of men on a mass scale is necessary, an alteration which can only take place in a practical movement, a revolution; this revolution is necessary, therefore, not only because the ruling class cannot be overthrown in any other way, but also because the class overthrowing it can only in a revolution succeed in ridding itself of all the muck of ages and become fitted to found society anew. (Marx, *The German Ideology*)

Chapter Ten

Marx and Human Self-Creation

Long, long ago, when I was young, socialism was very simple. A small minority of greedy rich people exploited the mass of poor people, those who produced the wealth of the world. If we, the vast majority, got ourselves organized, we could easily take the wealth into our hands, along with the means to produce it. Then centralized planning would ensure a rising standard of living and all major problems of social life could be resolved.

Of course, there was the little problem of how the transition would begin. Some of us thought that the majority could elect their representatives and form a socialist government. Others believed that wouldn't work, because of the violent resistance of the rulers: more drastic measures would be required. It seemed self-evident that dedicated socialists like us, if we tried hard enough, could set up a new way of living for all. Other people would soon see how right we had been.

Such notions have gone forever. The twentieth century tried out every possible solution to these problems, and demonstrated that each of them was infeasible. The leaders of the labor movement have several times formed elected governments, which all collapsed in corruption and betrayal. The outcome of the most important attempt, the 1917 revolution, was the most monstrous tyranny. Socialism, however we understood it, was a failure. No wonder that, especially after the collapse of the Russian Revolution, nobody thinks in such terms anymore. Of course, the old words remain, but "socialism" is nowadays little more than another name for bureaucratic state ownership, perhaps flavored with a bit of social welfare.

Meanwhile, the continued existence of capital entails an ever-increasing series of appalling social crises. The money relationship, taking hold of areas of life we could not have imagined, eats away at the brain and heart of society and the state, destroying culture, nature, and humanity. A handful of multibillionaires control huge multinational corporations and thus the world's productive system, while billions of people starve.

All this is well known, but finding a way out appears impossible. When the global "anticapitalist" movements erupted, they generated renewed hope. It was good to see how boldly they broke from decrepit formulae. But, so far at any rate, they have shown unbounded confusion, and sometimes seem to have made a virtue of not going too deeply into what they are aiming at. Many of these young people see the problem as the bad behavior of "uncontrolled" multinational corporations which, they imagine, might be embarrassed into being better behaved. Others, struggling to avoid the alternatives of the domination of inhuman "market forces" and a corrupt centralized bureaucratic state, try to envisage a return to a time before capital, or even before civilization.

Some of my earliest memories are of serious arguments about how we could persuade people to work in a collectively organized manner. Skeptics were always asking: "Who would look after the sewers?" (Sanitation seemed to concern them a great deal.) If there was plenty of everything for everybody, why should anyone work? We had our answer, of course: although, under present conditions, people were understandably selfish and competitive, driven to fight each other for scarce means to live, once we had (very kindly) provided them with a decent way of life, they would soon learn better ways. Our opponents said repeatedly—always as if they were the first to think of it—that socialism seemed a good idea "in theory," but that, human nature being what it is. . . . We answered with the assertion that human nature was not a constant and that we were sure we could fix it.

Such an all-embracing social engineering project needed a basis in a social physics, and the only candidate for this position was called "Marxism." But, at a fundamental level, what we called "Marxism" was *not just different from the ideas of Marx but their direct opposite*. The theoretical framework called "Marxism" purported to be a doctrine, sometimes even a "complete and integral world outlook" (Plekhanov, Lenin). When we "Marxists" claimed to be "scientific," we had in mind an analogy with the certainties of the natural sciences. We saw ourselves as inheritors of the tradition known as the Enlightenment, which in the eighteenth century had fought so bravely against the old ideas of religion and superstition, laying the basis for the modern rational science of nature and for liberty, equality, and fraternity.

The "Marxists" explained that those eighteenth-century thinkers were not quite able to attain a scientific view of history, but that "Marxism" had provided that extension. There was developed a "theory of history" called "historical materialism," an "economic doctrine," sometimes referred to as

"Marxist economics," and a philosophical outlook, called "dialectical materialism." None of this was to be found in the writings of Karl Marx and when, in the 1960s, important texts of Marx were studied for the first time, the most strenuous efforts failed to reconcile them with "Marxism."

Marx works to demonstrate that living humanly, in a manner "worthy of and appropriate to our human nature" (*Capital*, Vol. 3), would mean a free association of human individuals, an association in which "the free development of each individual is the condition for the free development of all" (*Manifesto*). He shows that individuals are "alienated", dominated by the relations between them which they themselves have made. A truly human way of life is incompatible with private property, wage-labour, money and the state, but is actually in accord with nature, and the way that humanity, at whose heart lies free, creative, social activity, emerged from the blind activity of nature.

Marx is not responsible for a "doctrine" of any kind, neither a teaching about what the world ought to be, nor an explanation of the way the world works. He conceives of humanity as socially self-creating, and this clashes with anything which purports to be a "doctrine" or "theory" of any kind. For "doctrine" means separating the "teacher" from the ordinary person being taught, a separation which is itself a symptom of the sick, fragmented way of life of modernity. Today, entities like money, capital, and the state are crazily accepted as subjects; at the same time, we treat each other and ourselves, not as free, self-creating subjects, but as if we were *things*. That is how we necessarily cut ourselves off from understanding ourselves.

While human freedom means that humans—all of us—consciously create their own lives under mutually agreed relations, socialism sought the rearrangement of a given collection of humans by a self-appointed set of rearrangers. Marx is after something quite different: "the alteration of men [*Menschen* = humans] on a mass scale." What might this mean? Clearly, he is not talking about each individual changing him- or herself, one at a time, for he shows that the essence of humanity is "the ensemble of social relations": history is the process in which *we all make each other*. Marx's aim is nothing less than a collective struggle by all of us to remake our world, our social relations and ourselves: self-creation. This is what he means by freedom. The notion that some people, the socialists, will remake the world on behalf of everybody else, has nothing to do with Marx.

What does it mean to make something? It generally implies, among other things, that the object made will exist outside you when it is done, and will be compared with the aim which preceded the job. So what can it mean to make *yourself*, as a consciously planned outcome? Each attempt to fulfill your aim will lead to changes in yourself, both as subject and as object, and thus the aim. Even harder: how could this include the conscious making of the social relations between the makers? But Marx, acknowledging his debt to Hegel, was attempting to express nothing less.

So this idea of self-creation is not a simple one. Perhaps it would be easier if we first thought about creation in general, just the deliberate act of bringing something into being which did not exist before. Aristotle gave this question some attention. Surprisingly, he seems to have been the last philosopher to do so for over two thousand years, and even he could not consider the creation of social relations. Since his time, it has been God's act of creation of the world, rather than human production, that has received most of the attention. So we can't avoid turning to religion to illuminate our question.

Of course, over the millennia, there have been many types of religious accounts of the world, communal attempts to understand how humans relate to nature and to each other, and the story of Creation was usually central to them. *Chambers English Dictionary*, for example, defines religion like this:

> Belief in, recognition of, or an awakened sense of, a higher unseen controlling power, with the emotion and morality connected therewith: rites or worship: any system of such belief or worship: devoted fidelity.

The etymology is also worth recalling: "perh. conn. with *religare*, to bind." The process over the past few centuries in which religion took a reduced role in Europe, was certainly accompanied by the weakening of this binding function.

Over the past few thousand years, intellectual and political activity has largely taken religious forms, and this ought not to be ignored. Perhaps we can distinguish two main versions. In the mainline monotheistic religions, God is the Almighty Father, Creator of Heaven and Earth, and human activities are strictly secondary. God made the world as he willed it to be, and there's nothing you can do about it. But this is not the only way of thinking and might even have been a minority view. Other mystical and religious accounts give quite different answers. For varieties of Buddhism, for example, the question does not arise: the world has always existed, and always will.

But there have also been a wide variety of mystical religious standpoints, most of them heretically clashing with the established outlook. While a divine power was involved in creating a world, they taught, the result remained incomplete. To finish it, human activity had to collaborate with the divine. Such ideas give human beings a starring role, and this makes a big difference to the relation between nature and humanity. Nature is seen as an active unity, in which human purposive activity plays a part. In this category, we shall mention Jewish Cabbalists, Islamic Sufis, and some Christian heretics, entwined with Gnosticism, Neoplatonism, and Hermetism. For such thinkers, divine creation of the world was *self*-creation, God making Himself through Nature and through us.

And that will bring us to Hegel. Describing his own kind of "speculative philosophy" as mysticism, Hegel drew on the work of that long line of mystics. After Aristotle, he seems to have been one of the few philosophers—as opposed to straight theologians—to look at the problem of human and divine creative process, and, through his concept of Spirit, explicitly to bring them together. Only after examining his relation to the heretics will it be possible for us to return to Marx and his critique of Hegel. Then we shall see that, grasping humanity as self-creating, Marx is opposed to every attempt to consider humanity and its destiny from inside a closed or complete intellectual system. He never forgets that he is a human being talking about human beings. That is why "Marxism," which found this quite distasteful, was so hostile to the real ideas of Marx.

But we have missed something out of this story. Starting in the seventeenth century, and especially in eighteenth, all such questions, intensely important to previous centuries, seemed to fade away. Armed with the advances of science and technology, many thinkers opposed the oppressive political and intellectual authority of the Church. But this led them simply to dismiss as "superstition" the ideas of thousands of years, with the aid of which people have struggled with some of the central questions of existence. What was left made little or no attempt to ask how individuals related to each other, to the community as a whole or to the natural world in which they lived and died. For the new rational-scientific outlook, making something new meant rearranging bits of the existing world.

So freedom could mean no more than the removal of some obstacles to the will of the isolated individual. Society could be nothing but a discrete collection of such individuals, and the individuals could not be seen as more than grains of subjectivity whirling around inside a mindless, indifferent, deterministic nature machine.

I want to show that Hegel, followed by Feuerbach and Marx, had to reconnect with those older, "heretical" traditions to do their work, rediscovering them and giving them a modern form. This entailed breaking through the barrier of the Enlightenment and its successors, like, for instance, nineteenth-century positivists. Only then can freedom and self-creation be brought to light in the conditions of modern life. Of course, we don't reject the powerful contribution made by rationalism and empiricism, or their great struggles for individual freedom. Without their conquests and their limitations, we couldn't begin to move forward. But we have to go beyond them. Only then can Marx find out how we must struggle to make them a reality.

(The critique of the Enlightenment made by Hegel and Marx has little to do with that made by the postmodern fashion. As we shall see, Marx's critical standpoint is that of "human society or social humanity," and Hegel's is what he calls *Geist*. Since I do not speak the language in which the postmodernists communicate their thoughts to the world, I am not able to say what their standpoint actually is.)

My first task, then, is to look at a long line of thinkers, mainly religious mystics, whose work feeds into that of Hegel. (I have left out lots of others, about whom he says nothing, while including one or two who, while they are not actually mentioned by him, directly connect with those who are.)

"HUMAN PRODUCTION AND DIVINE CREATION"

1. Aristotle

Although Aristotle's *Metaphysics* was one of the most influential of philosophical documents over the past two millennia, his attempt to discuss the nature of human productive activity (*poesis*) had no successor for most of that time. In Book *Zeta* (*Met*. VII, 7 and 8), the Philosopher explains three kinds of "things that come to be or are generated, some by nature, others, by art; still others, 'automatically.'"

> It is by art that those products come whose form dwells in the mind, where by "form" I mean what it is to be that product, its first or primary being. . . . [I]t would be impossible for anything to be if nothing were present previously. . . thus, the material part is essential, since it is in process, and it is this material that comes to be something.

So we have three elements in production: agency, form, and material. Aristotle has nothing to say about where the first and third of these come from, and on the second, form, he says:

> [T]he form, or whatever we want to call the shape in the perceived object, is not produced; nor is there ever any production of it; no intrinsic nature is ever made.

The production of, say, a bronze sphere, consists of a workman, who has the spherical form in his head, putting some bronze into the shape of the sphere. Aristotle follows this with a careful discussion of many other aspects of form, for example, how wholes and parts are related. When production is completed, something new has come into being. For Aristotle, form was the active generator, the father, while matter was the feminine, the passive and so—quite obviously to him—inferior.

In his *Poetics*, he discusses the production of poetry, the only kind of making that later philosophers thought elevated enough to merit philosophical interest. By defining it as "imitation of action," he is able to include it within his general idea of *poesis*. Aristotle can never ask how sociopolitical relations are "generated," because for him they have no history. Nor does he need to ask how the world as a whole is generated: his world is eternal. His "Unmoved Mover," the original cause of all motion, is indeed "divine," but "the divine" and its life are "the activity of mind . . . life unending, continuous and eternal."

> And thought in itself deals with that which is best in itself, and that which is thought in the fullest sense with that which is best in the fullest sense. And thought thinks itself, because it shares the nature of the object of thought; for it becomes an object of thought in coming into contact with and thinking its objects, so that thought and object of thought are the same. For that which is capable of receiving the objects of thought, i.e. the substance, is thought. And it is active when it possesses this object. Therefore the latter rather than the former is the divine element which thought seems to contain, and the act of contemplation is what is most pleasant and best. If, then, God is always in that good state in which we sometimes are, this compels our wonder; and if in a better, this compels it still more. And God is in a better state. And life also belongs to God; for the actuality of thought is life, and God is that actuality; and God's essential actuality is life most good and eternal. We say, therefore, God is a living being, eternal, most good, so that life and duration continuous and eternal belong to God; for this is God. (Aristotle, *Met*, xii. 7)

This passage was given by Hegel, as his summing-up of the whole of philosophy (End of *Encyclopedia: The Philosophy of Mind*).

2. Divine Creation

Many centuries later, when Aquinas roped Aristotle into the service of the Catholic Church, he had a hard job reconciling the pagan philosopher with the Christian story of Divine Creation. How could you reconcile God creating the world from nothing (*ex nihilo*), the official Catholic view since Athanasius, with the principle that "nothing comes from nothing" (*ex nihilo nihil fit*), or even with Greek belief in the eternity of the world?

Humans have been trying to understand the world and their own place in it for a long time. They have generally expressed their efforts in terms of some kind of religious or mythical account. This has helped to shape the way people lived because it was a way of explaining the unity of the world, including the natural and the social world, as well as the relation between the two.

How people thought about their lives, their origins, and their destiny could not be separated from a story of the way the world got started. (Jews and Romans, for example, have a conception of history beginning after this starting point, while Greeks didn't think much about the question of creation at all.) In modern, more "enlightened" times, the attempt is made to explain the world without such stories, which are dismissed as mere superstition. It is hoped that a phrase like "Big Bang" will make the thing go away. The problem that keeps recurring is that God is the eternal, infinite, and unchanging Creator, but his creation is finite, changeable, and imperfect. Does creation occur *in* time, or does time itself only begin when everything else begins? Modern "Big Bang" stories, are, of course, much more sophisticated, but still stumble on the same difficulty. But that leaves the big question unanswered: In what kind of world is it possible for conscious humanity to exist? All the discussion of how the world started is really about this issue, I believe.

In some accounts of Creation, God has to work a bit like a human producer. Creation takes time and effort. Each of the six days' output has to be checked to see if it was good. (Luckily, it was.) In the orthodox versions of the three big monotheistic religions, Almighty God, who is bound up with the almighty powers on Earth, produces the whole show and writes the script. If you complain about how dreadful it is for most people to live in, you are fobbed off with a story about free will; this is God's alibi, a Divine trick to put all the blame on us mortals. But the problem refused to disappear. What are we to make of the existence of evil doing, pain, disease, famine, violence, greed? Are these part of God's willful design? But if so, what chance do we have of making the world a decent place to live? The Catholic Church in particular fought for centuries against dualist answers to this conundrum, those conceptions that saw the world as a product of both Good and Evil, "matter" being the evil part.

3. Plato and After

After the Greek language had been forgotten in Western Europe, the dialogue *Timaeus*, one of Plato's later works, was the only part of his output to be remembered. It is also the only place where Plato considers questions of cosmology and cosmogony. Like other Greek texts, it was known only to Arab scholars, and then in Latin translation. Earlier, it had formed the basis for the Neoplatonism of Plotinus (205–270). By the way, that had nothing to do with Zeus and the other Greek Gods. Unlike the orthodox Judeo-Christian tradition, the Greeks believed in Gods who were themselves created, following on from Titans and other older entities.

Significantly, Socrates begins the *Timaeus* by outlining his ideal society. His friend Timaeus then proceeds to explain that the cosmos must have had a beginning and a constructor, because it is perceptible by the senses, and so changeable. Its maker was the Demiurge, the divine workman, who, says Timaeus, was good and so "had his eye" on an ideal and unchanging blueprint, which was a living being.

> God therefore, wishing that all things should be good, and so far as possible nothing be imperfect, and finding the visible universe in a state not of rest but of inharmonious and disorderly motion, reduced it to order from disorder, as he judged that order was in every way better.

That is how he came to make the world a living being with "reason in soul and soul in body." Timaeus goes on to describe the construction of the physical world and the human soul. For example, because it was perfect, it had to be spherical and "a single complete whole."

Accounts like this are much, much older than Plato, of course. About 2,000 years earlier, the Egyptians had the story of how the ordered cosmos emerged from chaos which had always been there. Sometimes, this was the work of the Sun god Ra, ably assisted by his secretary, the Moon god Thoth. A sort of cosmic project-manager, Thoth was not just important for setting the show up, but also for keeping it going. (We shall meet him again, but under the Greek name Hermes and the Latin Mercury.) Even before this, the Mesopotamians had a similar creation myth, in which the Demiurge has the benefit of many assistant gods and the opposition of a mass of disorderly demons. In all of these accounts, cosmic order involves the struggle of opposites and is bound up with political order.

When Plotinus built up his highly complex world picture on the basis of the *Timaeus*, the ultimate reality was the One, an unknowable, unchangeble Being which was also the Good. Matter, which was Evil, was not real. Emanating from the One, as light emanates from the Sun, were the Intelligences (*nous*), and from them the Soul. Individual souls were eternal, migrating from body to body (*metempsychosis*).

> But how is Evil recognised? It is owing to the thought turning away from itself that matter arises; it exists only through the abstraction of what it is other than itself. What remains behind when we take away the Ideas is, we say, matter; thought accordingly becomes different, the opposite of thought, since it dares to direct itself on that which not within its province.

For Proclus (412–85), who systematized Neoplatonism, these individual souls were drawn to return to the One. By philosophically contemplating the One, they could get back to Square One, completing the loop.

4. Gnosticism

Now we must turn to several varieties of mysticism, which we shall need to talk about Hegel, and thus Marx. Thomas Aquinas defined mysticism as "the knowledge of God through experience." Many mystics seek, not just knowledge, but "mystical union with God," Each variety of mysticism is characterized by the particular set of religious views and particular conception of God inside which it develops.

Gnosticism was a term used by the heresy hunters in the early Church to refer to a cluster of unorthodox notions, which had to be tidied away if a unified state outlook were to function efficiently. Similar ideas were also to be found among the Jewish and Christian-Jewish sects that abounded in the first and second centuries and connections can also be made both with Neoplatonism and with Eastern religions. These trends also believed that the material world was made by a Demiurge, but they identified him with the angry God of the Old Testament. Evil was his work. The true God was far above him and was unknowable. Christ was the messenger of the true God, who only appeared to take human form, so that the Crucifixion was merely apparent. The world and its history were driven by a war between Good and Evil, with angels and demons carrying out the work of the Demiurge. Only through the internal spiritual work of the individual believer, the "pneumatic," was the Kingdom of God created. Thus God needed those people to complete his work.

The founders of the Church tried very hard, and with true Christian brutality, to eliminate these ideas, but could never quite succeed. Until fairly recently, our knowledge of these groups was only via the writings of their enemies the heresy hunters. Only after the discovery of a cache of Coptic translations in 1945 in Nag Hammadi in Upper Egypt was it possible for us to read actual Gnostic writings. Medieval heretics often held Gnostic conceptions, as we know from their recorded statements to the Inquisition before they were burnt. Bogomils, Cathars (Albigensians), and Waldensians, rebelling against the orthodoxy of the Church, all espoused dualist, Gnostic ideas. Traces of these were still current in the peasant movements of the Reformation.

5. Cabbala

A Hebrew word meaning "the tradition," Cabbala covers a long history of Jewish mystical teachings. These texts were believed to be very ancient, conveying the wisdom imparted by God to Adam, and then to Moses. In fact, they seem to have originated about two millennia ago, beginning as a mixture of Jewish Gnosticism and Neoplatonism. However, Cabbalists were always confronted with the impossible task of reconciling their ideas with the strictly monotheistic Rabbinical conceptions of God.

Two events in the history of European Jewry prompted the flourishing of Cabbala mysticism as we know it now. First, at the start of the second millennium, centuries of murderous Christian barbarism known as the Crusades erupted. Second, at the end of the fifteenth century, the defeat of the Muslim civilization led to the expulsion of the Jews from Spain. Each of these catastrophes brought the problem of evil into sharp relief: if God is both good and omnipotent, and if the Jews were indeed his chosen ones, how could He let such things happen to them?

From twelfth-century Provence, where the influence of Catharism might have added its contribution, Cabbalism moved into Spain. The thirteenth-century "*Sefer ha-Zohar*" ("Book of Splendor") comes from the town of Gerona in Catalonia. At the time of the expulsion, the Center moved from there to Safed in Upper Galilee. Here worked, among others, Moses Cordevero (1522–70) and his student Isaac Luria (1534–72), "the Ari." It is their later Cabbala with which we shall be mainly concerned.

The Rabbis had prohibited inquiry into what happened before Creation: you were not allowed to ask God for His CV. And this was precisely the enquiry in which the Cabbalists were engaged, as they sought to understand the origin of Evil. Each aspect of the mystical account of Creation, and what went on before it, was the subject of fierce controversy, but a rough outline involves the following. Corresponding to the Neoplatonist "One," we have the *Ein-Sof*, the Infinite, absolute, and undifferentiated perfection, which is completely unknowable. Even the mystic who engages in deep meditation can only glimpse it through its manifestation in material Creation. *Ein-Sof* emanates the whole of existence through a complex system often elements called the *Sefiroth*. All things come from the One, which breaks into the many. Thereafter, all things yearn for reunification. But this is a cyclic process, for God also yearns to create, and so Cosmogony—the origin of the universe— is at the same time Theogony—the origin of God. The Divine both conceals and reveals itself in a continual process of self-creation.

In the very beginning, the *Sefiroth* are in a state of perfect equilibrium. In the account developed by Luria and his followers, Creation is a violent crisis that disrupts this delicate balance. Only in this catastrophe does the Divine reveal itself. For example, before the crisis, Power (*Gevurah*) or Judgment (*Din*), is balanced with Beauty (*Tiferet*) and loving-kindness (*Tifereth*).

But after the catastrophe of Creation, the imbalance of this system turns each fragment into a source of evil. Since Creation, the world has been alienated from its source, *Ein Sof*. In the theory of Luria, Contraction (*Zimzum*) was the convulsive movement in which the Divine pulls itself into itself and away from the world. In its following expansion, the Divine light fills the *Sefiroth* as "vessels," and smashes them, causing sparks of divinity to scatter into the material world. How is this to be put right? Humans must carefully gather up these "sparks" and reassemble the original perfection. This mending (*Tikkun*) is the responsibility of the Jews, whose righteousness is essential if the world is to be redeemed.

(I must reveal my own feelings here: I am immensely impressed with the struggle of Cabbalists to express very difficult notions of universal importance. At the same time, I am repelled by the narrow ethnocentricity of their work.)

6. Magic and Mysticism

I have so far omitted an important aspect of Cabbalism which it would be wrong to ignore. "Practical Cabbala" or magic, not only plays a vital part in its influence, but also links it to many other mystical trends. Every culture and religious scheme has known the idea that wise men and women could find out how to predict the movements of natural forces and influence them in favor of human interests. (For all our "enlightened" ideas, new forms of this notion are with us still!) The Cabbalist outlook is naturally favorable to the notion that, by means of prayer, incantation, interpretation of dreams, contemplation of mystical symbols and so on, those who know the workings of reality can control it in some way. The world, being divine and, moreover, still under construction, contains angelic and demonic forces which might be commanded by people with special knowledge. In particular, since God created the world out of the twenty-two letters of the Hebrew alphabet, manipulating these letters and their numerical equivalents in the text of the Torah, especially the names of God, would give inside information of the divinity. If you did it right, it might grant the practitioner magical power.

When Christian scholars found the way to read the Hebrew texts of Cabbala, it was often this aspect which attracted and excited them. Even before the expulsion of the Jews from Spain in 1492 brought these texts to the attention of Latin and other translators, Giovanni Pico della Mirandola (1463–94) had read some of the *Zohar* and connected it with his humanist and Neoplatonist ideas, and especially with his work on magic. This great Renaissance thinker wanted to integrate the whole of religion and philosophy, linking Islamic, Jewish, and Christian sources. This got him into trouble, both with the Church and with the Cabbalists. (The former got him to spend some time in the dungeons of the Paris Inquisition.)

His famous defense, the *Oration on the Dignity of Man*, begins like this:

Most esteemed Fathers, I have read in the ancient writings of the Arabians that Abdala the Saracen on being asked what, on this stage, so to say, of the world, seemed to him most evocative of wonder, replied that there was nothing to be seen more marvellous than man.

And that celebrated exclamation of Hermes Trismegistus, "What a great miracle is man, Asclepius," confirms this opinion. This Hermes Trismegistus ("Thrice Great"), quoted thus as an acknowledged authority, plays an important part in Renaissance attempts to bring Jewish, Christian, and Islamic ideas together. Toward the end of the fifteenth century, translation of Greek authors, preserved until then only by Islamic scholars, opened up new ways of thought. The writings attributed to Hermes were widely studied as a body of work whose roots are extremely ancient. The manuscripts are now known in fact to be Gnostic texts of the second century, many from Roman Egypt. Together with Cabbala, they had for centuries formed the basis for alchemy, astrology, and natural magic, and did in fact continue a tradition of even greater antiquity. (Moses was sometimes believed to have been an early worker in this field, having learned his craft from the Egyptian Hermes, identified with the Egyptian god Thoth, with the assistance of Jehovah.)

Lorenzo di Medici set Pico's colleague Marsilio Ficino (1433–99) to work translating these writings, as well as the *Zohar*, even instructing him to give this job priority over the translation of Plato. For the next three centuries or more, this tradition was the background to the thinking of the leading figures in European thought in the run-up to modernity. It was this intellectual world that actually saw the birth of modern science.

As a scientific picture of the world, many of the results obtained by the alchemists and magicians look somewhat bizarre today. But the undoubted triumphs of modern scientific rationalism can blind us to what is important in the world outlook of the Hermeticists. First of all, they saw that the contrasts and oppositions between the divine and the human, like those between spirit and nature, were not unbridgeable. The cosmos was a whole, its parts held together by a series of internal relations, correspondences, and "sympathies." The most important of these is the connection between humanity and nature, in which the human individual is a microcosm whose physical and mental structure corresponds to that of the macrocosm, so that each individual included the whole world within itself. "As above, so below," as the opening words of the *Corpus Hermeticum* put it. This was an active connection. When God created the world, he had not completed the job, and to rectify the remaining imperfections required human subjective activity. Indeed, the question: "Why did God create the world?" could only be answered in terms of His need for humanity to do this work.

Alchemy is often presented as the attempt to get rich quick by making gold out of lead. But the Renaissance practitioners were scornful of such tricks, calling those who pulled them "puffers." The work of serious alchemists was concerned with the transformation of matter through the application of ancient knowledge of creative activity. Through his own personality and imagination, the Magus called down cosmic forces, which his knowledge enabled him to direct. Thus the Magus himself participated in person in the Great Work of Creation, and so identified himself with the world, even with God. (You had to be careful: in the wrong hands, this knowledge could bring demons instead of angels into the picture: big trouble. So to become "adept" required a long apprenticeship, in which false ideas were purged. This is what Goethe's poem, the "Sorcerer's Apprentice," is about.) So whatever the oddities of the results of particular experiments, they were founded on a pattern of united activity in which mind, hand, and matter all participated.

7. Some Christian Heretics

All of these people have in common a conception of Creation as self-creation. For them, God, in bringing the world into being, including humanity as a special part, also brings Himself into being, and conscious human productive activity has the starring role. Moreover, God puts Himself into his work, so that Nature and humanity are aspects of the divine. That is why these people were certain that knowledge of nature and humanity were possible only to those who achieve mystical union with God. All these people think of human history as being a product of two interlinked processes: on the one hand there is God, a spiritual being who creates the world as he thinks fit; on the other, humankind, divided into finite individuals. This might continue, until there is sufficient wisdom in existence to make all divine. Thus, we shall look at a series of thinkers, drawn from the late Middle Ages and Renaissance, who have in common that they were all a kind of Christian condemned by the Church.

We meet with John the Scot, Eriugena (born in Ireland), only after he was adopted by Charles the Bald, grandson of Charlemagne. (Most of the biographical "facts" reported about him apart from that are invented!) Eriugena worked as a teacher of Greek, as did some other of his fellow Irishmen. That was at a time when the split between the Greek and Roman wings of the Church had not yet been clarified, but which was beginning to be seen. Eriugena read the Greek Fathers of the Church like the pseudo-Dionysus, Gregory of Nyssa, Maximus the Confessor, and others. (Gregory is known to have commented that "all the arts and sciences have their roots in the struggle against death.")

The masterpiece of Eriugena, *Periphyseion: On the Division of Nature*, was written in Latin and was condemned and burned in the Vatican for pantheism three hundred years after the author's death. On being translated in the seventeenth century it was instantly put on the Index of banned books. But for a thousand years, it was circulated in a semi-clandestine manner.

It is a dialogue of a Teacher and a Student, the former quite clearly Eriugena, the latter being an orthodox, although a thoughtful, theologian. The Teacher is perfectly aware that his ideas will be controversial, although he tries to make them seem in line with orthodox opinions by pretending to quote Scripture and people like Augustine, often misquoting them. He talks about this method of scriptural exegisis as "allegorical." He is one of the first to speak of God as someone who is the Creator along with his collaborator, man.

On the first few pages of the *Periphyseion* he propounds two main ideas.

1. He introduces the notion that his subject called "*natura*"—nature—is the total of objects in the world, both those which are known and those which are unknown, and he does not regard the former as fixed.
2. He regards these objects as divided into four groups: (i) those which are uncreated but which create; (ii) those which are created and which create; (iii) those which are created which do not create; and (iv) those which neither are created nor create.

The Student thinks he is prepared to accept all of these propositions except the last. He does not see all of subtle and startling conclusions to be derived from them.

As a devotee of Neoplatonism, Eriugena is able to derive from his way of dividing up the world a vision of God and His creation. (He bases himself initially on the pseudo-Dionysius, Maximus the Confessor, and other Greek Fathers of the Church.) First of all, he is clear that what are known in the world—things like rocks and trees—are far outweighed by the infinite number of things which are unknown. And the boundary between them is certainly not fixed, but is continually moving.

The four divisions form a circle. The uncreated creator is in the first place God. Then comes the whole of creation, minus one thing: us. That is the third, the driving force of nature. But the fourth and crowning achievement is the return to God, and man's reconciliation with God.

The question is the relation between creation and knowledge, and that means the relation between nature which is unknown and the transformation from the unknown and the known. In Eriugena, of course, God is all in all, the Creator of everything, but not all at once. In the meantime, in the third division, there is the process through which man gets to know the world. God only becomes Himself when man knows him. Then, at the end of time, man becomes God.

Everything finite is contained within his infinite nature and returns to it. Nature is an active process, "*natura naturata*." Man began this process when he was in Paradise. At the start of time, man sinned and fell. Now, he works his way back, making God in the process. If I have got this right, the condemnation by the Church is not surprising; if anything, it was long overdue.

Joachim of Fiore was born in Calabria, the very toe of Italy, in about 1135. Leaving the service of the Norman bureaucracy, he traveled to Palestine and then became a monk. After a time as a Cistercian, he left them and became abbot of his own order in Saint John of Fiore. Here he died in 1202. He was noted as a prophet in his lifetime, being consulted on such matters by Richard I of England, Philip Augustus of France, and the Emperor Henry VI.

But it was not these worthies whose respect is our chief concern. Joachim's fame as a prophet rests largely on the devotion which they inspired in the hearts of humbler folk. For centuries after his death, rebels against the feudal order were describing themselves as "Joachimites." Indeed, we only know of them largely because the Inquisition recorded the trial statements of these millenarians before it condemned them to the flames. Some of their ideas are still echoed in the radical writings which abounded in seventeenth-century England.

Some doubt whether this reputation was deserved, but this was how Joachim was remembered. His account of the unity of truth and ignorance and his conception of Divine Knowledge anticipates Hegel in many ways. Joachim believes that God is *knowing* and self-revelatory. He identifies the structure of the Trinity with three stages of divine history. The third of these stages, identified with the Holy Spirit, was about to begin at any time now, when the ending of the corruption of the Church would usher in a thousand-year Utopia, a communal life of poverty and humility. This was to happen *in* time, *not at the end* of it, and it was for everybody, not, as with the Augustinian doctrine, a prize in the spiritual lottery called "God's grace."

But Joachim's reputation rested not on his works alone, but on what he was *supposed* to have said. In 1254, a certain Gerard of Borgo San Donnino, a Franciscan, published a summary of Joachim's works. This not only went beyond anything which he wrote, but went as far as to say that the third age was to possess a third gospel, the "Eternal Evangel," which would make the Old and New Testaments redundant. Gerard was imprisoned and ended his days there. There was a great scandal, which involved the resignation of the Minister-General of the Franciscan Order, John of Parma. By the end of the thirteenth century, the Spirituals, the most radical of the Franciscans, were suspected of Joachite sympathies.

Thomas Muentzer, the Taborites, and the Anabaptists were only three examples of those who referred to Joachim in their revolutionary statements.

And even after the Reformation, there were Puritan sects during the English Revolution who still looked forward to the Third Age of Joachim.

Meister Eckhart (1260–1327), a German monk, was the first to develop the terminology of philosophy in German, translating and adapting Latin terms. All his life he was a Dominican, one of the Friars Preacher, and it was in this capacity that he became famous as an academic theologian, both in Germany and in Paris. It was in this connection that he lectured to Beguines. These were nuns, who were suspected of including amongst their ranks some heretics of the Free Spirit. When he was first investigated in 1325—the only Dominican ever to suffer this indignity—it was suggested that he was soft on this tendency. Eckhart defended himself with great energy, but without success. He died while the case was going through its appeal, but even that did not suffice to get it off his back, the Pope insisting that it reach finality.

The heresy of the Free Spirit were some of many within the Church who argued that, since Christ died for our sins, all bets were off now that the Crucifixion was accomplished. Eckhart did not agree with this antinomianism, but this issue was so sensitive that even the suggestion that he was not 100 percent on it was suspect.

Like Eruigena and Joachim—he was acquainted with *Periphyseon* despite the ban—he was devoted to the Greek fathers, and this colored all his ideas. For him, God becomes conscious of himself only within his creation, which took place through the "creative ideas" in his Son. Christ is continually reborn within each believing soul. Each soul derives its essence from God and so is not merely finite. It contains within it a "tiny spark" (*"Funklein"*), which enables the individual soul to play its part in the existence of God. Eckhart also argues that Divine Knowledge is "the negation of negation."

> The One is a negation of negations. Every creature contains a negation: one denies that it is the other. An angel denies that it is any other creature; but God contains the denial of denials. He is the One who denies of every other that it is anything except himself.

The chief characteristic of Eckhart's God is his oneness. Of course, the nature of creation involves that of multiplicity. But at the same time all things are united in God. The detachment (*Gelassenheit*) of the liberated man is only the other side of his unity with God.

The combination of Christianity with Neoplatonism in Eckhart is like German idealism, both Hegelian and Schellingian. Imagine Hegel's delight when he found in Eckhart's sermons:

The eye with which God sees me is the eye with which I see Him; my eye and His eye are the same. . . . If He did not exist, nor would I; if I did not exist, nor would He.

It turns out that this startling statement, which Hegel picked up half a millennium later, was actually a Sufi saying, a *Hadith*.

Nicolas of Cusa (1401–64) (*Cusanus*) was born in Kues, near Trier. He was a leading Church lawyer, at a time when the papacy was in difficulties. A grateful Pope was happy to make him a cardinal. But his importance for our account is his philosophical work. He was a Neoplatonist and follower of Eriugena and Meister Eckhart, and as such he was attacked as a pantheist, seeing God as united with his creation. He was also influenced by Raymond Lull's mystical mathematics, and he quotes Hermes Trismegistus extensively.

Nicolas seems to have been the first to use the word "absolute" to refer to God as unconditioned by anything else. His famous book, *Of Learned Ignorance*, works out some implications of God as absolute subjectivity. Everything in the world is God, and God *is* everything. Each individual thing reflects everything else, and is reflected in it. "Everything is in everything." The universe, including the human being, must be divine, and therefore infinite, says Nicolas, with its circumference nowhere and its center everywhere. This "coincidence of opposites"—(*concidentia oppositorum*)— preceded Copernicus (1473–1543) by a century, who prudently published his rather scaled-down version of Nicolas's idea only on his deathbed.

Henry Cornelius Agrippa von Nettesheim (1486–1535) was a German nobleman who was educated in Italy. He aimed to unify the knowledge of his time as a combination of Christian Cabbala, Neoplatonism, and Hermeticism. He held up publication of his main work, *The Occult Philosophy*, for over twenty years, rightly fearing the attacks which it would attract from the Church. His version of Aristotelian physics includes the influence of "occult virtues" from the World Soul, which, if we were clever enough, would enable us to move objects as we desired. Cabbala would make it possible to gain power over demons and angels by means of operations on letters and numbers. He always insisted, however, that this White Magic was in cooperation with God and His Angels, and had nothing at all to do with demonic Black Magic.

Theophrastus Bombastus von Hohenheim (1493–1541), known as Paracelsus, is often referred to as the founder of modern medicine and chemistry, and he did indeed aggressively pioneer the rejection of the old Aristotelian and Galenic ideas which still held those fields in an iron grip. Typically, he dramatized his criticism by throwing the works of Galen onto a bonfire in the course of a public open-air lecture. He opened up the use of herbal and chemical substances in the cure of many illnesses, drawing on the wisdom of peasant men and women. He was also the first to study an occupational disease, in his work on the ailments of miners. Erasmus of Rotterdam wrote him a letter, thanking him for his successful medical advice.

But he was also an alchemist and Hermeticist, keenly interested in magic. In his medical work, Paracelsus took very seriously the Hermetic formula "as above, so below": the human had the same structure as the cosmos.

> What else could fortune [*Glück*] be than living in conformity to nature's wisdom? If nature goes well, that is fortune; if it does not, that is misfortune. For our essence is ordained in nature.

He saw the work of the physician as a practical activity which drew from his own imagination to tune in to the physical problems of the patient. Intuition, not logical reasoning was the heart of medical science. For Paracelsus, astrology was mistaken only in that it concentrated on the influence of the stars on the human individual, and ignored the reverse influence of the magus and his imagination on the stars. Imagination for Paracelsus is not a passive depiction of the world, but an active power to change it. Pathological symptoms exhibit the "signatures" of an out-of-balance in nature and the magus has to correct this by his art.

An opponent of both the Church hierarchy and of Luther, whose oppression of the peasants offended him deeply, he was a firm Neoplatonist and student of Cabbala. So his world is an emanation of the One, produced by the "separation" of the elements from "Prime Matter," and this individuation is a "fall" of nature and of man. The purpose of human activity is to perfect an imperfect world, and this is the role of alchemy and magic.

From the stars to the human individual and from angels and demons to the mind, the world is a unity which has become divided. Everywhere, Paracelsus shows us a loop from the One to the multiplicity and back, with human conscious and imaginative activity bringing about the return journey.

> No-one sees what is hidden in him [the human being], but only what his works reveal. Therefore man should work continually to discover what God has given him.

Giordano Bruno (1548–1600) was an advocate of the ideas of Copernicus, but went much further. Bruno was certainly not influenced by Copernicus' caution: he openly flaunted the most heretical implications of Nicolas's ideas and took them as far as they would go.

Born at Nola, near Naples, Bruno had joined the Dominican Order, but soon quarreled with it, and spent the rest of his life as a wandering scholar, annoying the established authorities wherever he went. Eventually, he was arrested by the Inquisition and burned after several years of torture. (The

Holy Fathers of the Inquisition were determined to complete this job: they took Bruno's burned bones out of the fire and smashed them up with hammers.) If you go to the Piazza Campo dei Fiori in Rome, the place where he was burned, you will see his statue, erected in the 1860s to celebrate his importance as a martyr for modern science. In fact, this idea of him was quite misleading.

Strongly against the Aristotelian stranglehold on cosmological ideas, his development of the Copernican cosmology led him to some very modern ideas about the universe. Doing away with Copernicus' belief in a center of the universe, he propounded his conception of an infinite world. He influenced people like Kepler—a fellow Neoplatonist—and perhaps Galileo too. He was ahead of them in his rejection of the necessity of planetary orbits to be circles, for example, and anticipated many of Galileo's arguments for the movement of the Earth.

But his outlook combined Hermeticism and Neoplatonism with ideas derived from the *Zohar*. Although he seems not to have known Hebrew, he studied several of the Cabbalist texts, which were by his time causing great excitement among Renaissance scholars. Perhaps we should not include him under the heading of *Christian* Cabbalism, because it is not at all clear that he was a Christian. His overt religious views actually hide the fact that he is much more an adherent of what he thought was the ancient Egyptian religion. He thinks he has found this in the Hermetic manuscripts, and from this source he knows that the Earth is alive and moves itself round the Sun. In general, matter is permeated with life and form, which are processes of continual self-transformation.

> The universal intellect is the most intimate, the most real and the most proper faculty and partial power of the world soul (*anima mundi*). This is one and the same thing which fills whole, illumines the universe and directs nature to produce its various species as is fitting, and has the same relation to the production of natural things as our intellect to the parallel production of rational concepts. . . . I call it intrinsic cause because as efficient it does not form a part of the things composed and the things produced. I call it intrinsic cause in so far as it does not operate around and outside of matter. (*De la causa*, 1584)

The Brunonian cosmology is very modern, in that the infinity of the universe was ahead of scientific cosmology until Hubble's discovery of the galaxies in 1928. But his physics is not at all modern: he derives the movement of the particles from the pressure of the *anima mundi*. The unity of this movement is that "everything is in everything."

Above all, his studies ceaselessly strive to probe the deepest relationships between humanity and the movements of the material world.

> To recognise the unity of form and matter in all things, is what reason is striving to attain to. But in order to penetrate to this unity, in order to investigate all the secrets of Nature, we must search into the opposed and contradictory extremes of things, the maximum and the minimum.

All souls are unified in the transmigration of souls (*metempsychosis*), which he finds in "*cabalah-telogica-filosofia.*" Not only "everything is in everything," but "everybody is in everybody." This is hidden at present, but it will become manifest to the Cabbalists of the new religion.

Jakob Boehme (1585–1624) was a shoemaker of Görlitz, a town of Lusatia, between Silesia and Bohemia. He had only an elementary education, but in 1600 he began to write a huge mystical manuscript, which he only finished twelve years later. Despite orthodox disapproval, he went on writing for the rest of his life. Amid the troubles of Europe at the beginning of the Thirty Years War, he struggled to reconcile the ordered cosmos with freedom.

He brought into this work that combination of Neoplatonism, Gnosticism, Cabbala, and Hermeticism we have found in earlier writers. He used the language of alchemy to express his human-centered conceptions of the world, which, as with those of Paracelsus, linked God, Nature, and individual psychology. He is Keplerian, in that he defiantly places the sun directly at the center of the solar system, contrary to Lutheran agreement. "Thus, I intend to write correctly, according to my intuition, and to heed the authority of no one," writes the cobbler.

Creation is not *ex nihilo*, from nothing, but *ex Deo*, from God. That is how God reveals Himself.

> The book in which all secrets lie hidden is man himself; he himself is the Book of the Essence of all Essences. . . . He is like unto God. . . . Why do you seek God in the depths or beyond the stars?. . . Seek him in your heart, in the centre of your life's origin. There shall you find Him.

Boehme struggles all his life with the problem of evil. He poses the question of how evil arises in a world that God has made. The answer lies in the equal presence of mercy. Many of Boehme's notions, often expressed with great obscurity, may also be linked with the Islamic mystics, the Sufis. All three, Christian, Jewish, and Islamic heresies, maintained a centuries-long collaboration and dispute. "Nature is God's body," writes Boehme. Only with great difficulty does he avoid saying outright that God must therefore be the source of evil. "For all life is steeped in poison and the light alone withstands the poison, and yet is also a cause that the poison lives and does not languish."

Boehme, like his co-thinkers, continually quotes Holy Scripture, but picks and chooses which bits to he wants, and even then "interprets" the pieces to suit his purposes. Thus, in showing how the Creator set about producing Adam from a handful of dust, he stresses that this is not a sign of man's inferiority. The *materia* out of which he created him was a *massa*, a *quinta essentia*, out of the stars and elements. Stressing that Adam was like God, Boehme writes:

> And *Adam* knew all of what every creature was, and gave every one its name, according to the quality of its spirit. As God can see into the heart of all things, so could *Adam* also do, in which his perfection may very well be observed.

It is therefore no surprise that Boehme is also an inspiration for many other writers, notably for the poet Blake, and in the twentieth century for Jung and the surrealists. Hegel devoted thirty pages of his *Lectures on the History of Philosophy* to Boehme—John Locke gets about half as much!—and this is not surprising when you read passages like this one:

> Nothing can be revealed to itself without opposition: For if there is nothing that opposes it, then it always goes out of itself and never returns to itself again. If it does not return into itself, as into that from which it originated, then it knows nothing of its origin. (Boehme, "The Way to Christ." Quoted by Hegel, *op cit*, Vol. 3, 203)

(Another character ought to appear on our cast list of heretics, but doesn't. Isaac Newton [1642–1727] is the most famous name in the history of Hermeticism, but Hegel, like most of us until quite recently, did not know this. Newton kept completely secret the facts that he spent much of his working life as an alchemist, had the largest collection of Hermetic literature in his library, and translated some key manuscripts in the *Corpus Hermeticum*. His lifelong studies of the Book of Daniel and the dimensions of the Great Pyramid seemed to be unconnected eccentricities. Only toward the end of the twentieth century has the real story been uncovered, in the work of Betty-Jo Dobbs. Meanwhile, learned authorities still insist on gibbering about "the Newtonian mechanical universe." There is still a problem about Newton, however. He was secretly an Arian, who downplayed Jesus in relation to the other members of the Trinity, and it is not clear what the significance of this was—at least, to me.)

8. Islamic Mysticism

I can only mention the Islamic contribution to our story very briefly, but I think it will be seen to link up with many other episodes. Even more sharply than either Judaism or Christianity, Islamic orthodoxy would seem to be hostile to the trends we have been discussing. Allah's distance from the material human world is of a still higher order of infinity than that of Jehovah and the Christian God. But ideas cannot be separated from each other, even by the efforts of the most ferocious dogmatism.

Quite early in the history of Islam, the orthodox upholders of tradition had to fight to combat other influences, especially that of Greek philosophy. It was a losing battle. Neoplatonic and Aristotelian strands began to be interwoven with the concepts of the Koran, until, by the ninth, tenth, and eleventh centuries, Arabic philosophers were the only ones to maintain the traditions of Greek thought, and to transmit them to the West. All of the problems which beset the other religions recur, of course, above all, the problems of evil and of human free will. Mystical ideas, often influenced by Zoroastrianism, Taoism, and Hinduism, also begin to be combined with Islam throughout the Muslim world, sometimes in opposition to the Greek influences. Despite the vast gulf between Allah and the human, the mystic seeks unity with God. In 922, the great al-Hallaj met his death, executed for declaring—at least according to his accusers—"I am God!" Centuries later, in 1191, al-Shurawadhi faced death in Aleppo for similar crimes. He had set himself the task of rediscovering the theosophy of ancient Iran, linking Plato with Hermes. Muslim mystics (Sufis) had to exercise great ingenuity in avoiding charges of polytheism and pantheism, finding support wherever they could in quotations from the Koran and the *hadith*. Even the ascetic denial of marriage by some of them raised difficulties not faced by their Christian counterparts: it could be taken as criticism of the Prophet, who was definitely married.

But despite all these obstacles, Sufi teachings gained many followers and their writings in poetry and prose flourished. It is important that Avicenna (Ibn Sina) (980–1037) and Averroes (Ibn Rushd) (1165–1240), the greatest scholars of their times, responsible for preserving and developing the works of Aristotle, were also involved in the mystical speculation of Sufism. Islamic mysticism is concerned chiefly with the spiritual journey of the individual soul. Contemplating the Divine, the Contemplator is himself the Contemplated, and the seeker is himself a particle of the Divine Light that he seeks. At the endpoint of this journey, the individual souls are all united. The Sufi teachers attempt to describe the course of the journey and the visions which mark its stages, often making use of alchemical terms. Some of these descriptions center on the colors which the visionary sees. These ideas recur centuries later in the color doctrine which Goethe, with the enthusiastic support of Hegel, counterposed to the theories of Newton—or at least, those attributed to Newton by the Newtonians. The "Newtonians" wanted color to be a function of an objective phenomenon called light, while Goethe and Hegel, who were well aware of the mystical background to this discussion, insisted that it was simultaneously objective and the result of subjective activity.

In our time, Sufism has made a surprising entry into the literary world of the United States. In 1995, when a translation of the poetry of Mevlana Jelauddin Rumi was published, it became a major best-seller. Rumi (1207–1273), born in what is now Afghanistan and living in Anatolia in Turkey, was a leading Sufi scholar and poet. Founder of the Mehlevi order of dervishes, the so-called "whirling Dervishes" (*darwish* = "poor in spirit"), Rumi tried to express the mystical experience in poetry, together with the ideas he learned from Ibn al-Arabi (1165–1240). Hegel is also said to have encountered a translation of some of Rumi's poems and to have been very impressed by them.

9. Enlightenment versus Magic

The word "enlightenment" usually refers to the thought of the second half of the eighteenth century. However, while the differences among the thinkers of two centuries 1600–1800 are, of course, very significant, the term does capture that fundamental shift in thinking which took place—from Descartes to Kant—as modern bourgeois society was taking shape. What is important here is that these scientific, rational ideas which came to predominate in the seventeenth and eighteenth centuries, tended to brush aside all the questions we have been discussing.

In his 1784 essay "What Is Enlightenment?" Kant sees the essence of the new way of looking at the world lying in the freedom of individual thought.

> Enlightenment is man's leaving his self-caused immaturity. Immaturity is the incapacity to use one's intelligence without the guidance of another. . . . *Sapere aude!* Have the courage to use your own intelligence is therefore the motto of the enlightenment.

Thus advanced thought took for its standpoint "the single individual in civil society." Its exhilarating declaration of independence challenged all authority of Church and State. But already, Kant, Rousseau, and others begin to explore the problems this raises. There is no doubt that thinking is indeed inseparable from the activity of the individual brain. But it is at the same time completely social, involving language and categories of thought, all products of society and history. Moreover, no thinker can separate his intellect from emotion and will, which are at once individual and social in nature. And so the excellent exhortation to "think for yourself" can, taken by itself, be very misleading.

From the point of view of each social atom, the natural world and society look like collections of discrete bits and pieces, machines made up of smaller machines. When the "single individual" thinks about this mechanical world, he sees himself as yet another machine, quite unchanged by interaction with the other machines. In trying to think about these assemblies of atoms, many problems arise, and the best way to answer these is to isolate each one and break it into separate, smaller subproblems. One way of grasping this vast array of particles is to count them and relate the numbers. Of course, there is no end to such a process of subdivision. Infinity, just one darn thing after another, is an unimaginable collection of bits.

The individual gets his knowledge of the world by logically decoding the messages conveyed to him through his senses. (Who is doing the decoding, though?) Otherwise, the knowing subject and the object of knowledge are utterly different and separate from each other, as are Nature and humanity. Freedom, which for this outlook means the removal of "external" restrictions on the individual, is not to be found in nature, where all movement is rigidly determined. To be "objective" you have to expunge everything subjective, like quality, feeling, will, or free, creative activity. This is how reason, the equipment of each individual human, worked in opposition to all kinds of superstition.

This outlook made possible modern natural science, and the earlier history of science, which was inseparable from magic and alchemy, was expunged from the record. The fact that it had been the Hermeticists who had borne the brunt of the fight against scholasticism was forgotten. After the battle had been won, rationalism falsely claimed the sole credit for victory. Although the power of the Churches was courageously challenged by the Enlighteners, atheism was actually rare. The predominant belief was in a benevolent Deity, who didn't interfere with the workings of the material world. That great upholder of Jacobinism, Immanuel Kant, got into a lot of trouble for his 1793 *Religion within the Limits of Reason Alone*, but he concludes that courageous work with his aim of an "ethical commonwealth," whose concept was that of "a people of God under ethical laws." A rational conception of God took the place of earlier ideas of the Lord of the World. Miracles were rationally explained away, and the laws of matter came to be assumed as paramount. God was demoted, just an affair of "the heart," a matter for the individual conscience.

And what did the rationalists have to say about human society? For them, humanity was an aspect of a blind rushing about of particles. Whether humans were put here by an absent Deity, or got here by chance, their social relations could only be understood as external to their subjectivity. Political economy, and later, sociology, studied a social machine, made up of atoms driven by self-interest, while the social order and its history were governed by laws as fixed as those which ruled the solar system. This outlook encouraged its devotees to attempt to remake social relations to bring them into line with what was self-evidently rational. This was how American rebels who drafted their Declaration of Independence in 1777, and soon after them the Frenchmen with their Rights of Man, came to see their work. When the outcome of the French revolution could be discerned a little more clearly, the idea of extending such ways of thinking to transcend the rights of private property gave rise to various socialist schemes.

Deep inside all these sets of ideas was the separation of people from each other, from society as a whole and from the world of nature. Rational thought and emotions were not just separate but totally opposed to each other. Creation was inexplicable and self-creation inconceivable for such a world outlook. Most important, this way of thinking could not explain itself.

HEGEL

G. W. F. Hegel (1770–1831) takes account of the advances of the Enlightenment with respect, but stands in fundamental opposition to its basic conceptions. What is often played down is that, while the *philosophes* either attempted to rationalize religion, or to disregard it entirely, Hegel places theology—but only his own special brand—at the center of all his work. After grappling with Christianity in his student years in the Tübingen Theological Seminary, his turn to philosophy or "Science" (*Wissenschaft* = "knowing craft" or "knowing-hood") is inseparable from his peculiar views on God. It is not only "Marxists" for whom this poses a problem. Even when some of them bring themselves to peep into Hegel's system, they just can't handle Hegel's religion. It is particularly comical to see Lenin's superstitious panic, in his *Notebooks on Hegel's Science of Logic*, every time Hegel mentions God. Georgi Lukacs, who knew rather more about such things, treats Hegel's religious views as a shameful secret.

The fragmentation of eighteenth-century social and intellectual life in a world increasingly dominated by money and capital is the key to the ideas I have called "the Enlightenment." Although in Germany such changes spread much more slowly than in Britain and France, by the end of the century many German intellectuals were reading with alarm about the effect that commercialization and industrialization were having in England, Scotland, and France. Comparing their not very brave new world with the idealized picture they had of ancient Greece, people like Goethe, Schiller, and Herder looked urgently for ways in which Germany might bypass such developments.

The young Hegel, together with his fellow students Hölderlin and Schelling, welcomed the French Revolution with enthusiasm. At first it seemed to offer an alternative to the fragmentation of modernity. Together, the three adopted as their slogan the Neoplatonic motto *"Hen Kai Pan,"* "One and All," which they saw as summing up their opposition to the Enlightenment. Then the dream of 1789 faded. Hölderlin's poetry and his novel *Hyperion* had combined his yearning for the harmony of the Greek ideal with a romantic pantheism. Eventually, disappointment at the failure of these dreams played an important part in his madness, which lasted for half of his lifetime.

Of these three young men, the leader is undoubtedly the youngest. Friedrich Wilhelm Joseph von Schelling (1775–1854) is just fifteen when he is admitted to the Tübingen Seminary and eighteen when he begins to produce his massive output of books and articles. At twenty-three, Schelling is a professor in Jena. Throughout his life, his work expresses a series of outlooks which continually strive to discover the fundamental unity of reality. Where Enlightenment thinkers separated Nature and humanity from Reason, Schelling strives to deduce them *from* Reason. Nature is Mind or Self in the process of becoming. Art unites the poles of consciousness and unconsciousness, and the universe itself is a work of art. He has a deep relationship with his contemporaries the romantics. (For example, compare him with the pantheism of Wordsworth.)

In his 1804 dialogue *Bruno*, Schelling makes Giordano the protagonist for his own views. By now he has studied enough of Boehme to decide that the world originates from God by a nonrational leap. Nature is sin and unreason, while history is Nature striving to return to reason. All of these ideas are clearly related to the tradition of Boehme and to Cabbala. Schelling's God is "not a System, but a Life." In his *Philosophy and Religion* (1809), he is able to write that:

> History is an epic composed in the mind of God. Its two main parts are, first, that which depicts the departure of mankind from its centre, up to its farther point of alienation, and second, that which depicts the return. The first is the *Odyssey* of History, the second, its *Iliad*. In the first, the movement is centrifugal, in the second it is centripetal.

Schelling's Absolute, the unconditioned, is the One from which the world begins. At the creation, it falls into the Many, and, from then on, strives to get back to the One.

By the time when, in 1841, the sixty-five-year-old Schelling is called to occupy the Berlin chair, which Hegel had held until ten years before, he has drawn the most reactionary conclusions. Now a defender of religious orthodoxy, he has become the Prussian establishment's answer to the pernicious influence of that dangerous "atheist" Hegel.

Hegel never ceased to celebrate the achievements of the French Revolution, but devoted his work to grasping the meaning of its limitations and those of the Enlightenment which had been revealed by it. Until his thirties, Hegel follows many of the ideas of his brilliant younger friend. But then the gap between them widens, as Hegel's vast system matures inside his head. Only in 1807 does his first book appear, the *Phenomenology of Spirit*. His conception of Spirit or Mind, *Geist*, central to all his work, is Hegel's attempt to counter the atomization which bedevils Enlightenment thinking at every level. Thus the *Phenomenology* expounds the autobiography of Spirit, and the 1830 edition of the *Philosophy of Spirit (Mind)*, the third and final part of his *Encyclopedia of the Philosophical Sciences*, is among his last publications.

Geist has a wide range of meanings for Hegel. He wants it to unite individual psychology—"subjective Spirit"—with history and the State. But above all *Geist* has religious connotations as the Holy Ghost (*der heiliger Geist*), the third Person of the Christian Trinity, which reconciles the opposition of the first and second, Father and Son, Creator and Created. The *Phenomenology* aims to recount the many "shapes" through which the experience of cultural, social, intellectual, artistic, and religious life have passed, summarized in the last chapter, "Absolute Knowing." Each of these "shapes" moves the sequence forward, as it both shows humanity as a whole *and* reveals the inadequacy of any one shape to express the whole story. Each shape is the result of past human activity, and yet confronts individuals as something given, a task to be carried out, an obstacle to be overcome, a problem to be solved.

The sequence continues until philosophical science has transcended itself as absolute—unconditioned—knowing. Then, *Geist* is the whole process, the approach to freedom, the community, "the 'I' that is 'we,' the 'we' that is 'I.'" You could think of it like this: "we" observe the self-development of Spirit, through all its shapes, until "we" discover that "our" observation is itself part of the movement. Spirit is us, and we are Spirit observing itself. Hegel is then ready to describe his entire system, Logic, Nature, and Mind, which ends with "Philosophy," the last Section of the *Philosophy of Spirit*. Thus Hegel's Absolute, in opposition to that of Schelling, is both a *result*, the outcome of the entire experience of history and the development of culture, as well as the implicit *starting point* for the whole movement.

Kant—both as Enlightener and as a critic of the Enlightenment—had attempted to show how Reason could overcome the fragments of society in a unity of social and intellectual life transcending experience. But Hegel tries to show how Spirit, which is immanent in the world, moves *itself*, from the standpoint of simple sensation all the way to religion and "Absolute Knowing." We, the readers, "look on" at this self-development. Each whole differentiates itself into many forms, which then exhibit their essential reconciliation, returning to the whole. Thus *Geist*, under its own steam, *develops itself* into higher and more comprehensive forms. Spirit *makes itself* from within itself. We are not forbidden to know the whole of truth, but nor can we know it immediately. It reveals itself only through the entire contradictory historical process. The Enlightenment thought that each rational individual had only to clear priestly mists of superstition and mysticism out of the way to be able to get a clear view of the truth. Hegel shows that the craft of knowing (*Wissenschaft*) unfolds itself in what is simultaneously the education of the individual, the contradictory movement of history, and the logical development of nature. The truth reveals itself *through* mystery.

That is why Hegel must be taken as a whole. "The True is the Whole," he says in the preface to the *Phenomenology*.

> But the whole is nothing other than the essence consummating itself through its development. Of the Absolute it must be said that it is essentially a *result*, that only in the *end* is it what it truly is; and that precisely in this consists its nature, viz. to be actual, subject, the spontaneous becoming of itself.

Another important idea follows from this. "Knowledge is only actual, and can only be expounded, as Science or as *system*." Any tendency to pick out odd bits which look interesting, episodes from his rich texture, misses the point of what he is trying to do. (Don't forget: this is Hegel, not Marx. It is humanity as *Geist* which is self-creating here, and this is not the same as what Marx will call humanity.)

Hegel's last years in Berlin, 1819–31, are crucial for what we need from him. This includes his work (a) on the State (1821); (b) on the history of philosophy; (c) on Aesthetics; (d) on the philosophy of religion; (e) on the philosophy of history. In each of these fields, as with each of his earlier works, Hegel stresses the centrality of God.

So, when Hegel frequently professes his Lutheran convictions, this is not, as some Young Hegelians supposed, just an attempt to stay within the bounds of respectability and keep his job. He really means it. Hegel does not conceive of the Christian Trinity as belonging to particular events in history. God the Father, the Creator, does his work all the time, putting Himself into His Creation. He is also identified with Logic, "logos," "the Word" of the Fourth Gospel.

> The world is something produced by God, and so the divine idea always forms the foundation of what the world as a whole is. (*Lectures on the Philosophy of Religion*)

God does not create the world and humanity within it out of free choice, but because he has to. He *needs* his creation, for without it "God is not God." Without our conscious activity, God is not self-conscious. This is how Hegel regards Christ, who is also Nature. Only through the world of the Son does God the Father become conscious of Himself. The Holy Spirit is this process of ascent to self-knowledge, taken as a whole. Hegel agrees that the Trinity is a mystery, and identifies his own "speculative philosophy" as "mysticism." But this does not imply that its truth must remain hidden: on the contrary, it is *through* mystery that God reveals himself, to himself as well as to us. So— following Aristotle here—Hegel sees his own system as "the self-thinking Idea," which is at the same time the self-consciousness of God.

Hegel faces the problem of Evil in a manner which entirely separates him from orthodoxy, while resembling closely the heretical ideas of the alchemists and mystics. For Hegel, Evil is a part of God's creation. (Compare this with the magnificent debate in Heaven between God and the Devil, before the action begins in Goethe's *Faust*.) Indeed, the contradiction between Good and Evil is the driving force of all movement and development, and without it, there is no humanity. Thus Hegel's account of the Fall, which resembles some Gnostic versions of the Mosaic Story, tears apart the *Book of Genesis*. As he explains:

> The myth does not conclude with the expulsion from paradise. It says further, "God said: Behold, Adam is become as one of us, to know good and evil" [*Genesis*, 3:22]. Cognition is now something divine, and not, as earlier, what ought not to be. So in this story there lies also the refutation of the idle chatter about how philosophy belongs only to the finitude of spirit; philosophy is cognition, and the original calling of man, to be an image of God, can be realised only through cognition. (*Encyclopedia*, para 24, Addition 2)

Hegel's entire system is penetrated by this view of religion, which places him close to the Hermetic tradition and in opposition to the Enlightenment. It might be compared with the ideas of Hegel's fellow Boehmian and contemporary, William Blake (1757–1827). The *Song of Liberty* which ends his *Marriage of Heaven and Hell* declares, for example, that "The road of excess leads to the palace of wisdom," that "the tygers of wrath are wiser than the horses of instruction," that "Energy is Eternal Delight" and that "Everything that lives is Holy." Hegel never refers to Blake, nor Blake to Hegel, but such is the power of Blake's ideas, that we never *need* the direct reference.

Look again at the triadic divisions which abound throughout Hegel's system:

Subjective Mind, Objective Mind, Absolute Mind;
Logic, Nature, Mind;

> Universal, Particular, Individual;
> Being, Essence, Concept;
> Abstract Right, Morality, Ethical Life;
> Family, Civil Society, State.

Each element of each triad is itself a triad. But each of these is an expression of the Holy Trinity: Father, Son, and Holy Spirit. The relationships among the members of each triad cannot be properly appreciated unless this is grasped. At every level, Hegel is showing how these three "Persons" actively create and determine each other. Finally, Hegel sees God creating and being created by humanity, in the religious community. (The picture by M. C. Escher called "Drawing Hands," in which each of two hands draws and is drawn by the other, might be a helpful illustration here.) In each triad, the third term both reconciles the opposition between the first two, and contains and preserves it. (The word "synthesis," often murmured in relation to Hegel, doesn't really fit the bill here. See, for instance, the last few paragraphs of the *Encyclopedia Philosophy of Mind*, including the final quotation from Aristotle's *Metaphysics*. Compare Hegel's concluding three syllogisms, relating Universal, Particular, and Individual, with the syllogisms of the Holy Trinity, a few paragraphs earlier.)

The third member of each triad both arises from the contradiction between other two and reconciles them, as, for example, Spirit reconciles Father and Son. Hegel's last book, the *Philosophy of Right*, reaches its climax in the State, which brings together in this way family and civil society, despite, or, rather, *through*, the contradictions he finds in them. Thus he highlights the conflicting relations between people in a world of private property and money. (In the *Phenomenology*, he savages this world as "the Animal Kingdom of Spirit.") But in the development of the concept of State, he finds the way these battles can be philosophically overcome. So Marx will put his finger on Hegel's inability to criticize political economy, and this involves him in a critique of Hegel's notion of the State and his dialectic as a whole.

Thus Hegel turns both the Enlightenment conception of Reason and its religious opposite inside out. Hegel's Reason, is identified with divine wisdom. It does not merely exist passively in human history: that history expresses itself as "purposive activity."

> In our knowledge, we aim for the insight that whatever was intended by the Eternal Wisdom has come to fulfilment—as in the realm of nature, so in the realm of spirit that is active and actual in the world. (*Reason in History*, 19)

(In Hegel, *Wirklichkeit* should not be read as "reality," but as "actuality," something like Aristotle's *entelechia*: it *acts*.) But in Hegel the "Eternal Wisdom" is not a divine script which humanity is forced to perform, for the Spirit "that is active and actual in the world" is the individual and social activity of humanity. History is the coming to be of freedom. But the consciousness of an individual human ("finite spirit") is no more than a fragment of the whole story, which is only found in the Self-consciousness of Spirit. This is an alias for the Self-consciousness of God, worked out only through human history as a whole. (By the way, Hegel has no use for the immortality of an individual soul, "finite spirit": only the Infinite, the World Spirit, is eternal.)

Let us look again at that word "Freedom" in Hegel's system. Every systematic move is a step toward the inevitable endpoint, from Subjective Spirit, to Objective Spirit, to Absolute Spirit. Absolute Spirit is Art, Religion and Philosophy, so Philosophy is the pinnacle: Freedom. Hegel stresses that the world of Nature knows nothing about being free; only spiritual beings, those who are self-conscious, can know freedom. So every philosopher before Kant is certain that individual humans are the subjects of philosophy. Kant himself thinks that every philosophy must run into contradictions if it attempts to ask about Freedom. Hegel, on the other hand, shows that this absolute knowledge *can* be achieved, but only as a result of hard work, by special people called "philosophers." Freedom can at last be attained, but only by students of philosophy.

(This attitude to Freedom does not prevent him from being pro-slavery. Unlike the Enlightenment thinkers—in fact unlike most of his contemporaries— Hegel repeated most of the propaganda put out by the slave owners, in all its crudity.)

Spirit is self-developing, simultaneously consciousness and self-consciousness: it *is* its own history.

> [T]his development of the spirit, considered historically, is the history of philosophy. It is a history of all the self-developments of the spirit, an exhibition of these decisive moments and stages as they have followed one another in the course of time. . . . Consequently, the history of philosophy is identical with the system of philosophy. (*Introduction to the Lectures on the History of Philosophy*)

If Hegel's account of the development of history did not include *itself*, it would be in contradiction with itself. In making itself "what it truly is," Spirit is at the same time writing its autobiography. That is one reason I support with enthusiasm the contention of Magee, in his remarkable book *Hegel and the Hermetic Tradition*, that Hegel is best understood, not as a philosopher, explaining a world external to him, but as part of the Hermetic tradition.

Ludwig Feuerbach (1804–72) is perhaps the most important of Hegel's immediate followers. In 1824, he abandons his theological studies and decides—against parental disapproval—in favor of philosophy under the

Master in Berlin. Soon, at the end of the 1830s, the Hegelian school starts to disintegrate. After writing some Hegelian books on the history of philosophy, Feuerbach begins to break away from the Hegelian system, and is soon the leader of the "Left" or "Young" Hegelians. In 1841, he publishes his chief work, *The Essence of Christianity*, followed by *Preliminary Theses for the Reform of Philosophy* and *Foundations of the Philosophy of the Future*.

Like the other Left Hegelians, Feuerbach is first of all concerned with religion. Unlike some of his fellow rebels, however, he does not merely denounce religion, which he describes as "the first and indirect self-consciousness of man." Where his teacher Hegel had made human self-consciousness the way that God is conscious of Himself, Feuerbach sees "what man knows of God" as an upside-down form of "what man knows of himself." Religion takes what is best of humanity, "the human essence," human feeling, willing, thinking, love, and projects it on to something which appears as other than human, the product of imagination (*Phantasie*). But this is the root of human enslavement.

> Man—this is the mystery of religion—projects his essence into objectivity and then makes himself the image of this projected image of himself thus converted into a subject, a person; he thinks of himself as an object to himself, but as the object of an object, of another being than himself. (*Essence*)

Feuerbach sees the demystification of this process as the way to freedom: "What in religion is a *predicate* we must make into a *subject.*" Describing Hegel's "theological idealism," he says that "man's consciousness of God is the self-consciousness of God. . . . Thus does absolute philosophy externalise from man his own essence and activity" (*Principles*).

Feuerbach's target is Theology rather than religion. When it formalises the study of God, theology becomes "the worst enemy of the awakened spirit." In his earlier writing, Feuerbach had quoted Boehme's personal understanding of God with approval. Now, he praises Boehme for understanding that God has His material body in nature. But his aim is to get behind all forms of mystification. In *Essence* . . . he devotes chapter VIII to the mystery of Divine Creation and chapter IX, "Of the Mystery of Mysticism, or of Nature in God," to Jakob Boehme.

His critique of Hegel is that the formal reasoning of the Hegelian system is actually disguised theology which excludes the personal. But in this, Feuerbach is criticizing the whole of philosophy, philosophy as such. That is what he means by "the new philosophy."

> Just as theology transforms the determinations of man into divine determinations—through depriving them of their own determination by which they are what they are—so also in precisely the same way does philosophy deprive

them. . . . So does absolute philosophy externalise and alienate from man his own essence and activity. Hence the violence and torture that it inflicts on our minds.

The new philosophy makes man—with the inclusion of nature as the foundation of man—the unique, universal and highest object of philosophy. (*Principles*)

As he famously explained himself: "My religion is—no religion. My philosophy—no philosophy."

Does Feuerbach represent a step backward from Hegel toward the Enlightenment? Yes and no. Perhaps it is more of a *sideways* move. The only social relation Feuerbach knows is the "love"—what kind is unspecified!—between two characters called "I" and "thou." While he does not ignore Hegel's critical attitude to Kant and his predecessors, he still denies its religious implications. Effectively, he reestablishes the Enlightenment's view of the human as an isolated individual.

Marx

When, in 1837, Karl Marx (1818–83) transferred to Berlin University, it was with the intention of continuing his study of law. But, despite his best intentions, he was inexorably drawn into the study of philosophy in general and the Hegelian philosophical system in particular. A decade earlier, this would have meant adhering to the unified outlook which had come to dominate thought in Prussia. But by the late 1830s, that outlook was in a state of decomposition. So the young Marx was inevitably embroiled in the vehement, noisy and highly alcoholic arguments among the "Young Hegelians," focussed largely on what they saw as the radical political and religious implications of Hegel's work.

Many of these students affected an abstract "atheism." They wanted to show that Hegel also was really an atheist, whose open religious ideas were little more than a pretence, just accommodation to the establishment. Marx had little patience with such attitudes. As he explained in a letter to Arnold Ruge (November 30, 1842):

I desired that there be less trifling with the label "atheism" (which reminds one of children, assuring everyone who is ready to listen to them that they are not afraid of the bogy man), and that instead the content of philosophy should be brought to the people. (*MCEW*, Vol. 1, 395)

Marx's chief interest at that time was the history of Greek philosophy, particularly the period after Aristotle. He saw the appearance of schools like Stoicism, Skepticism and Epicureanism as analogous to the situation in German philosophy after Hegel. He took as the topic for his doctoral dissertation the relation between the philosophies of nature of the atomists Democritus and Epicurus. Hegel had regarded the work of Epicurus as containing little new, but Marx respectfully disagrees. While the atoms of Democritus fell in straight lines in the void, those of Epicurus swerved from the rectilinear. In this "declination," thinks Marx, Epicurus and his Roman disciple Lucretius were approaching an understanding of human freedom. "Repulsion is the first form of self-consciousness."

In his notebooks to prepare for the dissertation, Marx writes:

> The modern rational outlook on nature must first raise itself to the point from which the ancient Ionian philosophy, in principle at least, begins—the point of seeing the Divine, the Idea, embodied in nature. (MECW, Vol. 1, 423–24)

Marx is seeking ways of understanding nature which will grasp its unity with human life. He thinks that Epicurus, for all his limitations, gets closer to this than Democritus, and that Hegel had overlooked this advance. This leads him to see more clearly the significance of philosophy and its attitude to the world in his own time. Philosophy and the world condition each other. Hegel's philosophy had "sealed itself off to form a consummate, total world." Meanwhile,

> The determination of this totality is conditioned by the general development of this philosophy, just as the development of this philosophy is the condition of the form in which philosophy turns into a practical relationship toward reality. . . . The world confronting a philosophy total in itself is thus a world torn apart. (MECW, Vol. 1, 491)

So, from an incidental disagreement with Hegel over an episode in the history of ancient Greek philosophy, the twenty-one-year-old Marx arrives at the necessity for the practical activity of philosophy in healing the divisions in a world "torn apart." Dr. Marx then realizes that he will never find an academic job, becomes the editor of a newspaper, gets into a running battle with the Prussian Censorship over the freedom of the press, and finds himself unemployed—and married—at the age of twenty-five. In this situation (in the house of his mother-in-law), he begins to write a detailed critique of one part of Hegel's *Philosophy of Right*, the section on the State.

But he is able to embark on this work, in 1843, only because he has been convinced by Feuerbach's criticisms of Hegel. Although his enthusiasm for Feuerbach only lasts a couple of years, it opens up a new attitude to Hegel, increasing the confidence with which he declares his independence from his

"great teacher." As he recalls sixteen years later, in the famous 1859 preface
to his *Contribution to a Critique of Political Economy*:

> The first work which I undertook to dispel the doubts assailing me was a critical
> re-examination of the Hegelian philosophy of law. . . . My enquiry led me to the
> conclusion that neither legal relations nor political forms could be comprehended
> whether by themselves or on the basis of the so-called general development of
> the human mind, but that on the contrary they originate in the material conditions
> of life, the totality of which Hegel, following the example of English and French
> thinkers of the eighteenth century, embraces within the term "civil society"; that
> the anatomy of this society, however, is to be sought in political economy.

So from the critique of religion, which Marx found in Feuerbach, Marx
moves to the critique of the State and thence to the critique of political economy. This progression, from God to State to economy, is a movement deeper
into the nature of humanity and its mystification, especially the mystification
of human productive activity.

It is important to bear in mind the meaning which Marx gives to the word
"critique" by this point in his development. Occurring in the titles of almost
all his works, critique does not mean rejection of—and certainly not mere disagreement with—secondary features. Critique implies demystification, not
by rejecting mystery, but by tracing its origins to the reality of social life. I
used to place Marx's critiques of political economy and of socialist Utopia on
the same level as the critique of Hegelian dialectic, but I now want to place
this third critical operation on a separate plane, for it includes and underlies
each of the other two.

Marx seeks to probe the connections of each object to the essence of humanity. His critique uncovers the inhuman ways that humans deny their humanity inside the very forms of life they themselves have made. Shut inside
these forms, they struggle to think about themselves, both truly and falsely. In
the *Critique of Hegel's Philosophy of Law*, Marx charges Hegel with mystification on several occasions, even of "logical pantheistic mysticism." But as
he moves steadily through Hegel's sometimes apologetic analysis of the
State, he shows how Hegel has succeeded in reflecting mysterious—that is to
say hidden—aspects of political life.

This is most clearly expressed in the only part of this *Critique* published by
Marx, the *Introduction*. In its most famous—and most misquoted—passage,
Marx clarifies what he means by "critique."

> The basis of irreligious criticism is: Man makes religion, religion does not make
> man. Religion is the self-consciousness and self-esteem of man who has either
> not yet found himself or has already lost himself again. But man is no abstract
> being encamped outside the world. Man is the world of men, the state, society.

This state, this society, produce religion, an inverted world-consciousness, because they are an inverted world. Religion is the general theory of that world, its encyclopaedic *point d'honeur*, its enthusiasm, its moral sanction, its solemn complement, its universal source of consolation and justification. It is the fantastic realisation of the human essence, because the human essence has no true reality. The struggle against religion is therefore indirectly a fight against the world of which religion is the spiritual aroma. Religious distress is at the same time the expression of real distress and also the protest against real distress. Religion is the sigh of the oppressed creature, the heart of a heartless world, just as it is the spirit of spiritless conditions. It is the opium of the people. (*Critique*, Vol. 3, 175.)

Of course, Marx does not want us to cling to religion, but neither does he throw it away, or denounce it, or deny its mystery. His task is to find out why religion exists, to trace the roots of mystery in humanity's inhuman way of life. So, from religion, the *Introduction* proceeds to examine with great savagery the contemporary position of Germany.

If the speculative philosophy of law, that abstract extravagant *thinking* on the modern state, the reality of which remains a thing of the beyond, if only beyond the Rhine, was possible only in Germany, inversely the *German* thought-image of the modern state which disregards *real man* was possible only because and insofar as the modern state itself disregards *real man* or satisfies the *whole* of man only in imagination. (181)

Now, for the first time, Marx can speak about the proletariat as the most important emancipatory force, "a class with radical chains" (186). "As philosophy finds its material weapons in the proletariat, so the proletariat finds its spiritual weapons in philosophy" (187).

Spurred on by Engels' brilliant 1843 essay *Outlines of a Critique of Political Economy*, Marx now embarks on his life's work. Somehow, he still imagines himself a follower of Feuerbach, and remains so for almost a year longer. But already in reality he has gone far beyond that much cruder form of "critique." From the mystery of religion, via the mystery of the state, Marx now confronts the central mystery of modernity, what he would later call the secret, "fetish" character of commodities and commodity relationships which permeates and dominates all our lives.

Some time in May, 1844, now an exile in Paris, Marx reads and comments on a French translation of James Mill's *Elements of Political Economy*. Seeing Mill's banal characterization of money as "the medium of exchange," Marx brings to bear everything he has learned on this disciple of Ricardo.

The *human* social act by which man's products mutually complement one another, is *estranged* from man and becomes the attribute of money, a *material thing* outside man. Since man alienates this mediating activity itself, he is active here only as a man who has lost himself and is dehumanised. . . . His slavery therefore reaches its peak. It is clear that this *mediator* becomes a *real God*. (212)

We might say that this analogy between God and money occupies Marx for the rest of his life. Unless we connect it with Marx's relationship with Hegel's mysticism, the deepest significance of this analogy is hidden.

To illuminate just how far Marx has already surpassed Feuerbach, albeit unknown to himself, let us look briefly at the respective receptions of Anselm's so-called ontological proof of God's existence by Kant, Hegel, Feuerbach, and Marx. Tidied up by Descartes, this "proof" says that, since God is the most perfect being we can conceive, and since perfection must surely include existence. . . . Kant famously and unceremoniously knocked this on the head: if I think I have 100 talers in my pocket, that is not the same as actually having them! Hegel is not impressed with this wisecrack. "When we speak of 'God,' we are referring to an object of quite a different kind than one hundred talers." "The true cognition of God begins with our knowing that things in their immediate being have no truth." Feuerbach (*Principles*, para 25), however, wants to reestablish Kant's argument against Hegel's mockery.

But Marx takes this argument to an entirely different plane. First, with Hegel, he points to the parallel between God and money as "alien mediators" between individuals. But then he leaps from this critique of what appears to be the most mundane of topics, money—"Everybody knows what money is," declares the learned professor of economics—to nothing less than *the nature of humanity*.

Since *human* nature is the *true community* of men, by manifesting the *nature* men *create*, produce, the *human community*, the social entity, is no abstract universal power opposed to the single individual, but is the essential nature of each individual, his own activity, his own life, his own spirit, his own wealth. (217)

Now, Marx can begin to ask what it would be like to live in a truly human world, in which we "carried out production as human beings." Without the "alien mediators," private property, money and state, "my work would be a free manifestation of life" (228). Marx has discovered his own conception of communism.

The content of these few scribbled pages is so rich that its elaboration occupies Marx for the rest of his life, with many ideas left untouched. Soon he is at work on those pages, given by their Moscow editors the most misleading title: *Economic-Philosophical Manuscripts*. (To the original edition in 1936, these bureaucrats added an even more baffling title about "the foundations of historical materialism.") Through an investigation of some economists, Marx gets to the heart of the nature of labor in its *alienated* form, in the production of commodities for sale, and thus to the nature of human creative activity as such and of human sociality.

> The animal is immediately one with its life activity. . . . Man makes his life activity itself the object of his will and of his consciousness. . . . An animal's product belongs immediately to its physical body, whilst man freely confronts his product. . . . In degrading spontaneous, free activity to a means, estranged labour makes man's species-life a means to his physical existence. . . . Estranged labour turns thus *man's species-being*, both nature and his spiritual species-property, into a being *alien* to him, into a *means* for his *individual existence*. It estranges from man his own body, as well as external nature and his spiritual aspect, his *human* aspect. (276–77)

So, through his analysis of alienated, estranged labor, Marx is able to discover the way in which to be a human individual means participation in three linked processes: making humanity, making the human social-historical, and even making the natural world. Only within estrangement, this is hidden, and we are imprisoned by this very act of making. This is how Marx can deal with religious argumentation:

> Any questions about the creation of the world and of humanity "*ex nihilo*" are based upon an abstraction, the assumption of the non-existence of the world and thus of the questioner. Looked at concretely, such problems vanish.
>
> But since for the socialist man the *entire so-called history of the world* is nothing but the creation of man through human labour, nothing but the emergence of nature for man, so he has the visible, irrefutable proof of his *birth* through himself, of his *genesis*. Since the *real existence* of man and nature has become evident in practice, through sense experience, because man has thus become evident for man as the being of nature, the question about an *alien* being, about a being above nature and man—a question which implies the admission of the unreality of nature and of man—has become impossible in practice. *Atheism*, as the denial of this unreality, has no longer any meaning, for atheism is a *negation of God*, and postulates the *existence* of man through this negation. (305–306)

The last of these *Paris Manuscripts*, "Critique of the Hegelian Dialectic and Philosophy as a Whole," begins with some of Marx's most fulsome praise of Feuerbach. And yet the ideas Marx begins to develop here leave Feuerbach far behind. Marx enters into a detailed critical discussion of the last chapter of Hegel's *Phenomenology*, "Absolute Knowing." Philosophy transcends "Revealed Religion," which, Hegel says, is defective only in that it has not made "its actual self-consciousness the object of its consciousness." Having learned from Feuerbach that Hegel makes the human being "the same as self-consciousness," Marx is able to transform Hegel's upside-down picture into an understanding of man as a "human natural being," and that means, not an isolated individual, but a social being.

> As everything natural has to come into being, man too has his act of origin—history—which, however, is for him a known history, and hence as an act of origin, is a conscious self-transcending act of origin.

Within his inverted philosophical picture,

> Hegel conceives labour as man's act of self-genesis—conceives man's relation to himself as an alien being and the manifestation of himself as an alien being to be the emergence of species-consciousness and species-life. (333)

So instead of Aristotle's self-thinking Idea, or Hegel's self-creating Spirit, Marx places the self-developing creative powers of the total social human being, what he sometimes calls "productive forces." (The misunderstanding of Marx by "Marxism" is epitomized in its insistent identification of this phrase with machinery, occasionally adding "and labor power," which only serves to make the misunderstanding worse.)

Toward the end of 1844, Marx works with Engels on a book, the *Holy Family*, which attacks the positions of some of the "Left Hegelians," especially Bruno Bauer. It clarifies a number of ideas, in particular the character of Marx's communism and his conception of the proletariat.

> Since in the fully-formed proletariat the abstraction of all humanity, even of the *semblance* of humanity, is practically complete; since the conditions of life of the proletariat sum up all the conditions of life of society today in their most inhuman form; since man has lost himself in the proletariat, yet at the same time has found not only theoretical consciousness of that loss, but through urgent, no longer removable, no longer disguisable, absolutely imperative *need*—the practical expression of *necessity*—is driven to revolt against this inhumanity, it follows that the proletariat can and must emancipate itself. But it cannot emancipate itself without abolishing the conditions of its own life. It cannot abolish the conditions of its own life without abolishing *all* the inhuman conditions of life which are summed up in its own situation. . . . It is not a question of this or that proletarian, or even the whole proletariat, *regards* as its aim. It is a question of *what the proletariat is*, and what, in accordance with this being, it will historically be compelled to do. (*Holy Family*, Vol. 4, 37)

"Marxists," including for example Georgi Lukacs, took this to imply that those privileged to know about this historical necessity, while the ordinary proletarians do not, will be obliged to act on their behalf. As we have seen, this is not what Marx was saying at all.

Marx's Break with Feuerbach

By the beginning of 1845, Marx can no longer avoid the conclusion that his critique of Hegel is quite different from Feuerbach's. As part of his preparation for the joint work with Engels called *The German Ideology*, the first part of which is entitled "Feuerbach," Marx, now expelled from Paris to Brussels, scribbles the famous eleven points known as the Theses on Feuerbach. These were discovered by Engels and published in an edited version in his *Ludwig Feuerbach* in 1888. I want to analyze briefly some of the ideas contained in Marx's original form of this manuscript.

The last of the Theses are among the best known of Marx's aphorisms:

Thesis 11. Philosophers have hitherto only interpreted the world in various ways; the point is to change it.

It is engraved on the statue which surmounts his tomb in Highgate Cemetery. (The word "but" or "however" [*aber*] which often appears between its two phrases is an editorial insertion by Engels and should be disregarded.)

The meaning of this neat pairing should not be taken for granted. Engels' addition has, only too often, suggested that Marx wants us to change the world *instead of* interpreting it. The question is: *How* are we to change the world? By what means and according to what criteria? Interpretation and change must be connected. But how? Somehow, they must both take place inside "the world."

One remark might be worth making at the start: in every one of Theses 1–10—Marx separates Thesis 11 from the rest—he only attacks one particular philosophical "interpretation": materialism. The old story about "the materialist Marx" is just one of the ways that people have been misdirected before they even begin to read what he writes.

Thesis 3 is a good example.

Thesis 3. The materialist doctrine that men are products of circumstances and upbringing, and that, therefore, changed men are products of changed circumstances and changed upbringing, forgets that it is men who change circumstances and that the educator must himself be educated. Hence this doctrine is bound to divide society into two parts, one of which is superior to society.

The coincidence of the changing of circumstances and of human activity or self-change [*Selbstveränderung*] can be conceived and rationally understood only as *revolutionary practice*.

This clear rejection of anything like Utopianism was often praised by "Marxists," who failed to notice that it was aimed precisely at them! They (we!) thought that "revolutionizing practice" referred to their own limited forms of "political work." It is important to see how, instead, it is rooted firmly in Marx's basic conception of self-emancipation. He never had any time for transformation brought about by people at the top, well-meaning chaps who could be trusted to look after the interests of the little people. For Marx, "human activity" *means* "self-change" (*Selbstveränderung*). They are *synonyms*. An activity which is not self-changing is not human. By the way, this crucial word, "self-change," is actually missing from Engels' edited version, the only one we had until much later. (In English, not until 1938.) It implies the mutual transformation, indeed, identification, of an active subject, which does the interpreting and changing and an object which is interpreted and changed.

Theses 4, 6, and 7 all deal with religion and Feuerbach's attempt to understand it.

Thesis 4. Feuerbach starts off from the fact of religious self-estrangement [*Selbstentfremdung*], of the duplication of the world into a religious, imaginary world, and a secular [*weltliche*] one. His work consists in resolving the religious world into its secular basis. He overlooks the fact that after completing this work, the chief thing still remains to be done. For the fact that the secular basis lifts off from itself and establishes itself in the clouds as an independent realm can only be explained by the inner strife and intrinsic contradictoriness of this secular basis. The latter must itself be understood in its contradiction and then, by the removal of the contradiction, revolutionised. Thus, for instance, once the earthly family is discovered to be the secret of the holy family, the former must itself be annihilated [*vernichtet*] theoretically and practically.

This is an elaboration of Marx's earlier hostility to "abstract atheism," which leaves untouched the *real* problems expressed by religious belief. The Thesis must also be taken as an illumination of the phrase "educating the educators" in Thesis 3.

Thesis 6. Feuerbach resolves the essence of religion into the essence of man [*menschliche Wesen* = "human nature"]. But the essence of man is no abstraction inherent in each single individual. In reality, it is the ensemble of the social relations. Feuerbach, who does not enter upon a criticism of this real essence is hence obliged:

1. To abstract from the historical process and to define the religious sentiment regarded by itself, and to presuppose an abstract—isolated—human individual.
2. The essence therefore can by him only be regarded as "species," as an inner "dumb" generality which unites many individuals only in a *natural* way.

What unites human individuals is not their biological—these days we might say "genetic"—similarity, but their entire historical, cultural, and social character. Indeed, they only become individuals through productive activity inside this set of relations.

> Thesis 7. Feuerbach consequently does not see that the "religious sentiment" is itself a *social product*, and that the abstract individual that he analyses belongs in reality to a particular social form.

Here Marx pits his—and Hegel's—understanding of the social nature of humanity against the incompleteness of Feuerbach's break from Enlightenment individualism. We can also see most clearly the close connection between Marx's conceptions of humanity and of critique.

The word "practice" ("*Praxis*") occurs in nearly all the Theses. It does *not* just mean "activity," but carries a two-sided reference both to the human relation with nature and to human relations within society.

> Thesis 2. The question whether objective truth can be attributed to human thinking is not a question of theory but is a *practical* question. Man must prove the truth, ie the reality and power, the this-sidedness [*Diesseitigkeit*] of his thinking, in practice. The dispute over the reality or non-reality of thinking which is isolated from practice is a purely scholastic question.

The odd word "*Diesseitigkeit*" might carry a bit more weight than is sometimes imagine. It is chosen as the opposite of the much more common "*Jenseitigkeit*," "other-worldliness" or transcendence.

> Thesis 5. Feuerbach, not satisfied with abstract thinking, wants sensuous contemplation [*Anschauung*]; but he does not conceive sensuousness as practical, human-sensuous activity.

> Thesis 8. All social life is essentially practical. All mysteries which lead theory to mysticism find their rational solution in human practice and in the comprehension of this practice.

Marx's conception of practice, meaning "human life activity or self-change," is central to his world outlook. As his discussion of materialism makes clear, he is not concerned with "epistemology," a "theory of knowledge" standing outside his conception of humanity and of productive and self-productive activity. Such a "theory," explaining a subject standing outside its object, is the highest symptom of the alienated way of life of the modern world.

> Thesis 9. The highest point reached by contemplative [*anschauende*] materialism, that is, materialism which does not comprehend sensuousness as practical

activity, is the contemplation of single individuals and of civil society [*bürger-lichen Gesellschaft*].

Thesis 10. The standpoint of the old materialism is civil society; the standpoint of the new is human society or social humanity.

It is "civil society," Hegel's "battlefield of private interest" (*Philosophy of Right*), which is expressed in the fragmented, contemplative outlook of isolated individuals.

But the sharpest opposition between Marx on the one hand, and "Marxism," "dialectical materialism," "historical materialism," and the rest on the other, is displayed right at the start of Marx's summary:

> Thesis 1. The main defect of all hitherto-existing materialism—that of Feuerbach included—is that the Object [*der Gegenstand*], actuality, sensuousness, are conceived only in the form of the object [*Objekts*], or of contemplation [*Anschauung*], but not as human sensuous activity, practice [*Praxis*], not subjectively. Hence it happened that the active side, in opposition to materialism, was developed by idealism—but only abstractly, since, of course, idealism does not know real, sensuous activity as such. Feuerbach wants sensuous objects [*Objekte*], differentiated from thought-objects, but he does not conceive human activity itself as objective [*gegenständliche*] activity. In *The Essence of Christianity* [*Das Wesen des Christenthums*], he therefore regards the theoretical attitude as the only genuinely human attitude, while practice is conceived and defined only in its dirty-Jewish form of appearance [*Erscheinungsform*]. Hence he does not grasp the significance of "revolutionary," of "practical-critical," activity.

"Marxism," including its inventor, Plekhanov and his eminent pupil, V. I. Lenin, could make neither head nor tail of this Thesis—so they wisely just ignored it. Its praise of idealism and its downgrading of materialism just didn't fit their understanding of Marx, nor did the prominence it gives to subjectivity. But look at the text in the light of our brief view of Marx's development. Marx criticises materialism as it had grown up in the eighteenth century, with its passive attitude to reality, and lumps Ludwig Feuerbach's materialism together with it. The defect of this outlook, Marx explains, is that it is able to grasp knowledge only in opposition to both the object of knowledge and the knowing subject. It is incapable of understanding the activity of knowing the world in terms of the rest of human social and individual activity, the simultaneously subjective and objective social process of self-change and self-genesis.

It was German idealism—not just Hegel's work but that of Fichte and Schelling too—which developed this "active side." We have been discussing the long tradition of heretical religious and magical thought associated with this achievement. As individuals and as a social whole, we are trying to get hold of the world, as ourselves parts of the world. The objects we find in it must be grasped as aspects of our subjective striving, not as mere obstacles to be overcome. Our subjectivity and our objective drive to change the conditions in which we live are two aspects of the same world. "Theory," when it views things in the world as separate from us and from each other, is the direct opposite. Material productive activity is only part of this "active side." It also includes the transformation of the social relations and conditions within which production takes place. Marx has by now discovered that freedom has to include the creation and continual transformation by humans themselves of the relations between them. This requires the closure of the gap between production and social relations.

A world in which individuals exist as free subjects must be one where each part of the world belongs with and changes all other parts and itself. Changing the world implies knowing about it in the process of changing it, and change implies self-change and self-consciousness. The goals and the methods of the productive process are altered as a result of the process itself.

In the estranged world, where humans are hostile to each other, to their own life activity and to themselves, all this is hidden from them. All they can do is to "interpret" it in various ways, powerless to alter the course of its movement. Have we met anything like this attitude before? Certainly! It is the outlook of the Enlightenment. Opposed to it is the outlook of those Hermetics and mystics. In demystifying mysticism without rejecting it, Marx shows how humanity can bring about its own emancipation.

Marx and Revolution

Marx considers himself a communist from 1844 and all his work from then on is a contribution to the communist revolution, which he thinks of as imminent in Europe. But the history of "Marxism," which over much of its history modeled its notion of revolution on the Russian events following October 1917, makes it necessary to reconsider just what this means.

Clearly, Marx does not consider revolution as a sudden overnight transformation, resulting from some kind of coup d'état, however violent it might be. He refers to the situation following a prolonged historical transition, when "in the course of development class distinctions have disappeared and all production has been concentrated in the hands of a vast association of the whole nation" (Communist Manifesto, Vol. 6, 504). Then, he anticipates, "the public power will lose its political character." The proletariat will have abolished its own supremacy as a class. In place of the old bourgeois society, with its classes and class antagonisms, we shall have an association in which the free development of each is the condition for the free development of all. (Manifesto, 506)

Marx believes that the first step is "to raise the proletariat to the position of the ruling class, to win the battle of democracy," and identifies the resulting state with "the proletariat organised as the ruling class" (Manifesto, 504). This is in clear contrast with all previous such social overturns.

All the preceding classes that got the upper hand sought to fortify their already acquired status by subjecting society at large to their conditions of appropriation. The proletarians cannot become masters of the productive forces of society except by abolishing their own previous mode of appropriation, and thereby also every other mode of appropriation. . . . The proletariat cannot raise itself up without the whole superincumbent strata of official society being sprung into the air. (Manifesto, 495)

The idea that the revolution is basically a transformation of "economic conditions" is quite different from Marx's conception of the abolition of private property.

Private property has made us so stupid and one-sided that an object is only *ours* when we have it. . . . In the place of *all* physical and mental senses there has come therefore the sheer estrangement of all these senses, the sense of *having*. . . . The abolition of private property is therefore the complete *emancipation* of all human senses and qualities. (Manifesto, Vol. 3, 300)

Just pause over that phrase: "The complete emancipation of all human senses and qualities." Yes, such a transformation must be spearheaded by the subjective action of the proletariat, the "universal class." But it implies far more than can be summed up as "the overthrow of capitalism," as if it just meant fixing up a new economic and political system. It involves a new way of living, in which individual and universal no longer collide. Marx sees this revolution as marking a major epoch in human history, which displays three main stages.

Relationships of personal dependence (which originally arise quite spontaneously) are the first forms of society . . . . Personal independence based upon dependence mediated by things is the second great form, and only in it is a system of general social exchange of matter, a system of universal relations, universal requirements and universal capacities formed. Free individuality, based on the universal development of the individuals and the subordination of their communal, social productivity, which is the social possession, is the third stage. (*Grundrisse*. Manifesto, Vol. 28, 95)

Capital and Mysticism

Most of Marx's life was devoted to a single, never-completed work, *Capital*. Looking again at Volume 1, the only part he was able to publish, we are struck by the number of times it speaks of "mystery," "secrecy," the "nonmaterial." Here are just a few examples from the prefaces and the first chapter:

> and it is the ultimate aim of this work to reveal [*enthüllen*] the law of motion of modern society. (Preface to the first edition, 92)

> In its mystified form, the dialectic became the fashion in Germany, because it seemed to transfigure and glorify what exists. In its rational form it is a scandal and abomination to the bourgeoisie and its doctrinaire spokesmen. (Postface to the second edition 103)

> Not an atom of matter enters into the objectivity of commodities; in this it is the opposite of the coarsely sensuous objectivity of commodities as physical objects. (138)

> in the expression of the value of the linen, the coat represents a supra-natural property: their value, which is something purely social.
> The table continues to be wood, an ordinary, sensuous thing. But as soon as it emerges as a commodity, it changes into a thing which transcends sensuousness. . . . The mystical character of the commodity does not therefore arise from its use-value. . . . The mysterious character of the commodity-form consists therefore simply in the fact that the commodity reflects the social character of men's own labour as objective characteristics of the products of labour themselves. (163–65)

And so on, in many other places.

Marx does not merely point to this secret, mysterious nature of the social forms which underlie the whole of modern social life. He also *reveals* this secret. The noun *Hülle*, sometimes translated as "integument," and the verbs *enthüllen*, to reveal, and *verhüllen*, to conceal, veil, wrap up, are very important throughout this book. The integument is a film which covers the embryo and is removed at the time of birth. So the secret, the concealment, is not externally imposed; it grows out of the organism itself, and is actually an essential part of its coming into being. No more than religion is it a "mistake," a wrong way of thinking. Likewise, the revelation which "unconceals" what was hidden, is not the result of a trick being exposed by a clever "theorist," but is itself an aspect of organic development.

This is strikingly seen when Marx considers briefly another social form, showing us an association of free men, working with the means of production held in common, and expending their many different forms of labour-power in full self-awareness as one single social labour force. (171)

Contrasted with this is "a society of commodity producers," for which Christianity, with its religious cult of man in the abstract, more particularly in its bourgeois development, i.e. in Protestantism, Deism, etc, is the most fitting form of religion. (172)

Both in discussing religious and social forms, Marx does not see the secret side as something to be got rid of, something which ought not to be, a "mistake." The rational can appear only *through* the mystery.

The religious reflections of the real world can, in any case, vanish only when the practical relations of everyday life between man and man, and between man and nature, generally present themselves to him in a transparent form. The veil is not removed from the countenance of the social life-process until it becomes production by freely associated men, and stands under their conscious and planned control. This, however, requires that society possess a material foundation, which in turn is the natural and spontaneous product of a long and tormented historical development. (173)

Marx's task is to see how modern forms of private property like money, wage labor and capital, both conceal and reveal the truth about themselves. When, in chapter 7, he examines the labor process in general, he sees that "in changing nature, men change their own nature."

But, when the products of labor are exchanged on the market, and when even our capacity to produce, our very life-activity as humans, itself is reduced to a commodity, this process of self-creation is perverted and hidden. In the "Results of the Immediate Process of Production" (the planned part 7 of Volume 1 which Marx decided not to include, usually known as "the missing sixth chapter"), Marx writes:

Hence the rule of the capitalist over the worker is the rule of things over man, of dead labour over the living, of the product over the producer. For the commodities that become the instruments of rule over the workers (merely as the instruments of capital itself) are mere consequences of the process of production; they are its products. Thus at the level of material production, of the life-process in the realm of the social—for that is what the process of production is—we find the same situation that we find in religion at the ideological level, namely, the inversion of subject into object and *vice versa*. Viewed historically this inversion is the indispensable transition without which wealth as such, ie the relentless productive forces of social labour, which alone form the material base of a free human society, could not possibly be created by force at the expense of the majority. This antagonistic stage cannot be avoided, any more than it is possible for man to avoid the stage in which his spiritual energies are given a religious definition as powers independent of himself. What we are confronted by here is the alienation [*Entfremdung*] of man from his own labour. (Pelican edition, 990)

Thus that alienation, cause of the suffering of billions of men and women, is also the source of their emancipation. The perversion of human creative activity, taking ever more insane shapes, continually meets the resistance of the human beings who are treated inhumanly as they bear its weight. That is what capital—and *Capital*—are about. The struggle between wage earners and their employers is not an optional extra, but is the very heart of capital. Its many forms contain the struggle of human beings to be human, that is, to be self-consciously self-creative.

Capital and Self-Creation

We have seen how humans make themselves by simultaneously creating not only the physical conditions of their own life, but also the social forms within which this creation occurs. Hitherto, these forms have been alienated and have grown up unconsciously. In the early sections of *Capital*, the Hegelian phrase "behind their backs" occurs more than once. In Hegel, it refers to the rise of consciousness, behind the back of self-consciousness. In *Capital*, Marx uses it when he describes the transformation of the division of labor from commodities to money and then to capital.

> But the division of labour is an organisation of production which has grown up naturally, a web which has been and continues to be woven behind the backs of the producers of commodities. (201)

The misunderstanding of this aspect has been intensified by Engels' mistitling of the English translation of Volume 1. Where Marx called his volume "The Production-Process [*Produktionsprozess*] of Capital," Engels allowed the translation to give "The Process of Capitalist Production." We are given the impression that Marx was describing a system of producing goods under the conditions of "capitalism," not of the continuing weaving of a web in which the producers are enmeshed. Marx never used the term "capitalism" and his subject matter is, in fact, something quite different: the way that the social relation capital produces and reproduces itself.

> Here we shall see, not only how capital produces, but how capital itself is produced. The secret of profit-making must at last be laid bare [*enthüllen*]. (280)

Humans create themselves, but imprisoned within a form in which it is *capital*, an inhuman power, which creates itself.

In a well-known passage in chapter 1, Marx expresses more generally the problem raised by his aim of criticizing political economy:

> Reflection on the forms of human life, hence also scientific analysis of these forms, takes a course directly opposite to their real development. Reflection begins *post festum*, and therefore with the results of the process of development ready to hand. The forms which stamp products as commodities, and which are therefore the preliminary requirements for the circulation of commodities, already possess the fixed quality of natural forms of social life before men seek to give an account, not of their historical character, for in their eyes they are immutable, but of their content and meaning. (168)

Those old mystics had probed the contradictory structure of self-creation, but only in its heretical-religious form. How could they do anything more under the conditions of their time? Hegel took this much further, attempting to systematize that knowledge. Marx, living in the last stage of alienation, is able, in his critiques of religion, the state, philosophy, and political economy, to pose the problem in the form in which its practical solution can be discerned: *the communist revolution*. Instead of the mystical loop, "God making humanity making God," Marx must express an even more sharply contradictory movement, that of "human activity or self-change": humans make their own conditions of life, which in turn make humanity what it is. In its estranged shape, labor produces capital, which in turn enslaves labor.

Marx's achievement is to succeed in stripping away from the process of production its inhuman integument, revealing its true, human structure as free self-creation. Perhaps we should rather say, he has expressed scientifically that which the domination of social life by capital has laid bare. At the heart of his description of the labor process in general (in chapter 7, section 1 of *Capital*), is his combination of the elements of Aristotle's *poesis* with the Hermetic understanding of imagination as an active power.

> Labour is, first of all, a process between man and nature, a process by which man, through his own actions, mediates, regulates and controls the metabolism between himself and nature. He confronts the materials of nature as a force of nature. He sets in motion the forces belonging to his own body, his arms, legs, head and hands, in order to appropriate the materials of nature in a form adapted to his own needs. Through this movement he acts upon external nature and changes it, and in this way changes his own nature. . . . A spider conducts operations which resemble those of the weaver, and a bee would put many a human architect to shame by the construction of its honeycomb cells. But what distin-

guishes the worst of architects from the best of bees is that the architect builds the cell in his mind before he constructs it in wax. (283–84)

Here is human activity, the activity of production which distinguishes the human being from the rest of the world, seen as free, conscious self-change.

The method of *Capital* had to express this contradictory movement. In the succeeding categories, Marx couches his critique of political economy. In this money negates and preserves commodity, capital negates and preserves money, and so on, demanding a logical movement which

> includes in its positive understanding of what exists a simultaneous recognition of its negation, its inevitable destruction; because it regards every historically developed form as being in a fluid state, in motion, and therefore grasps its transient aspect as well. (Postface to the second edition of *Capital*)

In a "doctrine," an indoctrinator sets out what is "correct," before his admiring—if somewhat obtuse—disciples. Marx's approach is the polar opposite, for he shows the actual development of a living process revealing itself. Thus money is very old, but its secret cannot fully develop until it is transformed into capital. Then it is possible to see money's essential inhumanity for what it is, but only through the self-destruction of the capital form in which the money form is a subordinate part.

"AN INCONCLUSIVE CONCLUSION"

The contrast between Hermetism and what I have called "Enlightenment thinking" centers on their opposing ways of regarding the relation of humanity and nature. For the scientific-rationalist, the material world and the world of human history are quite independent of each other, as are individuals and the social movement in which their lives are lived. Once humans have appeared, human reason, with which those beings are conveniently equipped, takes over and history can begin. As I have suggested, this view is not so far distant from that of the orthodox monotheist religions: if the natural and human worlds were freely created by God's will, there was no reason why these two aspects should fit together. From this basic conception flows the way social change is seen, those individuals in the know being given—or at any rate taking—the job of scientifically working out what the world ought to be like, and then setting about making everybody else fit into their scheme.

Socialism, including "Marxism," had a similar angle on this question, sometimes seeing the natural world in terms of mechanically interacting particles of matter, and humanity as a collection of individuals. Rather badly organized at present, humans might, if those qualified to do so think very hard, be found a better way to set up their mutual relationships. Relying heavily on the works of Engels, the "Marxists" attempted to formulate an account of nature and natural science which they called "dialectical materialism," and tried with great difficulty to make Marx fit into its patterns. In its Stalinist form, this was dogmatized into a kind of state religion. When, in the wake of the study of the early writings of Marx, some people began to pay attention to his early humanism, there was a tendency to keep this "Young Marx" rigidly separate from the "mature" or "scientific" Marx. The barrier between "man" and "nature" had to be left intact.

But this eliminates the very questions of the fundamental unity of humans with each other, and of all of them with nature. For the mystics, Hermetics, and magicians, the human is only an aspect of the natural and vice versa. "As above, so below," they read in Hermes. We have seen that Hegel takes the side of the magicians on this issue: the movements of nature, history, and psychology all express the unfolding of Spirit. But what about Marx? Does human self-emancipation, a task for humans to tackle in practice, require any specific conception of the universe?

In the inhuman shell of private property, money, capital, and the state, Marx discovers why self-creation appears as a mystery. Once that "integument has burst asunder," relations within a free association of producers, truly human relations, will be transparent and so will the relationship between nature and humanity as a whole. That is why he envisages—as a program for the future—a united science of nature and humanity.

> Natural science will in time incorporate into itself the science of man, just as the science of man will incorporate into itself the science of nature: there will be one science. (*MECW*, Vol. 3, 304)

Was this not, in essence, also the program of Hermetism?

But living inside alienated society this can only be perceived dimly and with great difficulty. The path to the emancipation of humanity from the inhuman shell in which it has imprisoned itself is hidden from us. Tearing aside the veil which conceals it is only possible through a series of false steps, each of which negates its predecessor. Not that these "errors" are simply wasted. Nobody can simply set aside the advances of the English and French revolutions—however hard some people try. But of course, a century and a half after Marx began this work it is deeply frustrating to see ourselves apparently back at square one. However, if we face up to the gulf which we have to cross to get from bourgeois society to a human way of life, could it be otherwise?

When the years of revolution 1848–49 seemed to many people to have passed without leaving a trace, Marx wrote in *The Eighteenth Brumaire of Louis Bonaparte*:

> Proletarian revolutions, like those of the nineteenth century, criticise themselves constantly, interrupting themselves continually in their own course, come back to the apparently accomplished in order to begin it afresh, deride with unmerciful thoroughness the inadequacies, weaknesses and paltrinesses of their first attempts, seem to throw down their adversary only in order that he may draw new strength from the earth and rise again, more gigantic than before, recoil ever and anon from the indefinite prodigiousness of their own aims, until a situation has been created which makes all turning back impossible, and the conditions themselves cry out: *Hic Rhodus, hic salta!* Here is the rose, here dance!

Each phase in the process of self-creation reveals new sides of the task of self-emancipation and poses it anew. That is why the scientific—in Marx's sense of this word—aspect of this process cannot be a complete, finished "theoretical system," which can then be "applied," like a sort of all-purpose theoretical tool. "Revolutionary critical activity" demands open self-critical thinking, the direct opposite of all dogma.

Of course, that implies that Marx's work must be seen as radically incomplete. For example, those who say that Marx did not completely understand Hegel usually mean to downgrade him by this remark. They are, of course, absolutely correct—and totally miss the point. Every great thinker must yield a mass of ideas which transcend, not only his own time and his own thought, but any particular reading of his work. That is why Marx continually returns to Hegel to win yet further insights and to criticise him anew. Naturally, similar considerations apply to any reading of Marx. Writing in the century before last, he could not have imagined the monstrous history of the twentieth century, or the depth of corruption of our time. I would only add that all future development must begin with his work. Taking it as the last word meant falsifying it, but ignoring it would have still more dangerous consequences.

At the start of the new millennium, any kind of fundamental transformation looks like an impossibility, a dream. Private property seems to be the only way to distribute wealth. Even class organization appears to be an appeal to self-interest, requiring special apology. A revolution would be a miracle. The billions who are merely "laborers" cannot be expected to act otherwise if their betters do no more than grab more than enough for themselves. And even if individuals here and there try to break the mold, what can they achieve as isolated humans in a sea of greed? But that leaves humanity without hope.

Marx's notions alone give grounds for optimism, but only if they are seen in the provisional context of the Hermetics, not the definite, predetermined way of "Marxism," but the open, self-conscious, forward-looking manner of Marx himself. Only this can provide us with a way of seeing, inside the monstrosities of the twenty-first century, the possibility of human life hidden within.

I began by recalling that socialism used to be easy to understand. Now I hope we can see that Marx's basic conceptions, like that of universal human emancipation and of the free association of individuals, are not complex, but go far beyond any particular account of them. Simply describing a world without private property or money, however important these might be, misses the point. We are facing instead the practical and scientific tasks of human self-creation, and these are necessarily unbounded and undefined.

"Communism is the riddle of history solved, and it knows itself to be this solution" (MECW, Vol. 3, 296–97).

Yes, but not as something completed, only as an unfinished task.

REFERENCES

Benz, Ernst. *The Mystical Sources of German Romantic Philosophy*. Allison Park, Pa.: Pickwick Publications, 1983.

Chittick, William C. *The Sufi Path of Knowledge: Ibn Al'Arabi's Metaphysics of Imagination*. Albany, N.Y.: State University of New York Press, 1989.

Cohn, Norman. *Cosmos, Chaos and the World to Come: The Ancient Roots of Apocalyptic Faith*. New Haven, Conn.: Yale University Press, 1993.

Corbin, Henry. *The Man of Light in Iranian Sufism*. Boulder, Colo.: Shambhala, 1978.

Goldner, Loren. *Vanguard of Retrogression: Postmodern Fictions as Ideology in the Era of Fictitious Capital*. New York: Queequeg Publications, 2001.

Hampson, Norman. *The Enlightenment: An Evaluation of Its Assumptions, Attitudes and Values*. New York: Penguin, 1968.

Holloway, John. *Change the World without Taking Power: The Meaning of Revolution Today*. London: Pluto, 2002.

de Leon-Jones, Karen Sylvia. *Giordano Bruno and the Kabbalah: Prophets, Magicians and Rabbis*. New Haven, Conn.: Yale University Press, 1997.

Magee, Glenn. *Hegel and the Hermetic Tradition*. Ithaca, N. Y.: Cornell University Press, 2001.

Pagel, Walter. *Paracelsus: An Introduction to Philosophical Medicine in the Era of Renaissance*. New York: S. Karger, 1958.

Preston, Antoinette Mann. *The Infinite Worlds of Giordano Bruno*. Springfield, Ill.: Charles C. Thomas 1958.

Scholem, Gershom. *Major Trends in Jewish Mysticism*. New York: Schocken Books, 1961.

———. *Kabbalah*. New York: Quadrangle Books, 1974.

Shokek, Shimon. *Kabbalah and the Art of Being*. New York: Routledge, 2001.

Smith, Cyril. *Marx at the Millennium*. London: Pluto, 1996.

Weeks, Andrew. *Boehme: An Intellectual Biography of the Seventeenth-Century Philosopher and Mystic*. Albany, N.Y.: State University of New York Press, 1991.

Yates, Frances. *Giordano Bruno and the Hermetic Tradition*. New York: Routledge, 1999.

——. *Lull and Bruno: Collected Essays, Volume 1*. New York: Routledge, 1982.

——. *The Occult Philosophy in the Elizabethan Age*. New York: Routledge, 1999.

Chapter Eleven

Marx and the Fourfold Vision
of William Blake

In the book by E. O. Abbott called *Flatland: A Romance of Many Dimensions*, the hero "A Square" tries to persuade his fellow two-dimensional beings — triangles, hexagons, and so on — that other dimensions are possible. William Blake lived in a four-dimensional moral world, and for that reason he was considered quite mad by ordinary citizens. He did not agree with them and is reported to have told a friend: "There are probably men shut up as mad in bedlam who are not so; that possibly the madmen outside have shut up the sane people."

When he was four years old, God frightened the life out of him by looking in at his window. When he was about nine, walking on Peckham Rye, he saw a tree whose branches were covered in Angels. His father, told of this observation, prudently threatened to thrash him for lying, but it doesn't seem to have done him any good. Half a century later, he told someone that he knew that Michelangelo was much better at painting angels than Raphael, even though he had never been to Italy to see their pictures. His certainty was based upon the opinion of someone who had visited him recently, and who should certainly have known if the likeness was a good one, for his informant was the subject of the picture: the Archangel Gabriel.

All his life, Blake knew that the world of imagination was the true world, while that of industrial revolution London was certainly false. In the world which his imagination saw so clearly, individuals freely created beauty. But the other, "fallen" world was a place where slavery, exploitation, self-interest, and hypocrisy were rife.

He explained the way he saw things in a letter to the Reverend Dr. Trusler, in 1799,

I know that This World Is a World of IMAGINATION & Vision. I see Every thing I paint In This World, but Every body does not see alike. To the eyes of a

213

Miser a Guinea is more beautiful than the Sun, & a bag worn with the use of Money has more beautiful proportions than a Vine filled with Grapes. The tree which moves some to tears of joy is in the Eyes of others only a Green thing that stands in the way. . . .To the eyes of the Man of Imagination, Nature is Imagination itself. As a man is, So he Sees. As the Eye is formed, such are its Powers.

That explains his view of the relationship of art and nature.

Men think they can Copy Nature as Correctly as I copy Imagination. This they will find Impossible, & all Copiers or Pretended Copiers of Nature, from Rembrandt to Reynolds, Prove that Nature becomes to its Victim nothing but blots and blurs.

In *The Marriage of Heaven and Hell* (1793), he tried to explain how people generally saw the world falsely: "For man has closed himself up and sees all things thro' narrow chinks of his cavern." For Blake, the inability of his fellow Londoners to see those visions which were so clear to him was the consequence of the false, unbalanced way that they lived, the self-imposed blindness which hid reality from them. They lived in a way whose inhumanity hid itself from itself. But this implied that it was possible for them to live in a different world and to see it differently.

Marx, of course, did not see visions. But he also believed that the ordinary world and the way it was seen were not truly human. Whatever their huge differences, each of these men saw the entire world—nature, history, and social life—as centered on the activity of the human social individual, enslaved but striving for freedom. Marx called the blindness that made it so hard for us to see the modern world truly, "the fetish-character of commodities."

"Marxism," of course, could not abide such a juxtaposition. Its "complete, integral world outlook," as expounded by Plekhanov, Lenin, and others, is a clear illustration of that one-dimensional outlook that Blake called "single vision," the enemy of imagination. The hostility to the individual which has been given the name of "Marxism" is totally opposed to the ideas of Marx. Those ideas, on the contrary, took forward Blake's "fourfold vision," which combined reason and imagination, sense and emotion. Marx both analyzed the fracture of this quartet and showed how its unity could be actualized in revolutionary practice.

The visionary artist and poet William Blake (1757–1827) and the revolutionary thinker Karl Marx, born sixty years later, were equally hostile to eighteenth-century individualistic materialism, the predominant way of thinking of their own times, and, in a cruder form, of ours. In an early work, *There is no Natural Religion* (1788), Blake attacked the outlook promoted by John Locke, whom he often linked with Bacon and Newton.

If it were not for the Poetic or Prophetic character the Philosophic and Experimental would soon be at the ratio of all things, & stand still unable to do other than repeat the same dull round over again. . . . He who sees the Infinite in all things sees God. He who sees the Ratio only sees himself only. Therefore God becomes as we are, that we may be as he is.

I believe this is precisely what Marx meant, in the First Thesis on Feuerbach—so disliked by "Marxists"—when he also attacked materialism for not conceiving the world as "human sensuous activity, practice [*Praxis*], not subjectively." Blake is unlikely even to have heard of his near contemporary, Hegel, so he did not know of that writer's assertion that "the finite has no veritable being." The appearance of the actual as limited and fixed could not be the end of the story. But Marx never forgot his "great teacher," and spent his life in continual struggle and agreement with him. For Marx, freedom, the essence of the all-sided human being, involves opening up what is concealed and perverted by the malevolent magic power of capital. But Marx also shows how the path to freedom could be discerned within this power itself.

But surely, isn't Blake a "religious writer," always talking about God? How can Marx have anything in common with him? Yes, but what kind of God? Blake's Jesus is within the human individual. When he was very old, Crabb Robinson asked him about his religious ideas. "Jesus Christ is the only God," said the old man. But he added: "And so am I and so are you." Jesus, he explains many times, *is* Imagination. The God of the Old Testament, on the contrary, is the wrathful God. This God who judges Adam, as Milton reported, and who is so gratified at the Crucifixion of His Son, is a cruel tyrant, the source of all cruelty and falsehood. In a notebook, Blake describes this monster with characteristic irreverence:

> Old Nobodaddy up aloft farted & belchd & coughd
> And said I love hanging & drawing & quartering
> Every bit as well as war & slaughtering.

This divine personage is linked by Blake with God the Father, with institutional religion and with state power. He is the source of all kinds of moral law, restrictive rules with which individuals are brutally forced to comply, and which destroy their humanity.

William Blake was a Londoner, who grew up as the city was taking its modern shape. When he lived in Lambeth, there was a high-tech, steam-driven flour mill, the Albion, at the end of his road. Later he lived in South Molton Street, close to the Tyburn gallows tree. Apprenticed to an engraver, he tried all his life—with little success—to make his living as an artisan. He also studied drawing and painting, and combined all these accomplishments in his life's work. (He is also thought to have sung his early poetry, but never learned to write down the melodies he composed.)

In the 1780s and 1790s, he was part of London's radical circles, including its radical religious life. His relations with the Swedenborgian New Church and the Muggletonian and other sects have been much discussed. One thing is certain: he was fiercely hostile to all state forms and established religion, associating it with oppression and slavery. In the *Book of Urizen*, he writes of "His ancient infinite mansion: One command, one joy, one desire, One curse, one weight, one measure One King, one God, one Law."

Until the end of the century, he was actively involved with support for the American and French revolutions and the fight to abolish slavery. In the 1780s and 1790s, he believed that the freedom he longed for was actually at hand, but later he was less optimistic. But he never "ceased from mental fight" against the prevailing ideas of his time.

Two aspects of seventeenth- and eighteenth-century thought are important here: the conception of imagination and the problem of good and evil. And Blake's approach to these two problems forms the axes of his entire work. Of course, a category like "The Enlightenment" covers a wide variety of ideas, and some of the most important figures who are included in this term had by the end of the eighteenth century begun to point out the contradictions within it, but there was a widespread notion that opposed what was imaginary to what was real.

Hobbes had thought the question of imagination important enough to devote the second chapter of *Leviathan* to showing how imagination is dependent on sensation:

> After the object is removed, or the eye shut, we still retain an image of the thing seen, though more obscure than when we see it. And this is it, the Latins call Imagination.

Locke, for whom all correct knowledge originated in sense impressions, took it for granted that anything imagined was "mere idea." And Hume put it like this:

> But though our thought seems to possess this unbounded liberty. . . it is really confined within very narrow limits. . . . All this creative power of the mind amounts to no more than the faculty of compounding, transposing, augmenting or diminishing the materials afforded us by the senses and experience. (*An Enquiry Concerning Human Understanding*)

Blake's entire outlook was founded upon his hatred for such notions. As he learned from the work of Paracelsus, imagination was an active, creative power. When he saw himself as a prophet, this for him was the same as being an artist. His work as a graphic artist and poet aimed to change the way everybody saw the world so as to open the way for freedom.

> For the cherub with his flaming sword is hereby commanded to leave his guard at tree of life, and when he does, the whole creation will be consumed, and appear infinite, and holy whereas now it appears finite and corrupt. This will come to pass through an improvement of sensual enjoyment.
>
> But first the notion that man has a body distinct from his soul is to be expunged; this I shall do, by printing in the infernal method, by corrosives, which in Hell are salutary and medicinal, melting apparent surfaces away, and displaying the infinite which was hid.
>
> If the doors of perception were cleansed, every thing would appear to man as it is, infinite. (*The Marriage of Heaven and Hell*)

Imagination was not a faculty possessed by a few talented humans. It was the essence of freedom, of the truly human, and potentially available to everybody. That is why poetry was not just a particular literary medium: along with painting, it was the only way the infinite of imagination could find expression. The unity of the imagined, envisioned work of art showed how we all might "see infinity in a grain of sand."

Enlightenment thinkers opposed the Christian belief in the radical sinfulness of human beings with the optimistic certainty that they were basically good. Even Kant's summary of the Enlightenment could not evade these conflicting views: he was sure that, at bottom, man was radically evil.

Blake was strongly against both views, both orthodox religious belief, and the Deism which sought to rationalize it. He fiercely attacks all the teachings of the State Churches that pain, suffering, and conflict are the products of human sin. With institutionalized religion he associates abstract Reason. Like Hegel, Blake studied Jakob Boehme ("Behmen," as he was called in the English translation), and through his work linked up with the Hermetic, Gnostic, Cabbalistic, alchemical traditions. He does not accept any one of these predecessors unconditionally, but he learned from them to see Creation as the same event as the Fall, not a one-off event, but one which continually happens inside the human heart. Blake is an Antinomian, heir to those centuries of persecuted heretics who believed that, when a merciful Jesus redeems us, the Law of the angry God is cancelled. Blake stresses especially the tyrannical nature of all law governing sexuality.

In *The Marriage of Heaven and Hell*, he begins to work out the implications of these notions, taking the Satan of Milton's *Paradise Lost* as his starting point. Satan represents Energy, without which there is no Creation. Revolting against the tyranny of the Wrathful God, Satan opens the way for all freedom. But this is also the revolt against Reason, matter, and law.

Without Contraries is no progression. Attraction and Repulsion, Reason and Energy, Love and Hate are necessary to human existence. From these contraries spring what the religious call Good and Evil. Good is the passive that obeys Reason Evil is the active springing from Energy.

The *Marriage* ends with a *Song of Liberty*, an account of the revolutionary victory of Imagination, which had begun in Paris. "Look up! Look up! O citizen of London, enlarge thy countenance! . . . For everything that lives is Holy."

Blake is not an irrationalist. What he rejects is the abstractly rational, that cold mechanical logic which excludes emotion, forgiveness, loving, sensuality. There has to be a *marriage* of the contraries. (For him, contraries are not negations, which are at perpetual war.)

The *Songs of Innocence and Experience*, also dating from the period of the French Revolution, containing some of the best-known poetry in the language, must be taken as a whole. Blake's "innocence," the uncorrupted outlook of childhood, is not yet a clear vision of the world, and "experience" is certainly not cynical disillusion. It only seems like this in the "fallen" world. These "two contrary states of the human soul" are *both* required for freedom. Look, for example, at the two "Chimney Sweeper" poems. The innocent one ends:

> And the Angel told Tom if he'd be a good boy,
> He'd have God for a father & never want joy.
> And so Tom awoke and we rose in the dark,
> And got with our bags & our brushes to work,
> Tho' the morning was cold, Tom was happy and warm,
> So if all do their duty, they need not fear harm.

But we know perfectly well that Tom had been sold by his parents to a life of climbing up chimneys, so that his childhood has already been destroyed. The corresponding *Song of Experience* ends:

> And because I am happy & dance & sing,
> They think they have done me no injury:
> And are gone to praise God & his Priest & King,
> Who make up a heaven of our misery.

"The Tyger," a Song of Experience, is coupled with "The Lamb," a Song of Innocence, and Blake wants *both*. That powerful sequence of hammer-blow questions addressed to the Tyger, includes a reference to "deadly terrors," because Blake is thinking especially of the French Revolution, whose wrathful energy is both destructive and liberatory. Each question forces us to the answer "God," culminating in the question: "Did he who made the lamb make thee?" Creation involved *both* the angry God Nobodaddy, and the merciful Jesus.

Many accounts of Blake stress, with good reason, the social criticism of London at the end of the eighteenth century. But that is not enough. Look, for example at the powerful Song of Experience called "London":

> I wander thro' each charter'd street,
> Near where the charter'd Thames doth flow,
> And mark in every face I meet,
> Marks of weakness, marks of woe.
>
> In every cry of every man,
> In every Infants cry of fear,
> In every voice, in every ban,
> The mind-forg'd manacles I hear.
>
> How the Chimney-sweepers cry,
> Every blackning Church appalls,
> And the hapless soldiers sigh,
> Runs in blood down palace walls.
>
> But most at midnight hour I hear,
> How the youthful Harlots curse
> Blasts the new-born Infants tear
> And blights with plague the marriage hearse.

These short lines bring together the misery and fear which dominate those city streets, exploitation, especially of children, the inhumanity of State power and religion and twisted sexuality and its terrible consequences, again, for children, both the newborn and the child prostitute. But notice that the "manacles" which bind all of these together are "mind-forg'd."

About 1800, Blake began his poem *Milton*. Its preface contains a sort of art manifesto:

Painters! On you I call! Sculptors! Architects! Suffer not the fashionable Fools to depress your powers by the prices they pretend to give for contemptible works or the expensive advertizing boasts that they make of such works.

Then follows the best-known and most ridiculously misunderstood of all songs in English: *Jerusalem*. (We ought to try to forget the patriotic music by

Sir Hubert Parry, and the orchestration by Sir Edward Elgar, but it is hard to do so! It was recently chosen in some poll as an alternative National Anthem.) It is true that "those dark, Satanic mills" are undoubtedly smoking factories, exploiting the labor of children and their parents. But they are also much more. The mill is for Blake a machine in which "wheel outside wheel, with cogs tyrannic moving by compulsion each other," express cold, emotionless logic, as well as a religion of unbending rules enforced by the State. So, when the ladies of the Women's Institute belt out Parry's melody, they don't know that they are condemning above all the established Church, and especially its fear and hatred of sexual freedom.

What follows is an attempt to "justify the ways of God to men." It takes the form of the return to Albion's shores of the poet Milton, whose earlier efforts to accomplish this task had dissatisfied him. Now, he has one thing in his favor: Blake. He can show the way

> To cleanse the Face of my Spirit by Self-examination.
> To bathe in the waters of life; to wash off the Not Human
> I come in Self-annihilation & the grandeur of Inspiration
> To cast off Rational Demonstration by faith in the Saviour.

Blake's hostility to rational demonstration was seen in his attitude to Bacon as "Satan's arsehole," illustrated in the margin of his copy of the writings of the English philosopher.

The last three decades of Blake's life were devoted to the elaboration of ever more complex structures. *Vala, or the Four Zoas* aimed to be the most comprehensive account, but was never finished. In his complicated story, Blake seeks to represent simultaneously the Cosmos, the social order, and the human psyche, all couched in terms of mythical characters called "Eternals." Blake insists that he is *not* going in for allegory, where abstractions are personified. This is *symbolism*, a vision of what actually *is*, what "eternally exists."

Eternity is a balanced association of four "Zoas": Reason, Creative Imagination, Emotion, and Sensation. Following the Cabbalistic story, there is a Creation-Fall catastrophe, in which each of them becomes a separate and hostile "fallen" being. Thus, for example, Imagination and Reason each persist in our "fallen world," but each of them is turned against itself as it is set against the other. Blake took a lifetime to tell their story and even then never finished it.

Urizen, who is abstract reason, self-righteousness, is exemplified in Newton, Bacon, and Locke. Urizen writes in brass-bound books with pens of steel. He is the enemy of Urthona, who is creative imagination, Luvah, emotion and love, and Tharmas, the senses. When Urizen's pride and jealousy of Man leads him to break out of Eternity, he becomes Satan, the jealous, angry God of this, the Fallen World. He creates a world of geometric regularity, suppressed sex, and oppressive law, going under the name of merciless, unforgiving Justice.

> Urizen's hypocrisy is an important aspect of his being.
> And his soul sicken'd! he curs'd
> Both sons & daughters; for he saw
> That no flesh nor spirit could keep
> His iron laws one moment,
>
> For he saw that life liv'd upon death
> The Ox in the slaughter house moans
> The Dog at the wintry door
> And he wept and called in Pity
> And his tears flowed down on the winds.

Eventually, in a Last Judgment, he is forced to realize his error and accept the need for all four to unite. He is then regenerated, along with the whole of the universe.

After the Fall, each individual element breaks into a female "Emanation" and a male "Specter," the latter being the rational entity.

> The Spectre Is the Reasoning Power in Man; & when separated
> From Imagination, and closing itself as in steel, in a Ratio
> Of the Things of Memory, It then frames Laws & Moralities
> To destroy Imagination!

Luvah starts as Love and is transformed into Hate and wars against Urizen, causing the Fall. Tharmas, identified with the senses, and especially with sex, is transformed from "the mildest son of heaven." He begets Los, Urthona's Specter, the artist, worldly expression of Creative Imagination. It is Los, who is usually Blake himself, who eventually brings about the redemption of humanity and the building of Jerusalem. In this task he is helped by his son Orc, the spirit of Revolution.

In Jerusalem, his last great narrative and longest poem, Blake tells of man's last push for redemption. Jerusalem is defined as liberty. But as in Vala and the Four Zoas, only after she has overcome many adventures does she reveal her ability to give man what he wants.

> Awake! Awake Jerusalem! O lovely Emanation of Albion
> Awake and overspread all Nations as in Ancient Time
> For lo! The Night of Death is past and the Eternal Day
> Appears upon our hills: Awake Jerusalem and come away.

Albion represents the ordinary man, whose fall and resurrection are the subject of the action. This is how Blake depicts the use of the labor of the young people of Albion's England:

> And in their stead, intricate wheels invented, wheel without wheel;
> To perplex youth in their outgoings, & to bind to labours in Albion
> Of day & night the myriads of eternity that they may grind
> And polish brass & iron hour after hour laborious task:
> Kept ignorant of its use, that they might spend the days of wisdom
> In sorrowful drudgery, to obtain a scanty pittance of bread;
> In ignorance to view a small portion & think that All,
> And call it Demonstration: blind to all the simple rules of life.

There is no need to repeat: Marx is not Blake. But while "Marxism" merely sought some changes in economic structure, Marx was concerned with "self-alteration" (*Selbstveränderung*), "the alteration of men on a mass scale." This question of self-alteration—the aspect which Marx has in common with Blake—is not an aspect but the whole point of Marx. (It is not surprising that Engels, who got this point confused, found it impossible to include it in his edition of Theses on Feuerbach, the only version we had until quite recently.)

As Marx says:

> *Communism* as the *positive* transcendence of *private property* as *human self-estrangement*, and therefore as the real *appropriation* of the *human* essence by and for man; communism therefore as the complete return of man to himself as a *social* (i.e., human) being—a return accomplished consciously and embracing the entire wealth of previous development. . . . Communism is the riddle of history solved, and it knows itself to be the solution. (*MECW*, Vol. 3, 296–97)

And a few pages later,

> The abolition of private property is therefore the complete *emancipation* of all human senses and qualities, but it is this emancipation precisely because these senses and attributes have become, subjectively and objectively, *human*.

Thus, achieving the overthrow of relations based upon private property in "an association of free producers," implies the total self-transformation of humanity, the "complete emancipation of the human senses." Blake would have felt at home in such a new moral world, as some of the revolutionaries of 1968 began to see.

This conception of an alternative way of life is central to all of Marx's work. In particular, it is the contrast with what exists which is crucial for Marx's chief work, *Capital*. He gives a *critique* of political economy, of the method of the work of Adam Smith and David Ricardo—always contrasting political economy with mere economics. He expounded his view of the system that they propounded. It is nowhere presented directly. Marx's method is to give it is as the opposite of all methods which do.

Marx, in another way that he unconsciously follows Blake, is intent on showing how the false ways life are inseparable from false ways of thinking. In *Capital* he follows Blake's hero Paracelsus in characterizing the labor process, the essential activity of the human species, as beginning with imagination. (See Volume 1, chapter 7, first section.) In political economy, everything starts with definition.

Marx was about half a century after Blake, half a century which saw the rise of the modern workers' movement. So whereas the first beginnings of that movement left Blake quite cold, Marx was able to link it with his conception of communism.

In the conflict between social relations of production and powers of production, which appears in this, the fallen world, we have to base ourselves on the unity of the two. The very elements which appear to drive them into opposition—and which do indeed so drive them to war between us human beings—have their resolution in the elements of harmony. This is the power of Marx's thought, and of that of Blake. In the battles which rage, the thinking of these two men, misunderstood by so many of their devoted followers, marks them out as the great prophets of unity.

Let me conclude with another "song of liberty," from *America: A Prophecy.*

The morning comes, the night decays, the watchmen leave their stations;
The grave is burst, the spices shed, the linen wrapped up;
The bones of death, the cov'ring clay, the sinews shrunk & dry'd.
Reviving shake, inspiring move, breathing! awakening!
Spring like redeemed captives when their bonds & bars are burst;
Let the slave grinding at the mill, run out into the field;
Let him look up into the heavens & laugh in the bright air;
Let the inchained soul shut up in darkness and in sighing,
Whose face has never seen a smile in thirty weary years;
Rise up and look out, his chains are loose, his dungeon doors are open.
And let his wife and children return from the opressors scourge;
They look behind at every step & believe it is a dream,
Singing. The Sun has left his blackness and has found a fresher morning
And the fair Moon rejoices in the clear and cloudless night;
For Empire is no more, and the Lion & Wolf shall cease.

REFERENCES

Aristotle. *De Anima*. III, 3.

Ault, Donald D. *Visionary Physics: Blake's Response to Newton*. Chicago: University of Chicago Press, 1974.

Beer, John. *Blake's Visionary Universe*. Manchester, UK: Manchester University Press, 1969.

Bidney, Martin. *Blake and Goethe*. Columbia: University of Missouri Press, 1988.

Bloom, Harold. *Blake's Apocalypse*. Ithaca, N. Y.: Cornell University Press, 1970.

Crehan, Stewart. *Blake in Context*.

Damon, S. Foster. *A Blake Dictionary*. Boulder, Colo.: Shambala, 1979.

Doscow, Minna. *The Humanized Universe of Blake and Marx*. In Bertholf and Levitt, *William Blake and the Moderns*. Albany, N. Y.: SUNY Press, 1982.

Erdman, David V. *Blake: Prophet against Empire*. Princeton, N. J.: Princeton University Press, 1969.

Frye, Northrop (ed.). *Blake*. Upper Saddle River, N. J.: Prentice-Hall, 1966.

Gardner, Stanley. *Infinity on the Anvil: A Critical Study of Blake's Poetry*. Oxford: Oxford University Press, 1954.

Gore, W. C. *Imagination in Spinoza and Hume*. Chicago: University of Chicago Press, 1902.

Keynes, Geoffrey. *The Letters of William Blake*. Oxford: Oxford University Press, 1980.

Lindsay, Jack. *William Blake: His life and work*. London: Constable, 1978.

Morton, A. L. *The Everlasting Gospel*. London: Lawrence and Wishart, 1958.

Pagliaro, Harold. *Selfhood and Redemption in Blake's* Songs. University Park, Pa.: Pennylvania State University Press, 1987.

Peterfreund, Stuart. *William Blake in a Newtonian World*. Norman: University of Oklahoma Press, 1998.

Pico della Mirandola. *On the Imagination*. Westport, Conn.: Greenwood Press, 1971.

Piper, H. W. *The Active Universe: Pantheism and the Concept of Imagination in the English Romantic Poets*. London: Athlone Press, 1962.

Punter, David. *Blake, Hegel and Dialectic*. Amsterdam: Rodopi, 1982.

Raine, Kathleen. *Blake and the New Age*. London: George Allen and Unwin, 1979.

——. *Golgonooza, City of Imagination*. Ipswich, UK: Golgonooza Press, 1991.

——. *William Blake*. London: Thames and Hudson, 1970.

Sabri-Tabrizi, G. R. *The "Heaven" and "Hell" of William Blake*. London: Lawrence and Wishart, 1973.

Thompson, E. P. *Witness against the Beast: William Blake and the Moral Law*. New York: New Press, 1993.

Vaughan, William. *William Blake*. London: Tate Publishing, 1999.

Index

Abbott, E. O., 213; *Flatland: A Romance of Many Dimensions*, 213
Adam, 166, 178, 215
Adeimantus, 64
al Hallaj, 179
al Shurawadhi, 179
Albion, 222
Altenstein, 112
Anselm, 194
Aquinas, T., 75–77, 163, 166
Archangel Gabriel, 213
Aristotle, 56, 59, 62, 63, 67, 68, 69, 70, 72, 75–77, 81, 92, 94, 96, 110, 115, 117, 118, 125, 146, 150, 152, 161, 162, 179, 186, 187, 190, 196, 206; *Metaphysics*, 162; *Poetics*, 163
Athens, 73
Augustine, 75, 171; *Periphyseion*, 171, 173
Augustus of France, Philip, 172
Aurelius, Marcus, 73
Auschwitz, 37
Averros (Ibn Rushd), 75, 179
Avicenna (Ibn Sina), 75, 179

Bacon, F., 214, 219, 220
Bakunin, 42; *State and Anarchy*, 42; *The Late Marx and the Russian Road*, 42

Berkeley, B., 15
Bhopal, 37
Blake, William, xi, 178, 186, 213, 214; *Book of Urizen*, 216; *The Marriage of Heaven and Hell*, 186, 217; *The Song of Liberty*, 186, 218; *Songs of Innocence and Experience*, 218; *There Is No Natural Religion*, 214; *Vala, or the Four Zoas*, 220
Blanqui, A., 28
Boehme, J., 177, 178, 183, 189, 217
Bruno, G., 175, 176; *De la Causa*, 176

Calvin, John, 78
Cephalus, 63
Charlemagne, 170
Charles I, 81, 90, 93
Charles the Bald, 170
Chrisippus, 72
Christianity, 73
Cicero, 73, 76
Citium, 72
Communist League, 27, 42
Copernicus, 174
Cordevero, Moses, 167
Cornelius, 86
Cromwell, O., 82
Cynicism, 72

About the Author

Cyril Smith was born in 1929 and, for most of his life, was a communist, a follower of Trotsky. Then, in the 1980s, he began to question all his previously dogmatically held beliefs. Written after he retired from his job as Lecturer in Statistics at the London School of Economics, *Marx at the Millennium* (Pluto, 1995) was his first attempt at rereading Marx, and this is the second.